Yoga and Yogic

About the Author

YOGI Gupta was born at Kanpur, United Provinces, North India, into an aristocratic and well-to-do family. As a youth he studied law, was admitted to the Bar, and practiced before one of the high courts of India. His legal career was dedicated to the service of humanity, but for the fulfillment of his mission on earth he took to the path of renunciation. After intense penance and mastering nine types of Yoga, with the divine blessings of his *Guru* (spiritual teacher), he lived the life of a wandering monk, helping people to achieve radiant health and spiritual development.

Yogi Gupta was the founder and president of the *Kailashananda* Mission, situated on *Manikoot* Hills, Rishikesh, Himalayas, India, surrounded by the Himalayan peaks and on the banks of the holy river Ganges.

The Yoga Health Sanatorium at the Mission in India, had accommodations to admit fifty patients and unlimited accommodations for out-patients. Yogi Gupta was the director in charge of this sanatorium, which was operated by his disciples and followers.

Yogi Gupta developed a great following in the United States of America and other Western countries. His headquarters was in New York City. He was the director of Yogi Gupta New York Center, New York City, where he personally taught the occult and esoteric wisdom of the East and provided personal guidance to the disciples on the Path, besides holding regular lectures and classes in Yoga Postures, Deep Breathings, Relaxation, Meditation and *Raja Yoga*. Yogi Gupta is the author of the renowned book, *Yoga And Long Life*, a profusely illustrated handbook that presents all the important principles of Hatha Yoga, the Science of Living, practiced and perfected in India throughout the centuries. It has thirty-five full page illustrations of the author, including Postures for Beginners, Main Postures of

Yoga, and Postures for Advanced Students. You can order the second (e-book) edition of his book, *Yoga And Long Life*, from:

Yogi Gupta Society, Inc. (yogiguptasociety.org) - PUBLISHERS

YOGA AND YOGIC POWERS

by
YOGI GUPTA

Yogi Gupta Society, Inc. - PUBLISHERS
yogiguptasociety.org

Dedication

To all who aspire for a deeper friendship between the two great democracies on the earth, The Republic of the United States of America and The Republic of India.

Copyright

© 2014 Yogi Gupta Society, Inc.

All rights reserved

ISBN-13: 978-0615838564
ISBN-10: 0615838561

Manufactured in the United States of America

Preface to the Second Edition

The effect of the mind on the body is greater than the effect of the body on the mind. There is subconscious mind in every part of your body. Without the activity of the subconscious, the functions of the physical body are not possible.

The majority of bodily dysfunctions are caused by inharmonious thoughts and feelings, by negative thoughts, which send impurities into your bloodstream, then chronic and destructive conditions come into the body. Negative thoughts can originate in you or in somebody else and may find their way to you. Also, it may be a thought from previous lives which has finally blossomed due to suitable circumstances. *Yoga and Yogic Powers* tells how to transform mental patterns into physical form. You learn how to re-educate your subconscious. You learn the principles involved to exercise psychic influence on yourself, on anybody, on anyone anywhere in the world.

Certain parts of the Indian Vedas have only been transmitted from mouth to ear – never committed to writing. Those who partake of that knowledge are not many. There are twenty books composing the Veda of Psychic Phenomena – but the most esoteric teachings have been passed from mouth to ear. At present it is important that these teachings should be made available to people, including the people of the West. It was for this reason that Yogi Gupta wrote this book on the creation of psychic phenomena. It is an authoritative text because it was written by a genuine knower of the highest truth, a self-realized saint who has access to the reality beyond the world of mundane reality, beyond the veil of Maya.

In the fifty years since it was first published, this book has never been surpassed in English, or in any language for that matter, in its exposition of the laws and principles that are inherent in the use of the higher, subtle powers of Nature which make it possible for human beings to become their own creators, capable of having Nature do their bidding, rather than being slaves of Nature and destiny.

Every human being can rise above his dependency on fate, and recreate his world as he sees fit. To do this one must know the techniques the yogis have devised and used since time immemorial for the use of psychic force, to make it responsive to their needs. How this happens is admirably illustrated by many examples in *Yoga And Yogic Powers*.

The wish by the saints of India to make these teachings available to seekers in the West does not mean that this book divulges all the secrets that one needs to know in order to successfully engage one's higher mind in the service of one's purposes and goals in life. The reason is simple. The techniques of Psychic Treatment open up the door to unlimited power, and therefore should only be made accessible to those who will use them wisely and for the benefit of mankind. Therefore the full course of study that lays the foundation for the student to become an adept in the creation of psychic phenomena, psychic healing, must be studied under the direct guidance of a fully qualified teacher. The publisher of this edition, the Yogi Gupta Society, can direct the willing student to such teachers, who have been authorized by the Master to pass His teachings on to the people. You may avail yourself of such an opportunity by contacting the publisher at yogiguptasociety.org.

Yogi Gupta held classes and gave lectures throughout the world, and since 1954, almost exclusively across the United States and Canada, until his passing through Maha Samadhi on May 6, 2011. He developed a deeply devoted following in the United States of America of a small group of stalwart disciples who are now beginning to continue his great legacy. He is also the author of the outstanding book, *Yoga And Long Life*, which together with the efforts of a number of his disciples helped pave the way for the tremendous revolution in health standards in America that we have today, with more than sixteen million Americans practicing Hatha Yoga on a daily basis. He predicted at the beginning of the 21st century that in the next fifty years it would become common to develop the ability to create psychic phenomena. The republication of this book is meant to aid that process.

The Publishers

Introduction to First Edition

by MR. AND MRS. E. BIGOS *Directors of the Radhey Raman Yogic Center U.S.A.*

JUST AS the West has developed science, physics, radio, television, etc., similarly, the Hindu Yogis developed by their inner research, psychic powers, telepathy, thought transference, and mental broadcasting.

More than ever before, the forces of nature are pressing for the need of a closer relationship between the two countries, the United States of America and the Republic of India. The exchange of culture is the first step to the establishment of a true and lasting friendship between the two nations. Yogi Gupta has written this book in a sincere effort to achieve this goal.

This book reveals to the people of the United States of America the innermost thoughts of millions of Hindus, their way of life, and their mystic experiences. This book will certainly make Americans know and understand better the people of India, and thus prepare them for an enduring friendship.

Just as the people of India are learning chemistry, medicine and physical sciences from the West, many of them being invited to this country to learn the Western sciences, similarly the people of this country may avail themselves of the opportunity to share the treasures of the culture of the people of India and their experiences.

This book explains psychic powers taught and practiced by the Great Masters for the last 6,000 years, and these miracles are explained by the author in a most impressive and scientific method, best suited for the West.

The Orient is the home of mysteries and inner knowledge. The wise men came from the East when Christ was born. From the East comes the light. The sun rises in the East.

And in the East, the Wisdom of the Orient is still treasured, and still taught by the few, and to the few.

It is not easy for a person, especially a foreigner, to be admitted into the inner circle where these occult teachings are treasured. A visitor from the West can hardly reach the people that treasure the esoteric teachings and occult knowledge because he does not know how to give the right knock, and therefore he can hardly ever be admitted into that inner circle of the Great Teachers. Such tourists hardly ever meet the true Masters. They meet the people on the street who have fallen down from the high rank of the Great Masters.

With the advance of time, people in the West have been showing more and more interest in the occult teachings and the development of psychic powers; as a result of which there have come into existence a growing number of organizations which try to propagate Mental Science, Science of the Mind, Divine Science, faith healing, and Rosicrucian teaching, which are all rooted deep in the ancient occult teachings, taught and practiced by the Hindu Yogis.

This is the first book of its kind ever written to give inner insight into the thinking of the Hindu Yogis. It will serve a useful purpose in preparing the two democracies on this earth, the Republic of the United States of America, and the Republic of India, to come closer to each other than ever before, and help tighten the bond of friendship between the two great nations.

Yogi Gupta has been holding classes and lectures throughout the world, and since 1954, across the United States and Canada, in order to create closer ties between the Eastern and Western hemispheres. The author has developed a great following in the United States of America and other Western countries. He is the author of the renowned book, *Yoga And Long Life*.

The author is also the Director of the Yogi Gupta New York Center, Box 158, Times Square Station, New York City. He personally teaches the occult and esoteric wisdom to the students who participate in his classes and lectures.

AUTHOR'S PREFACE

IT WAS IN 1954 that I came to the United States of America in response to the request from my *Guru*, who is no longer in a physical body (but can materialize into a human body at will). His guidance and instructions always come to me through an invisible source. It was on one evening in Gorakhpur, situated in the northern part of India, in the Himalayan range, that my *Guru* called me and told me that I should go to the Western Hemisphere, in general, and the United States of America in particular, to disseminate the true teachings which have been so far known to the few. My *Guru* stated that now the West is ready and these teachings should be fully imparted to them. He stated that people now have a strong will and desire for these teachings; and I must give them this light and instructions in the occult and esoteric, which they can use in their life.

For five years I studied the people of America, their way of life, their culture, and their needs, and it was in 1959 that finally I came to the conclusion that the people of the West should be freely initiated into these higher and occult teachings. Another reason for my decision to give these teachings was to set right certain truths misrepresented and wrongly interpreted in the West by many people who picked up scattered hints and fragments of true occult teaching, but did not succeed in grasping the true meaning and understanding of the esoteric teaching. I found that due to inadequate training many people were confused and harmed, rather than deriving any benefits from the little fragments of esoteric teachings which they learned here and there. I came to the conclusion that people should be initiated into the true teachings and the dangers of using scattered hints and fragments of esoteric teachings should be explained.

I found that many people derived their knowledge from various publications and articles, and did not have the first-hand opportunity of studying at the feet of a Great

Master. Personal instructions are an indispensable part of occult teachings because with the instruction goes the impulse from the teacher to the student, which books can never give. Without the living impulse and psychic give-and-take, a person can hardly succeed in mastering occult knowledge.

Only a part of these teachings have been committed to writing, and they are found in the *Atharva Veda* (Scriptures of the Hindus). This *Atharva Veda* is known as "The Veda of Psychic Powers". It deals with the various techniques for the development of supernormal mental faculties, senses and powers.

Most of these teachings have never been committed to writing, but passed from mouth to ear, from teacher to disciple, without adulteration from the outside. These teachings have been kept completely pure and unaffected by external influences. There has been an increased demand for a book which would explain my system of teaching for the development of psychic powers best suited for the West, and due to this reason I decided to write this book.

The book will serve the great purpose of building a bridge between the East and the West. Thousands of Americans have become closer friends of mine through the dissemination and exchange of culture. Similarly, I have become a friend of countless people of this country, and I myself feel a part of them, deep within the heart of them.

YOGI GUPTA

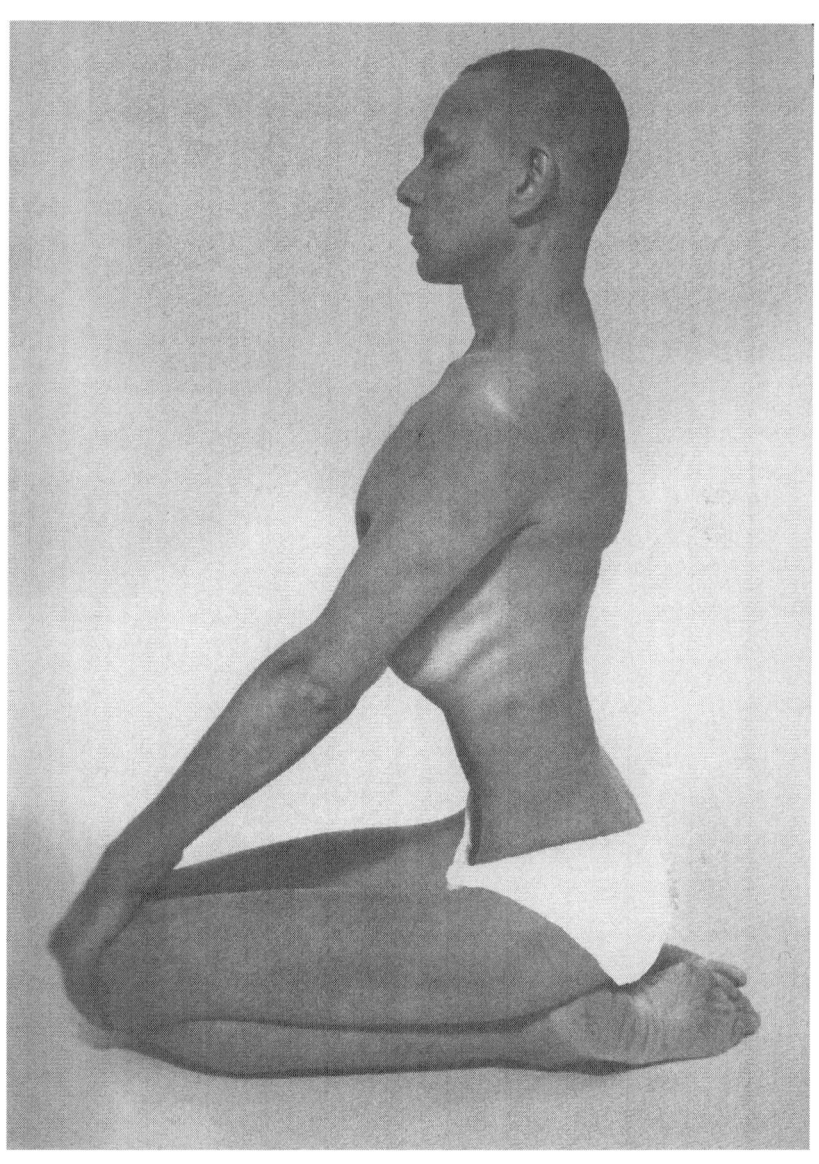

Illustration 1. *Vajrasana*: The Adamantine Posture.

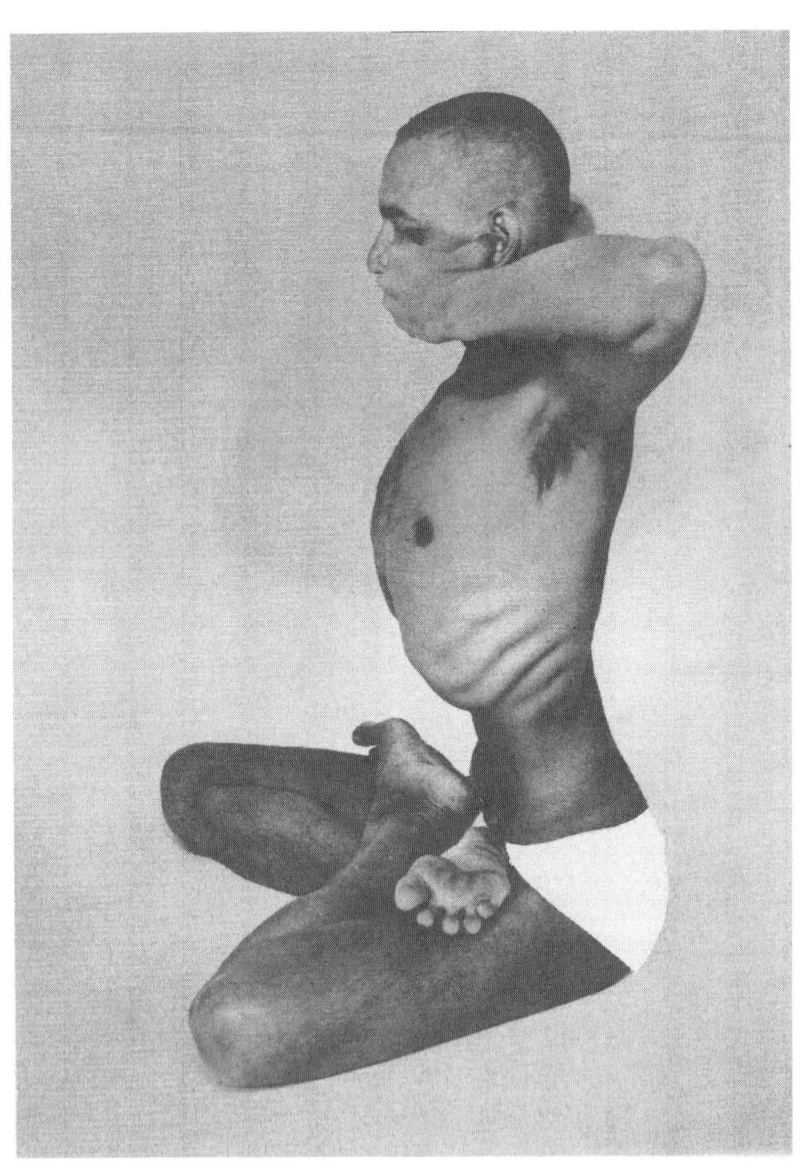

Illustration 2. *Nadi*-Vibrator *Pranayama*.

Illustration 3. The Author
a Wandering Monk.

Illustration 4. The Author a Missionary.

THE SIGNIFICANCE OF THE AUTHOR'S PICTURES

THE THREE STRIPES on the forehead and on the arm signify three states of consciousness. The waking state, the dream state, and the state of sleep.

In the waking state, the mind functions through the body and senses, and a person is aware of the world and his own physical existence.

The second state is the dream state. During dream, the mind functions independently of the body and senses, and as such, whatever you experience and see during dream appears true, and you are not aware of the existence of your body and the world during that period. When you awaken, you find that the dream was false and a delusion, and that only the world is true.

During the third state of sleep, you are neither aware of the world nor yourself, nor of the dream state; your consciousness is merged in ignorance.

All these three states of consciousness signify the changing phenomena created by the changing positions of the mind itself.

The rounded dart on the forehead signifies the fourth state of consciousness — the consciousness of Truth — by achieving which, you can watch and observe the three states of awareness while you remain detached from the changing phenomena. The fourth state of consciousness is unchanging.

The rosary around the neck of the author is an important item, given to him by his *Guru* at the time of his initiation, for the repetition of the *Guru Mantra*, which will be described in detail later on.

The begging bowl in the hand of the author signifies that he is a renunciate. A renunciate is a Hindu Yogi ordained into the Holy Order of *Sanyasa*. This begging bowl is made of the outer shell of a coconut. It is used to carry food and water, and also to accept alms from devotees.

The staff in his hand is carried by the author to help him climb the steep Himalayan peaks on which the *Kailashananda* Mission is located, and of which the author is the founder and lifetime minister-in-charge.

The author is returning after taking a bath in the Holy Ganges, which flows in front of the Mission, and practically surrounds the Mission on three sides amidst the scenic Himalayan panorama.

The orange robe which the author wraps around his waist and arms is the official dress of a Monk. The life of an ordained *Sanyasin* differs from that of worldly people inasmuch as he follows the path of renunciation (*Nivritti Marga*), while for the people of the world, the path of spiritual enlightenment is through *Pravritti Marga*, which means realization of the Truth under the guidance of their spiritual *Preceptor*, while living as a worldly person. At the time of renunciation a ceremony is held; an important part of it consists in the taking of certain vows by the renunciate, by which he has to abide during the rest of his life.

Below are a few of the vows taken by a renunciate. I am writing them with the idea of giving you an insight into the personal life of the author.

1. Do not cook your food, nor should it come in contact with fire.
2. Do not keep or possess such things as would bring about attachment to the world.
3. Initiate at least one disciple into the Holy Order of *Sanyasa*, after teaching him all the truths which were taught to you by your *Guru*. A monk may have more than one disciple, but he must ordain at least one so

that the ancient teachings may not die. Most of the esoteric and occult knowledge has been kept alive from teacher to student during the last 6,000 years without any adulteration. Most of the secret doctrines and teachings have been prohibited to be put into writing for the fear of being passed on to people who might misuse them, and therefore they have been remembered by adepts by heart, and in due course, passed on to their worthy disciples.

4. After the day of renunciation, do not keep any connection with relatives and parents.
5. Do not tell your age and your former name, or any information personal to you. At the time of ordination the disciple receives a new name from his teacher, which signifies that he is born twice. Twice-born means awakened into the awareness of Truth, and dead to the awareness of body. This is also known as the resurrection.
6. Lead the life of a *Parivrajaka* (a wandering monk) for some time in the beginning; then stay in one place, if so desired. The *Sanyasin*, is a ripe fruit, the product of the culmination of progress in discipline, refinement and culture of the early stages in his life, and therefore he is worthy of this mature and crowning state.
7. He should have a clean-shaven head, in order to save time used for stylish machine cuttings.
8. He should not sleep in another's house at night, and as far as possible after visiting, he should return to his own place to sleep.
9. Do not sleep on a soft bed, as it disturbs the healthy condition of the spine and body.
10. When accepting alms, do not touch the hands of the person who gives alms, in order to maintain the high degree of sensitivity, on which the vibrations of others will register.

11. He should not become a part of a social, political or any other secular organization.
12. He should not care for public opinion, or the advice of the devotees.
13. He should follow the command of his inner inspiration which comes from Divine Will.
14. He should not ask for advice or guidance from anyone, and should look for Divine Guidance within.
15. He should not be a permanent dependent upon a particular devotee, and should freely accept help from all who want to help his work—of course, without any strings attached to such help.
16. He should not show his psychic powers or power of psychic healing. Nor should he agree to give a treatment to anyone whenever anyone tells his troubles and sickness. Whenever he learns about the ailments of others, he should help them quietly.
17. He should not try to please anybody by doing a work which he himself does not approve of, although the devotee or such person may withdraw support to his work, or may stop giving alms.
18. He should not teach or advise anyone though he may need it, unless he comes to you and asks your advice and teaching.
19. He should not exhibit his psychic and spiritual powers.
20. He should abide in an awareness which is eternal and homogeneous essence of cosmic consciousness.

Contents

About the Author ii
Dedication v
Preface to the Second Edition vii
Introduction to First Edition x
AUTHOR'S PREFACE xiii
THE SIGNIFICANCE OF THE AUTHOR'S PICTURES xix

1	MIRACLES OF THE MIND	27
2	POLARIZATION	33
3	PHYSICAL CONDITIONS FROM MENTAL PATTERNS	41
4	SUPERSENSORY PERCEPTION	47
5	PSYCHIC ANESTHESIA	57
6	MATERIALIZATION OF OBJECTS	63
7	SAINTS WITH YOGIC POWERS	69
8	GREAT MASTERS MATERIALIZE AT WILL	77
9	THE YOGI PRECEPTOR	83
10	THE POWER OF MANTRAS	89
11	GURU MANTRAM	97
12	PRINCIPLES OF PSYCHIC PHENOMENA	105
13	THOUGHTS ARE THINGS	107
14	MIND OVER MIND	111
15	TAP YOUR SUBCONSCIOUS	117

16	PSYCHIC PERCEPTION AND ASTRAL SENSES	127
17	THOUGHT FORMS AND ASTRAL PICTURES	131
18	FAME AND FORTUNE BY PSYCHIC MEANS	139
19	PSYCHIC INFLUENCE TO WIN FRIENDS	145
20	MIRACLES OF PSYCHIC S.O.S.	151
21	YOUR PSYCHIC INCOME	157
22	PSYCHIC TELEGRAM	161
23	ETHERIC RECORDS	167
24	YOUR PSYCHIC ALARM CLOCK	173
25	ASTRAL TELESCOPE	181
26	WHEN YOUR THOUGHTS BECOME THINGS	185
27	PHYSICAL DISEASES AND MENTAL PROCESS	189
28	IMPULSIVE URGE FOR WRONGDOING	197
29	PROTECTIVE AURA AGAINST PSYCHIC ATTACKS	203
30	MENTAL PROJECTION AND PSYCHIC PROPULSION	209
31	THIS CAN BE THE MOST SUCCESSFUL YEAR IN YOUR LIFE	213
32	SECRET OF YOUR PROGRESS	219

33	EMOTION, THOUGHT AND MENTAL PROCESS	225
34	REVELATION OF ASTRAL JOURNEYS	231
35	YOUR GUARDIAN ANGEL	241
36	MIND'S AND SOUL'S LIFE IN SPACE	247
37	DO MASTERS CONTROL WORLD DESTINY?	253
38	FALLING IN PSYCHIC RHYTHM	261
39	TWO-MONTH COURSE IN PSYCHIC PHENOMENA	271
40	TWO YEAR COURSE IN DIVINE PERCEPTION	283

Chapter 1 MIRACLES OF THE MIND

THERE IS NOTHING in the world where mind does not exist. Mind is a subtle vibration not perceived by physical eyes. It is noticed only when it materializes into things, objects, actions, or physical conditions. Thoughts are as true as cars and houses. All objects—solid, liquid and gaseous—contain mind. Every cell in the body has life and mind. Wherever there is life, there is mind. Wherever there is mind, there is life. Wherever in your body there is blood, there is both life and mind.

The Yogis discovered in their inner research the existence of mind in everything, and that was the secret of the miraculous powers which they manifested not only in the control of matter, but also in the creation of phenomena. It is not a question of mind over matter, but it is a question of mind over mind. The difference in mind and matter is not one of kind, but only one of degree.

The human mind is positive, affirmative, and has the power of discrimination and making decisions. On the other hand, the mind in matter and the mind in the cells and organs of the human body, is negative, or an inferior mind. The secret of the power of mind lies in reaching the inferior mind and consciously controlling it and directing it consciously according to your needs and desires.

In the prebiotic age, there was no earth other than gases. Then came into existence the ocean, the earth and vegetation. According to scientific studies, life came into existence from matter. Human beings, animals, fish and reptiles would never have come into existence if matter had not existed before.

According to the research done by the Yogis in their inner communion, they discovered that life and mind always existed, even before the evolution of the world. Mind existed in a form invisible to the physical eye. It is this mind which has been constantly working and is still working and molding the world toward its ultimate pattern. The world is still in the process of being molded towards its final pattern. The visible world we see today is a counterpart of the invisible world which existed in the mind of the Great Cosmic Being. It is these higher forces of mind which help the creation and materialization of the world, and every minute of our life, these forces are molding the world towards its final destination.

According to a scientist, the earth is under the influence of outer space. These influences on earth act in the form of vibrations which scientists call by the name of actinic rays. The actinic rays are different from rays of light. Scientific studies have disclosed that these actinic rays make a seed grow into a plant, and subsequently into a tree to make flowers and fruits. The actinic rays are much more subtle than rays of light, and they continuously work on the whole phenomena helping it to assume form and shape according to the mental pattern of the earth which exists in the Great Cosmic Mind. The whole of space is filled with mind and intelligence.

When you know and understand the working process of the law of mind which is known as the law of psychic attraction, you will be able to reach the mind in the cells, the mind in parts of your body, and also the mind in physical and material objects. Only then will you be able to manifest the miraculous powers manifested by the Great Masters.

The law of psychic attraction is as good as the law of gravity or the law of electricity. If there is any will of God, then the law of mental attraction and the law of gravity are manifestations of the will of God.

Only recently has the West awakened to the power of the mind. The law of mental attraction has always existed and will always exist. If many people are not aware of the law of mental attraction and are not able to use the power of the mind, it does not mean that the law of mental attraction ceases to operate. If people cannot use the law of mental attraction, then this higher law of mind uses them. Just as the law of electricity always existed, if we had not discovered it, we would still be lighting our homes with candle light instead of electricity, but electricity would always be in the world. Similarly, the law of mental attraction is always operating, but we can only use it when we know how it works.

People who do not know and control the process of this higher law of mind, generally unconsciously, set into operation the forces of the higher mind in the wrong direction, thereby attracting to themselves wrong persons, objects and things, and similarly they are attracted to wrong persons and objects. It is for this reason that many people find themselves caught in adverse circumstances which they call misfortune, although it is the result of the wrong forces released by the person himself.

It is not a question of mind over matter, but a question of mind over mind. The only difference is one of kind. The brain mind is intelligent. It has the power of discrimination. It has the power to make decisions. On the other hand, the mind in the cells of your body, and the mind in matter, are inferior, and they can only work by instinct. The inferior mind cannot make its own decisions, but it can be very easily polarized to the human brain mind, and so it is very easy to direct and change.

All matter, all liquids, solids and gases have mind. According to a study of the prebiotic age, it has been revealed that living things were produced from matter. To an ordinary person it is unbelievable how life could emerge from matter. The true fact is that matter itself is full of life. Crystal formations are sound proof of the existence of mind in matter. Crystals form around the mental pattern prepared by the indwelling mind in the mother liquor. The crystalline substance materializes according to the pattern of the indwelling mind and the result is a uniform-shape production of crystals. It has also been discovered that this element of mind can be destroyed by putting harmful chemicals into the liquor. There is an element of sex in the liquor in which the crystal is formed, and by chemical treatment, sterilization can be achieved which prevents further formation of crystals.

Modern psychology informs us that the material particles in our brain are transformed, rearranged, reorganized, and set into motion and activity by our thoughts, and simultaneously, similar changes take place in the parts, organs and cells of your body. Thus, the thought pattern is reproduced into the mind of the cells in your body. As all matter has mind, the patterns of your thoughts are equally reproduced in the minds of objects and things which exist in this world. In order to explain the materialization of thought into physical phenomena, I would like to give the following example. If you place a handful of sand on the table in front of you and start to play a comedy on the violin, you can see through a magnifying glass that the particles of sand are picked up by the vibrations created from the sound emerging from the violin, and the particles of sand are rearranged, reorganized and set into a definite pattern. Then you start to play a tragedy on the violin and you can see the whole pattern of the particles of sand on the table being dismantled, rearranged, and reorganized into a different pattern. This is proof of living creation in matter through the power of mind expressed through the violin. Once you learn the process, it becomes simple to reach the mind in the cells of your body, as well as to reach the mind in matter, and thereby make changes in them. This is also known as the process of polarization.

There was once a big business man in Bombay, who due to poor sales in his grocery shop was on the brink of bankruptcy. When he learned and used the law of mental attraction, he was able to attract customers from far-off places. He was able to make the biggest sales of goods ever with which his store was stocked, and pay all his bills and his account books showed that all bills were paid and he had the greatest bank balance ever in the history of the store. Such is the power of your higher mind.

Another case to which I may refer, is that of a designer who could not get a financial backer for his work. By using the powers of mental attraction, he attracted the most suitable financier. It was the financier who found him rather than he searching for a financier. This was the cause of his success in life. To the Hindus, this knowledge is not new.

Teachings of psychic powers are not a part of religion or dogma, but deal with the process and techniques to evolve the powers of the mind in any person.

Chapter 2 POLARIZATION

THE POLARIZATION of the molecules or particles of matter from which an article is made arises from purely natural laws. This polarization takes its character from the property of your mind. Articles such as steel tools, razors, knives, etc., undergo a similar process of polarization because they acquire a certain character derived from their habitual user. This is the main reason why tools will do better work for their habitual user than for any other person. If the owner of an article, object, or tool, does not like your using that object, then the mind in the object itself shares the view of its owner, and therefore it would resist your using it. The mind in such object will react like the mind of its own master. This is the reason when a person uses an instrument or object belonging to another person, against his will, there is always a possibility of his being hurt in the process. For example, if you start shaving with a razor belonging to your friend, against his will, you may find more cuts and bruises on your face; while on the other hand, if you use it with the permission of the owner, you may have none.

The process of polarization is also called psychologizing. The Great Teachers sometimes polarize an ornament or piece of jewelry by their strong, and positive thought patterns. In the process of polarization, the thought patterns of the *Guru* are reproduced into the inferior mind of the gold and silver, or any other metal from which the piece of jewelry or ornament has been made.

When the jewelry has been polarized, it is known as an Amulet or Talisman, due to the miraculous magic-like powers which it contains. In many cases, a Talisman is polarized in order to exercise a specific type of influence for the well-being of the person for whom it is prepared. The Talisman is especially made to suit the personality of the person and to meet his particular requirements. Therefore it should be strictly used by the person for whom it has been made by the *Guru*. If the Talisman is used by a person other than the one for whom it was made, it would not work. A *Guru* may make a Talisman to help the disciple in his spiritual growth, or to protect his physical and mental health, by his spiritual powers. Talismans are also made for a disciple's prosperity and well-being. Talismans, due to the power of psychologizing which they have received from the *Guru*, can exert psychologizing influences upon other persons who come within the jurisdiction of the influences which radiate from the Talismans in the form of vibrations. A Talisman can prevent and neutralize the negative and harmful astrological influences upon a person, which sometimes bring disease, miseries, misfortune, loss of a friend, etc. The negative astrological influences radiate from outer space towards the person on this earth. Such influences are determined by the *Karmas* of the past lives of the person himself. These *Karmas* are the thought images and astro-mental images created in past lives, which still continue to exist in outer space, and exert good and bad psychologizing influences upon the person. These influences from outer space also come from the thoughts of your friends and enemies who do not exist any more in the physical body.

A Talisman is charged by the *Guru* with a specific formula to solve a specific problem and to bring a specific result for a specific person. Each formula is a thought energized by the *Guru* and seeded deep into the heart of the Talisman. The Talisman is like a friend who is alive and is always by your side no matter where you are, and is always ready to help you in adversity and in times of difficulty. Just as an electric rod which is fitted in a building prevents the destruction of the building from a thunderbolt by absorbing the electric shock in the rod and passing it deep into the heart of the earth, thus saving the building from complete destruction, exactly in the same way, a Talisman absorbs the harmful astrological influences from outer space, as well as the negative thought vibrations and influences from people and objects all around you, and keeps you in the sanctuary of positive and peaceful vibrations. The Talisman attracts, absorbs, and finally neutralizes all the harmful influences which are directed at you from any source. A Talisman is prepared by a *Guru*, who is also known as a Spiritual *Preceptor* or a Spiritual Guide.

As influences, good and bad, come from outer space, they similarly come from your environment and persons and objects amid whom you live and work. For example, if you start to live in an apartment which was occupied by people full of negative thoughts and criminal intentions, you will find yourself very uncomfortable. The particles in matter such as the wall, furniture, beddings, lamps, all absorb the criminal intent and negative thoughts from the persons who occupied the apartment, and then they radiate to you. The result is that you may find yourself in the tight grip of negative thoughts, and you may have an irresistible urge to do the wrong thing. Numerous crimes, suicides, murders, robberies, etc., are committed by innocent people when they are under the grip of negative thought waves which radiate from objects, persons, and matter. A Talisman can neutralize such harmful influences by creating a "protective psychic ring-pass-not" around you in the form of the vibrations radiating from the Talisman which has been especially charged for such results. You might have seen the searchlights on the high towers at airports and also on skyscrapers which continuously radiate rays of light in order to dispel the darkness. The positive vibrations emanating from the Talisman radiate psychologizing influences to neutralize the harmful thought vibrations, and thus they help your safety, health, and long life. The person who is protected by a Talisman lives under the wings of the Talisman just as a little chicken is protected under the wings of the mother hen.

The heart of the Amulet is the most sacred part and should not be disturbed or opened due to curiosity by the person to whom it is given. Just like a novice or a layman can disturb the functioning of the inner machinery of a radio or a watch by opening it, similarly by opening the heart of the Amulet its process of radiation can be disturbed. The heart of a Talisman is very sensitive and as such should never be opened and exposed to external vibrations and thoughts in order to let it function efficiently.

When I had perfected the nine types of Yoga, I was ordained as a Swami (Monk) of the Holy Order of *Sanyasa*. When I was ready, my *Guru* initiated me into the process of polarization and preparation of a Talisman. When I achieved self-realization, I became an intimate disciple of my *Guru*, and he treated me as his close friend and associate. Since then, I became very casual with the *Guru* and treated him as my companion. When I was alone with the *Guru*, all the codes of strict religious disciplines were relaxed. I always learned from the presence of my *Guru*, rather than from books. My *Guru* always lit the love of God in the chamber of my heart by his very presence, from the very beginning when I started to study with him. My soul and spirit would be brightened in his holy company. Before I became a friend of my *Guru*, I would not even dare to think of treating him as my friend and committing frivolities in the presence of a Great Maker, especially when I had the proof of his great powers and the miraculous things he was able to perform in a split second by his mere wish.

When the *Guru* took me into his confidence, I used to help him in his spiritual work. At the request of my *Guru*, I would take charge of his followers across the world who were seeking his spiritual guidance and enlightenment, and I would maintain mental contact with them continuously.

Just as a rocket can be released to travel into space by remote control, similarly, thoughts are released by the mere power of will, to penetrate the layers of ethereal substance which occupy space, and establish contact with the desired person. Thoughts, once released into space, continue to maintain a magnetic invisible contact with the person whose thoughts they are, and also continuously exert influence upon the person towards whom they are directed. Mental contact between the *Guru* and disciple plays a very important part in the spiritual evolution of the latter.

My *Guru* used to prepare Amulets for the successful accomplishment of desired objects, to overcome obstacles in prosperity, to win over enemies, to gain immunity from unnatural death, to counteract evil psychic influence, to develop individual talents, for the attainment of worldly desires, for plenty of wealth and material prosperity, for relief from disease, death and danger, for attainment of *Atama Jnana* (spiritual enlightenment), for success in business, etc., to help his followers and guide them on the spiritual path once their bare necessities of life were satisfied. Many times the *Guru* would ask me to help him in the preparation of Amulets for the protection of his followers.

The *Guru* would give an Amulet only to those followers, who were very sincere and devoted, and the *Guru* would ask them not to tell others, because he never liked publicity about his miraculous psychic powers. The *Guru* would prepare Amulets for persons who were primarily interested in spiritual development and only secondarily in the attainment of material things, which they wanted to use to achieve their spiritual goals. The *Guru* always stressed that attainment of material success, prosperity and material gains should be used as a means for spiritual ends and to seek wisdom values in life, and not as an end in itself.

I learned *Yantra* Yoga because it enabled me to understand the use of the higher forces of Nature in the preparation of Talismans. In the preparation of a Talisman, the Psychic Formula, which is made of energized thoughts, is condensed into a psychic pattern which is embedded deep into the heart of the Amulet from where it continues to function and help the person to whom it is given, in the attainment of his desires. As a matter of fact, the result is embedded inside the heart of the Amulet in a subtle form, and by using the finer forces of Nature, it continues to materialize the energized thoughts into physical material forms and objects in the outside world, thus helping the person who owns the Amulet in the acquisition or physical possession of objects, created for him by the power of the Talisman.

A disciple must get thorough training in *Mantra* Yoga in order to be ready for initiation into the secrets of *Yantra* Yoga. In the preparation of the *Yantra*, the psychic pattern of the thought is inscribed on a piece of metal instead of being reproduced psychically. The *Guru* selects the metal for the plate which is conducive to the specific person. It is sometimes gold, silver, copper, zinc, iron, etc.

The *Guru* designs the shape and form of the metal plate, to be cut in a triangular, half-circular, or any other shape which will serve the purpose of the *Yantra* for a specific person to help him achieve specific results.

Sometimes the *Guru* may write the *Yantra* on a piece of paper with an ordinary pen, simply by reproducing the subtle psychic pattern on the paper and polarizing it with his energized thoughts.

The psychic formula in the Amulet exists in a form invisible to the physical, because it stays in the thought form which is made of vibrations, and therefore is very powerful. The cause is always stronger than the effect. The subtle is the cause, and the material is the effect. The physical world is the reproduction of the invisible world, which exists in the form of thought. Every object in physical form in the world is a counterpart of the object as it exists in psychic form.

The Amulet is the creation of the object in the psychic form, for a disciple or a student, so that it may naturally materialize into physical form objects, conditions, environment, happenings and events to satisfy his needs and his desires in life.

Chapter 3 PHYSICAL CONDITIONS FROM MENTAL PATTERNS

MODERN SCIENCE supports and admits that mental states, feelings and emotions are materialized in physical conditions. Depressing thoughts can affect the glands and make them secrete poisons into the blood, thereby affecting circulation, respiration, digestion, assimilation, elimination and nutrition. The mental patterns control your body chemistry by accelerating, slowing down, or completely stopping the function of specific glands. Thoughts can retard or accelerate the process of circulation, respiration, digestion, assimilation and elimination.

In a healthy condition, thoughts make the glands exude healthy secretions known as hormones, which help the person maintain his biochemical balance, and therefore enjoy sound physical and mental health and emotional stability.

Negative thoughts, such as thoughts of hatred, jealousy, fear, anger, insecurity, etc., make the glands secrete poisons into the blood, thereby neutralizing all the healthy chemicals in your blood which you might have taken in the form of food or supplements. A person may take ample rest, may live in fresh air, and eat the best nutritive food and supplemental food, including plenty of fresh juices from fruits and vegetables, but negative thoughts can neutralize and destroy all nutritive chemicals in the blood in a very short time. A person may have healthy and nutritive chemicals in his blood before he went to bed, but in the morning when he wakes up he may find himself very weak, nervous, shaky and deficient in nutrition. Such things happen when negative thoughts arise from the mind of a person.

In many cases the harmful and negative thoughts are not original ones, but have been absorbed from other people.

Thoughts travel in space and they are contagious. Most mental sicknesses are contagious because the mental sickness travels from one city to another, from one person to another, across space, in the form of thoughts.

Once a mother, when she was under the spell of anger and her blood was poisoned with the secretions from the glands, suckled her baby, and the baby died instantaneously. The baby got poisoned through the mother, whose body was saturated with the poison created in her body by thoughts of anger. Thoughts work through involuntary organs and the sympathetic nervous system. Thoughts radiate vibrations which are picked up by the nerve endings and then transmitted to the internal organs and glands.

A thought of fear can make the mouth dry by retarding the function of the salivary glands. A thought of worry can make the sweat glands accelerate the flow of sweat. A thought of sorrow makes the lacrimal glands secrete tears. The functions of all glands are controlled by your thoughts. Glands are the foundation of your health because they are your inner factories which create the chemicals for your blood.

By operating on your thought processes, you can control and direct your physical condition as you wish it to be and thus enjoy vibrant health and perpetual youth, emotional stability and peace of mind. If you do not know the process of thoughts, which is closely connected with psychic powers, there is always a likelihood that you are living a life of chance. Whatever you do, you take a chance, either you hit or miss. You can be sure and confident of the results in your life, environment and your health only when you have learned the working process of your thoughts. In many persons, the power of thought is on reverse, and the result is that they get just opposite of what they expect. In many cases, a person expecting a big profit in business, may find a heavy loss at the end of the year. A person instead of finding a friend in someone, may turn him hostile due to the simple reason that the power of thought is on reverse and therefore, instead of the psychic powers helping him on his path, they are taking him in the opposite direction. If you are driving a car and you leave the gear shift in reverse, your car will start to move backward when you drive, rather than taking you forward.

The power of your mind is very strong—it can bring you success, prosperity, friendship, or loss, diversity and animosity. The power of the mind always works; if it does not work for you, surely it works against you, because it is never neutral. If you are driving a car, the car must go forward or backward, it cannot stay still when it is being driven. You can stop a car by stepping on the brake, but not the mental forces which continue to function even when you sleep. It is this power which makes your blood circulate, your heart beat, your respiration work, and your food digest and assimilate, even when you sleep.

For the reasons mentioned above, it is very important to control these higher forces of nature and the psychic powers of the mind, otherwise they control you.

Many people do not know the process of the higher power of the mind and its function, and the result is that unconsciously the power stays in reverse and they create their own difficulties in life by attracting to themselves wrong persons and things.

Mahatma Gandhi by the power of his mind was able to reproduce his thoughts and his will into millions of people across the world. His will and thoughts would become the will and thoughts of millions of people and all would start to think and like Mahatma Gandhi. Just as a cuckoo lays her egg in the nest of other birds and makes them believe that it is theirs and so makes them hatch for her, similarly, thoughts are reproduced into another person's mind and he will start to think for you, to speak for you, and finally to act for you. Due to the higher powers of the mind of Mahatma Gandhi, numerous people would have the hunch of cutting telephone and telegraph wires and disrupting the train and other postal services at one and the same time in various parts of India during the time of civil disobedience. This gave a hard time to the officials of the British government to send troops to restore order through normal means of communication and transportation at the same time in different parts of the country. The result was that finally India was given freedom from British rule.

Thoughts are as true as houses and buses and they have form, color and force, which are determined by the nature of thoughts. Scientists are trying to translate into language the waves of thoughts emanating from the brain, but success has not yet been achieved in this field. When scientists are able to translate thought traveling in space into language, then they will be able to know the thoughts before they reach their destination.

For example, if a person is thinking of breaking into his neighbor's house, the scientist could translate his thoughts into language and have the police arrest him before he is physically able to break into the house. This is the reason why Yogis discovered in their inner research that the real action takes place in the mind rather than the world outside. All external and physical actions are only a reflection and result of the internal thoughts.

Many persons have used this knowledge in their business affairs, thereby causing tremendous improvement and success in their business conditions. It is your mental pattern and thoughts which create things, by which you acquire physical possessions in the world, in your everyday life.

Only those persons who learn and practice the process of materialization can use it for improving their physical conditions as well as financial conditions. You can also use the power of the mind for improving position, better promotions, improving conditions in business and attracting to yourself persons, friends and events you want in your life.

I myself use and practice every day the law of mental attraction and psychic powers, otherwise I would not be able to accomplish so much of my work, especially when I do all the work by myself. I attend personally to the daily mail, and also telephone calls, besides my regular classes and lectures across the United States and Canada. I seldom write letters or make calls on the phone. Most of my calls are made mentally. Mental broadcasting is more effective.

For example, I will give you one of the instances out of the numerous which take place every day. Sometime ago I decided to advertise my book in one of the leading health magazines in the United States of America, Immediately the thought was broadcasted mentally and the result was that the next day in the morning mail I received a letter from the editor of said magazine requesting me to consider advertising my book in his magazine. He also sent me all the other information needed for the advertisement, plus a specimen copy of the magazine and the details of his rates, etc. Thus, time and energy are saved in thought transference, and you are able to reach the right person no matter where he is. What happened in this case was that my thought of considering his magazine to advertise my book was released from my mind and it traveled across space and was picked up by the mind of the editor in the form of thought waves. Then my thoughts became his thoughts and he had an irresistible urge to write to me suggesting that I place an ad in his magazine.

Chapter 4 SUPERSENSORY PERCEPTION

SUPERSENSORY PERCEPTION is no longer a fairy tale. Now it has become a reality. Supersensory perception is as real and popular as cocktail parties for those who are able to experience and practice it. Just as you have physical senses, similarly you have astral senses. When you are able to perceive through your astral senses without using the physical senses, that is known as supersensory or extra-sensory perception.

An ordinary person in the world thinks that only those things which he can perceive physically are true, but that is not the truth. For example, when you are in the dream state, you are perceiving things different than things which exist in the world, without using your physical senses. You believe as real the things you see in a dream, and the things of the wakeful state of your mind are no longer a reality. But when you are awake, you find that the dream was false, and the real things are only those which you perceive through the physical senses while wide awake. But while you are asleep, the objects of the state of dream, as well as the objects which you perceive in the wide awake state, both do not exist. A person's consciousness is completely merged into nothingness.

Did you ever give thought to these changing states of mind and to changing perceptions taking place in different states? Did you ever try to know which of these various states are true? Did you ever try to know what perception should be believed and what disbelieved? The inquiry and reflection on these subjects belong to the search into internal mysteries about you and your own reality. Your eagerness to know these mysteries of nature and high truths casts doubts and shadows upon your own belief as to whether you are a physical being, or a mental, emotional and astral entity, or a part of a soul and the Spirit. These truths have guided numerous people on the Path of Truth amid the distracting world.

Long ago, a well-known king in India was sitting in *Darbar* (Session of Parliament) on his throne. The ministers of his *Darbar* were all busy in the proceedings and heated debate. The king felt a little drowsy and entered into the state of dream as he relaxed on the throne. During this state he was absolutely unaware of what was going on in the *Darbar*. He was in dreamland. During the dream he thought he was a beggar who did not have enough money to purchase food and clothing. During the dream he was staggering in poor health across the road to beg for clothes to protect him against the bitter cold. As he was crossing the road he was run over by a car and was seriously hurt. Due to profuse bleeding he became exhausted and could not move from the scene of the accident. He saw a Yogi coming to him who picked him up and carried him to the nearest dispensary. The Yogi asked the doctor in charge to take good care of the beggar, and gave the doctor a little money which he had at that time, and promised to give him more when he came back. In order to save the life of the beggar, the doctor decided to perform an operation upon him. The pain on the operating table was so great that the king could not tolerate it and he cried out. This was all in dream; the king was still sitting on the throne in *Darbar* rather than lying as a beggar on the operating table. As the king cried, everybody started to look at him on the throne. His whole body shook and his crown tumbled from the throne and rolled to the other end of the hall. Due to the pain the king experienced during the dream, tears flowed unceasingly from his eyes, thoroughly wetting his cheeks and dress. His ministers in the *Darbar* asked the king what was wrong. They asked him why he was weeping when he had a large army to protect him and a treasury full of wealth to back his commands.

The king replied, "If the army and wealth could help me, why did they not help me a few minutes ago, when I was a beggar and was being operated on to save my life? Unless I know the truth, my mind and soul cannot be at peace."

The king immediately left his kingdom, throne and wealth, in search of a *Guru*, who initiated him into the inner mysteries and realities of Truth, and the process of supersensory perception. After knowing the truth, which was knowing his own reality, the king returned to his kingdom and ruled the kingdom together with his wife and children for a long, long time.

Real power to see is not in the physical senses. This fact has been corroborated by scientists. According to science, there are brain centers where the actual experiencing of hearing, seeing, tasting, and smelling takes place. When a person is able to receive these thought vibrations independently of the physical senses, he is experiencing supersensory perception.

Man himself is a being made up of thoughts and emotions in his everlasting journey across space. The physical body is a temporary vehicle for the use of the inner man. The inner man never dies. The inner man survives the fall of the body. Lincoln, Washington, Milton, Shakespeare, Mahatma Gandhi, Christ, and numerous other notable figures of the past have not gone into oblivion. They have only lost their physical vehicle and they continue to function in the finer vehicle of emotion and thought. A person can learn the use of his astral senses which are a part of the mental and emotional vehicle, while he is still in this world in a physical body.

Everything visual, physical and material is the counterpart of astral and mental form. When you learn psychic perception through the astral senses, you are able to perceive things in their thought form before they are able to materialize into physical and material form.

Supersensory perception takes place in mental space (*Chittakasa*). Just as the five elements exist in the physical form, they also exist within you in the subtle form, which is invisible to physical eyes, and this is known as elemental space. Dreams are seen and experienced in elemental space (*Mahakasha*).

When a Yogi achieves the highest spiritual evolution, he is able to perceive everything physical and material in the highest plane of consciousness, known as knowledge space (*Chidakasha*).

All physical perception is a reaction to action from the outside world. Such experience in mental space is transmitted to the body through nerve impulses, and the body reacts. In this way, thoughts materialize into physical reactions.

For example, if you happen to see in dream your girlfriend whom you met two years ago in Miami Beach, this perception is not original. You see the girlfriend and the beach and everything that happened between you and her, while you are still dreaming in your own room, while you lie on the bed. The girl on the beach is surely not present inside your room, so where did the perception come from? If this is not the original perception, then it must be a reproduction of same. Whatever you do in your everyday life, every single phenomena is imprinted in your mental body just as a picture is printed on film. Whenever this mental film is projected on the screen of your mind, you are able to experience and visualize the same phenomena. You see characters and personalities on the screen in a movie, many of whom are no longer alive, but they are imprinted on the film and as soon as the film is projected on the screen, you see them before you, and the result is that as you become a part of the movie, you either laugh or cry, according to the impression of the film, depending on whether it is a comedy or a tragedy. This will allow you to understand with perfect clarity that the picture of the whole incident with your girlfriend and Miami Beach was imprinted into the fluidic substance known as your inner body or thought body, which, truly speaking, is everlasting and survives even death. During the dream, the sight of your girlfriend and Miami Beach was nothing but the projection of the scenery from your thought body and you were able to experience the phenomena as the result of which your whole body reacted. Thus a dream is a perception from the reaction to the sensations of the outside world long ago, but which have remained coiled up in seed form within your mental body known as *chitta*. *Chitta* is situated in your spiritual heart close to your soul. Your spiritual heart is in the center of your chest, on the right side of your physical heart. Its size is equal to that of your thumb; it is also known as *Hridaya Guha*.

During a dream these coiled subtle impressions of the past known as your *karmas* start to rise from your spiritual heart and project toward your brain in the form of a beam of vapor mixed with tiny atoms of light. As the impressions on film projected on the screen of a movie, via misty beams of light, start to take the forms and shapes of objects and persons when they come in contact with the screen, in exactly the same way, the beams of vapor-like substance mixed with tiny atoms of light (your thought body) project from your spiritual heart into your brain. Each particle of light in your thought body represents an impression of one of your past memories returning to life. As soon as these thought memories reach your brain during a dream, the sparkling atoms of light start to assume the forms of persons and objects, and accordingly, you start to dream. Thus a dream is the materialization of your past memories. The amount of happiness or unhappiness arising from the dream, depends upon the intensity of the memory of a pleasant or unpleasant incident in the past. The intensity of memory, however, doesn't depend on the seriousness of an incident in your past life or lives, but on the intensity of your reaction to that incident.

For example, if your reaction to an unhappy incident of a very serious nature in the past was very weak, then you will not feel very unhappy when you perceive the same incident repeated in a dream. On the other hand, if you reacted very strongly to an unhappy event of the past that was not serious in nature, you will still feel greatly distressed and depressed when you perceive this ordinary sad type of event reproduced during a dream. The depressing effects of such dreams may last for hours or days, depending on the seriousness of your reaction. If your reaction was very strong and you were seriously affected, you will find yourself emotionally shaken up, during the dream, and the contents of hormones and enzymes in your bloodstream will be greatly reduced, badly jeopardizing your health. This explains the process by which your past incidents (*karmas*) direct and mold your actions and environment.

Just like a little movie film in your pocket contains a big story which will last for over three hours on the movie screen, similarly, your fluid-like mental body preserves in seed form incidents and happenings from hundreds and thousands of years of the past. The Yogis call it the seed of your *Karmas*, which may have their roots in previous lives. Just like persons now dead can be seen on a movie screen, similarly the impressions of past lives can be experienced in this life. The coiled-up sensations of the past when you met your girlfriend on Miami Beach stayed in your mental body, but during the dream they were stirred up, thereby causing motion in the in-carrying fiber-like nerves in your system. This movement in the in-carrying nerves simultaneously sets into motion the molecules of the brain thereby making the experience in dream of an incident which happened long, long ago. These perceptions of dreams take place unconsciously. When you can experience these perceptions consciously without using the physical senses and nerve currents which carry the vibrations from outside to your brain centers, you are experiencing extra-sensory perception.

When the sensations are carried through the astral channels, the perception is in mental space. When the sensations have gone beyond the astral channels which open into the brain centers, the perception is in the knowledge space. Your higher mind has the power to react and send news in the form of thought waves independent of your sympathetic and parasympathetic nerves, and similarly, it has the ability to receive thought currents, and this is the experience of extra-sensory perception.

An Adept can prevent things from happening in the future simply by changing the psychic pattern which would materialize into a physical phenomena. This is the reason that an Adept and a Yogi controls his environment.

He does not live the life of adjustment because he has the power to change happenings, events and things by changing the mental patterns which are the cause of physical conditions.

Man is the superior-most being on this earth because he is the only one who is endowed with psychic powers, although many people are not able to use them consciously. By the use of supersensory perception, one is able to discard the use of the physical as an instrument for perception. Due to this ability of man, he is respected and known as the image of God. The Highest Cosmic Intelligence created this world after its thought image so you can make or unmake the world, and change your destiny as you want it to be by the power of the higher mind and extra-sensory perception.

When a person perceives in mental space, his consciousness is in *Sushumna* (the astral channel in the spinal cord). When consciousness reaches the pituitary gland, the perception is in the knowledge space. When a person is able to experience in the knowledge space, all transcendental and intuitive knowledge comes to him.

The plane of consciousness changes with the rate of vibration of the mind. The pituitary and the pineal glands play an important part in determining the plane of consciousness. The pituitary and pineal glands contain brain particles which are similar to those of the sand particles and they continuously radiate vibrations, which register like sound, like short and long wave lengths. The change of wave length brings the change of awareness and attaches the mind to the plane of consciousness, the dream state, waking, sleep state, and extra-sensory perception.

Your perception of the thought waves that come in contact with the *Chitta* (the mind-stuff) of another person, thereby creating Vrittis (thought waves) in his mind-stuff, and reproducing the thought projected to him, is extra-sensory perception.

Thoughts are transmitted across space like electricity, light, heat, and radio waves. In India people understand very well the significance of being in the company of a Yogi and a Holy Man, because it brings them peace of mind and inner happiness. This result is due to the fact that a Yogi radiates waves of positivity, strength, joy and happiness, which neutralize the thoughts of sickness, emotional upsets and other negative outlooks.

The Yogis have developed a perfect science by which they can consciously transform, rearrange, reorganize, and set into motion and activity the brain particles by their thoughts, and thereby they are consciously able to change the plane of consciousness and enter into silence (*Samadhi*) and experience the peace that passeth all understanding.

The aroused state of mind brings a similar change into the physical condition. My patient in Bombay told me that since he was initiated into the truths of extra-sensory perception, he was able to arouse in his state of mind such a strong positivity, that it would neutralize the poisonous chemicals in his body, and he was able to discard his cancerous growth in a very, very short time. State of mind brings changes into the function of the glands, and thereby biochemical changes into your blood, causing health or disease, according to your state of mind.

Chapter 5 PSYCHIC ANESTHESIA

THE MIND is energy. The function of mind can be noted only when there are thoughts. In other words, mind is the process of thought registration. The mind cannot exist without thoughts, and thoughts are vibrations of energy which register within you.

When you control your thoughts, you can control your mind. Thoughts bring awareness. A man is aware of what he thinks. He experiences what he is aware of, and he lives what he experiences.

For example, if you think and become aware of an incident which happened ten years ago in your life, you can experience the whole thing again, and thus you can relive that period, or even part of your life. By this process, one can relive the sad or happy occasions of his life, again and again.

Yogis are able to discover in their inner research the effect of thoughts and their function within, and thereby they develop a scientific system of attaching and detaching the mind from one part of the body to the other, and from one part of the world to the other, consciously.

Pain in any part of the body is simply the awareness of the pain. If you can withdraw your mind from the ailing part of the body, you experience no pain. The conscious withdrawal of the mind gives one control over experiences, and also gives immunity to pain. If a person who is undergoing surgery on a certain part of his body consciously withdraws his awareness from that part of his body, he will never suffer the pains of the operation because he is able to stop the flow of impulses to and from the organ being operated.

The real suffering takes place in the mind rather than in the body. If the person did suffer in the body, he would still suffer when his body falls. A dead body does not suffer post mortem because the power which suffers, that is the mind, does not exist in the dead body—therefore it is immune to pain. The Adepts and Great Masters are able to withdraw their mind from the body and live in the awareness of their psychic and astral vehicle, and thereby they achieve immunity to pain.

When Christ was crucified, he did not suffer pain because he was dead to the awareness of the body, and he was awake to the awareness of the Spirit.

A person who has a pain in his leg will suffer while he is awake, but when he is asleep he does not suffer, simply because he is no longer aware of his physical body, and the pain is in the physical, not in his astral and psychic body, which is the true person within.

On a cold night you may be sleeping in a heated apartment under an electric blanket which keeps you fully warm, still in a dream you may be freezing in the icy-cold blizzard outside on the street. During the dream you may find yourself on the street and the result will be that although you are lying under an electric blanket, still your whole body will be affected as though you were exposed to the snow storm, and in the morning you will find that you are weak and exhausted as if you had been exposed to the storm. Such is the power of the mind. The mind was able to detach itself from your warm, heated apartment, and attach itself to the snow storm on the street, and thereby it made you suffer.

Pain and pleasure are all felt in the mind and not in your body. When you can withdraw your mind at will from the ailing part of your body, this is psychic anesthesia. Hypnosis is as different from psychic anesthesia, taught and practiced by the Yogis, as day is from night, as darkness differs from light, and heat from cold. In hypnosis a person's will power is overcome by another person of stronger will, thereby making the will of the subject weaker and weaker, day by day; while on the other hand, the Yogis develop their power of will and thereby are able to master their thought and mind. Finally they are able to attach and detach their mind from any part of the body, and also from the world outside, whenever they want.

Mind is just like electricity, which can be used for refrigeration, heating, air conditioning, cooking, shaving, dish washing, drying, cleaning, vacuuming, etc. When the mind is attached to the eyes, it starts to see, when attached to the ears, starts to hear, to the nose starts to smell, to the tongue starts to taste, when attached to the skin starts to feel hot and cold. Sometimes you might have noticed that you are not aware of the sound created by the steps of an incoming guest because you are absorbed in reading the newspaper or an interesting article in a magazine, because your mind was attached through the eyes to the newspaper, and was not attached to your ears which could not hear the sound created by the steps of the incoming guest.

An Adept can attach and detach his mind at will, and although he may be looking at the face of a person, he may still be looking at nothingness. A person may call such a look a blank gaze. Due to control of the mind, an Adept can consciously be at rest and bring on suspended animation of the heart or of any other involuntary organ of his body. The process of digestion, assimilation and elimination can be consciously retarded, stopped, or accelerated by the control of mind. Mind can be consciously detached from one's own body and projected into the body of somebody else across space. When you learn how to operate the mental switchboard, control of the mind becomes like the control of a switchboard.

The circulation of the blood follows your thought; where your thought goes, the blood follows, and the blood is the carrier of energy and awareness. For example, when somebody remarks to a girl that she is beautiful, the result is that she immediately blushes. What caused her cheeks to blush when she was addressed as beautiful? She immediately thought of her cheeks and face, followed by a big rush of blood to her face, making her cheeks blush. Similarly, the withdrawal of awareness from a part of the body brings automatic withdrawal of the circulation of blood and thereby the withdrawal of consciousness and awareness from that part of the body, and this is called psychic anesthesia.

When a part of the body does not have awareness, then it is never affected by the consequences which would affect it in ordinary circumstances of life when a person is aware of the incident.

Sometime ago, a person was repairing a straw roof as a precaution against the heavy months of rain in India. He was sitting on the straw roof and inserted a piece of rope into the thatch so that he could make a knot tying the straw thatch to the wooden pole below to prevent it from being blown by the monsoon storm. As he could not see the wooden pole which supported the thatch below, he inserted both hands through the thick layers of straw and was trying to feel for the wooden pole to fasten the rope. During his efforts, he unfortunately grabbed two ends of a big cobra hanging on the pole instead of the rope. He tied them tightly around the pole. During this period the cobra bit him three or four times, but the person was not in the least aware of the existence of the bite of the cobra. He attributed the bleeding caused by the bite of the cobra to the scratching of the dry straw. He continued to repair his straw roof for the full day and retired in the evening to his home. He continued to enjoy his happy family life for the next three years.

After three years the straw roof again needed repairing and he had to untie the ropes which fastened the thatch to the wooden poles under the roof. During his work, he found that he had used a live cobra as a rope to fasten the straw roof to the pole. He recollected the bleeding in his hand and realized it was caused by the bite of the cobra and not the scratches of the straw. Immediately, his awareness of this fact aroused a state of mind which brought a similar biochemical change into his blood. His whole system became poisoned and he died instantaneously. Such is the power of your awareness.

Due to unawareness, he was able to check the venom of the cobra from spreading into his system and causing him death; while the return of the awareness immediately caused the venom of the cobra to intensify its action, thereby causing sudden death.

Chapter 6 MATERIALIZATION OF OBJECTS

IN THE PROCESS of materialization, there is nothing supernatural. It is strictly based on natural laws and principles. Materialization is caused by using the higher and finer forces of Nature used by Cosmic Consciousness in the pre-biotic age for the materialization of this world on which we live.

The process of materialization appears to be supernatural to a person who does not use this process for the materialization of the objects he wants to acquire in this world.

A strong will power and creative thoughts together with the release of psychic forces help the materialization of thoughts into physical material objects. An Adept is able to hold his mental pattern with the power of his strong will in a firm position during the period of materialization.

One can make his thoughts materialize into the mind of another person making him speak and act in his favor. The person can use space as an instrument for materialization. The thoughts, combined with will power, attract and select the atoms and minute particles of the astral substance which fill space and give them shape and color to further their materialization into a physical object. Everything in this world is made of the ethereal substance which is finer than the ether known to science, and which fills all space. Everything — solid, liquid, and gaseous — is made from this ethereal substance.

If you take a piece of gold or a diamond and put it into specific chemicals, everything will be turned into smoke, and the gold or diamond will be converted back into ethereal substance. In other words, all matter, solid and liquid, is nothing but ethereal substance held together at certain rates of vibration which allow it to stay in the form of matter. Even scientists corroborate the fact that everything in the world, solid and liquid, physical and material, is nothing but vibrations. The difference between one object and another is not of kind, but of degree of vibration.

Will and thought power have the effect of making the ethereal substance more gross and material, or more subtle and rarefied. The grosser thoughts reacting upon the ethereal substance make it heavier, grosser and weighty, thus bringing it closer and closer to the earth, and helping its materialization into physical objects. Thoughts also cause the rarefaction and purification of grosser physical and material objects, transforming them into a more subtle state of substance.

The lenses which you use in your eyeglasses, are nothing but ordinary stone rarefied in a scientific process. Ordinary stone in the process of rarefaction helps you to see things clearer and bigger than what you are able to see without glasses, or through the gross piece of glass. Scientists have proven that if the matter from which the lenses are made is further rarefied, it would become very subtle and inflammable.

Science has been able to convert matter into energy, to convert uranium and other various metals into atomic energy. But an Adept and a Yogi and the Great Masters who know the process of materialization can materialize at will physical and material things from the invisible ethereal substance. An Adept who has mastered the higher forces of Nature which materialized this world from the ethereal substance, by using the same process, is able to materialize things by his power of will and thoughts.

When a flower fades and dies, the fragrance never dies. It stays in the ethereal in an invisible form, simply to materialize again in the Spring when flowers bloom due to the functioning of the laws of Nature. An Adept, by controlling and using the higher forces of Nature can accelerate the process of materialization. He can cause the fragrance to materialize in a form that a person can smell.

There lived in India a Saint who was known as the Perfume Saint simply because he used to create perfumes at will. People would come to visit him at his hermitage and would express their desire to smell a perfume. The Saint would ask them what type of perfume they wanted to smell. Each person would name the perfume of his own liking. The Saint would release his forces of thought to help materialize the ethereal substance into the perfume, and each one of the visitors would smell the perfume of his own liking.

To a Westerner it appears miraculous and unbelievable, but to a Yogi there is nothing amazing in the whole process. It is simply the use of the finer forces of Nature by which he is able to bring changes into the ethereal substance and out of them create the things and objects of his desire.

The West is showing more and more interest now in this process of materialization. Not long ago in the United States, some scientists were able to make solid sugar and protein from the rays of the sun through scientific instruments. An Adept and a Master Yogi use the powers of the mind as an instrument for transforming the ethereal substance into the physical and material object of desire.

Scientists, "Men of Action", use matter as a base for their knowledge, and to discover their connection with the invisible forces and intelligence which exists in matter in the form of energy. On the other hand, Yogis, "Men of Contemplation", first study and research during meditation the causes and the finer invisible forces which become matter. As a result of this inner research, an Adept is able to create matter from invisible energy just as a scientist creates energy from matter.

The process of the transformation of energy into matter is known as the process of materialization, which is known and practiced by Yogis and their disciples.

A visitor from the West may be surprised to meet an Adept in India who by the power of his will creates phenomena and materializes objects. These things happen due to his use of natural laws. A newspaperman saw an Adept in India who opened his fist and flowers started to fall from his hand and formed a big heap of flowers on the earth. The Adept said, "These are the flowers from *Rameswaram* (a holy place in south India)."

The same newspaperman met another Adept who opened his hand and a stream of water started to flow from it, and continued till the Adept stopped it. These things seem to happen miraculously, but it is really Nature's way of materializing things using the forces of Nature.

Once my *Guru* was invited to a big feast given by a Saint known as *Swami Khatkhatananda*. For this feast, people were sent invitations to attend. Also, the feast was announced in the neighboring villages and cities by the beat of drum, and anyone could join the feast.

At the time of the feast, people swarming in from neighboring places looked like a large ocean of humanity. People could not conceive how Swami would be able to feed so many people, the number of which was unknown. It was not long before the storehouse of eatables was exhausted, while large crowds were still waiting to dine. My *Guru* told me that Swami used his psychic powers and the food kept on increasing in the storehouse, and everyone was fed.

The clarified butter in which many of the items were being fried, completely ran out. The storekeeper and cooks were scared when they found out that there was no clarified butter, and wondered how they would be able to cook the food for the large crowd waiting to dine. When Swami heard the sad news, he told his disciples to follow him to the river with big empty drums. Swami plunged the drums into the river and told the disciples to carry them to the kitchen, and said, "That will be the butter." As the disciples carried those drums, they found that they all contained clarified butter. The Swami transformed the water into clarified butter by psychic powers.

Psychic power comes automatically to the Yogis and the Masters in their search for spiritual enlightenment. There have been many Great Masters, and still are, who possess psychic powers. *Babaji* is one of the Masters who would materialize things at will. Once he materialized a large mansion of gold studded with diamonds.

Many Masters live and move on this earth in their invisible mental body to guide and help people seeking their help. On many occasions these Masters, materialize into physical form. These Masters are known as the *Siddhas* (Yogis with perfected powers).

Chapter 7 SAINTS WITH YOGIC POWERS

IN THIS CHAPTER, I would like to give you an insight into some of the happenings caused by the psychic powers of eminent Yogis.

Sadasiva was a well known Yogi from south India. Once he was in *Samadhi* (Holy Communion) for many years on the bank of the River *Cauvari*. During the flood, he was covered by the water of the river, for a long time, in the rainy season. At the end of the rainy season, the river left high mud swells on its bank and no trace of Yogi *Sadasiva* could be found, because he had been buried in the mud. After a long time, people started to cultivate the land on the bank of the river. One day, when the land was tilled, the plough hit the head of the Yogi. The cultivator removed the mud, and pulled the Yogi out of the earth. The Yogi just walked away.

On another occasion, a Yogi was wandering at random and happened to enter the harem of a Moslem family. They thought he had entered intentionally, and therefore they attacked the Yogi with a sword and severed one of his arms from his body. The Yogi came out of the harem, touched his arm and a new arm grew out immediately. The person who attacked the Yogi fell on his knees and asked for forgiveness. The Yogi forgave him and also blessed him, and went away. These are the psychic powers of an Adept.

Kabir has a great following in India. His teachings were liked by people, from all walks of life. He used to give instructions in the form of songs while he roamed the streets of India. India is considered a country where Gods walk on the street with human beings. One day *Kabir* was standing on the sidewalk of a busy industrial crossroad. It was evening. Thousands of people were returning from their offices and jobs. As *Kabir* stared at the ocean of humanity, tears started to fall from his eyes. People seeing the holy man weeping, asked him the reason. He gently replied with the following song:

"*Chalti Maki dekh ker diya kabira roy; ya jag bhitar aayker, Linda bacha nakoya.*"

which means:

"*This whole world is like a mill, and night and day the wheels of this machine are grinding and human beings are the grain in the mill.*"

"As the wheat gets ground into flour when it goes into the grinding machine, similarly every human being who comes into this grinding machine, whose wheels are grinding day and night, constantly running, gets ground to death. As I watch this ocean of humanity I see them all ground as they march towards their death. Not a single person is able to escape from this grinding machine except those who stick to the axle. The wheat which sticks to the root of the axle of the grinding machine never gets ground, although the wheels keep on turning. While the wheat which goes away from the axle gets powdered into flour. Similarly, human beings who stay closer to the Soul and God, and take refuge in the Soul, which is situated in the center of the spiritual heart, can overcome death and achieve resurrection of the spirit in this life, while those who externalize into the world get ground to death."

His teachings were very touching and sensitive and had direct appeal to the heart and mind of the common people of the street.

When *Kabir* forsook his body, some of his disciples wanted to cremate the body, while others wanted to bury it. The disciples could not come to a compromise, and therefore they decided to divide the body in two, half to be cremated, and half to be buried. As the disciples removed the coffin to divide the body, the whole body was transformed into a large heap of flowers. The disciples divided the flowers; they buried half and the other half, they cremated.

These are the ways in which Yogis make things happen by their mere wish, which sets the psychic powers into operation. Just as you press a button and a whole machine goes into operation, simply by the mere wish of a Yogi, the forces of Nature start to function and make things happen.

Jnanadev had full control over the five elements, and therefore the elements could not affect him. He placed himself in fire and was not burned. Such miraculous things happen during the use of psychic powers. A few years ago, many people saw some Yogis in Lotus Pose travelling in space to attend the *Kumbha Mela* held on the bank of the the Ganges every twelve years, when seekers of Truth flock there in search of a Great Master who might accept them as his disciple. These Yogis were levitating by psychic powers; they achieved mastery over the elements, and as such, the law of gravity does not operate on them.

Another well known Saint in India who lived mostly in *Benares*, was *Trilinga Swami*. He was seen living for over 280 years. Through psychic powers he had achieved mastery over the elements, and he would go to meditate on the bed of the Ganges River; sometimes he would be meditating deep inside the waters of the Ganges for more than six months at a time.

Once, when India was governed by the British people, the Governor of the Province came to see the *Benares Ghat* (the place where people take baths in the Ganges). *Trilinga Swami* happened to be there and he took a dare. The Swami took the sword of the Governor and threw it deep into the Ganges River. The Governor became embarrassed seeing the great Swami throw his sword away. The Governor asked the Swami to give the sword back to him. The

Swami dived into the river and came up with two swords, and asked the Governor to take his own sword. Both swords were 100% alike and the Governor did not know which one to take of the two. Finally, the Swami gave him the one. Here, Swami materialized a sword exactly similar to that of the Governor simply by his firm wish and psychic powers.

When I was studying with my *Guru* in the deep Himalayas, I had the great privilege of attending to the personal work of my *Guru*. My *Guru* would eat only uncooked food, generally fruits, leaves and root vegetables, which were available in the Himalayan forest in the neighborhood of his hermitage. I used to keep his place clean, and bring firewood from the jungle to keep the *Guru* warm at night. Naturally, the *Guru* would have more time for meditation, while I spent most of my time on the personal work of my *Guru*, which did not appear to be connected with my spiritual training. Although my *Guru* would not give me much instruction in Yoga practice in those days, still I improved very fast spiritually, because I made more time available to my *Guru* for meditation by attending to the personal work, which otherwise the *Guru* would have to do for himself. I became a partner in his spiritual wealth, and as such, I was getting part of the benefits received by the *Guru* by his own *Sadhana*.

One day as I was returning from the woods, I saw a dead sparrow lying near the abode of the *Guru*. Most probably it was attacked by a bird of prey, which ate away the vital parts of its body. In the evening after my *Guru* had finished his meditation, he called me to accompany him for a stroll towards a nearby stream in the Himalayas. He happened to see the dead sparrow. On my inquiry, the *Guru* told me that he used his psychic power so that the sparrow came back to life. It flew up and perched on his hand. It fluttered a little, and looked towards the *Guru*. The *Guru* with a movement of his hand directed it towards the trees where it would spend the rest of its life, and the bird flew away.

Such is the power of Great Masters who can transfer life into a dead thing and bring it back to life.

Yogi *Matsyendranath* was a great Yogi possessing psychic power. The Yogi told one of his disciples that the disciple would be blessed by a son, but that the Yogi would like to have that son when the son reached twelve years of age as he would like to accept the son as his disciple for teaching the knowledge and wisdom of Yoga. The disciples (who were husband and wife) agreed to give the son to the *Guru* at the age of twelve, if they were blessed by a son. A son was born to them and they gave it to the *Guru*. *Guru Matsyendranath* taught him the Yoga practice and gave him a new name, *Gorakhnath*. *Gorakhnath* lived an ascetic life and performed great Tapas (Yoga Practice). For twelve years he lived only on air. *Gorakhnath* developed tremendous Yoga powers. Once in *Kumbha Mela* on the bank of the River Godavari, he gave food to all the pilgrims. He asked everyone what they would like to eat. Then he told them to sit down on the sandy beach. The food came flying from nowhere across the sky descending in front of each person. Everyone got the food that he wanted. This food was materialized for all the people by the psychic power of *Guru Gorakhnath*. He was a Perfected Yogi and had many *Siddhies* (psychic powers). One of his disciples was King *Bharthari*.

Swami *Krishna Ashram* lived in an icy region near *Gangotri*, the origin of River Ganges near Tibet. He lived in a nudist state. He was also in *Rishikeshi*. Once he went into an almshouse for food where all the Swamis and Monks are provided free food. As a matter of rule, every Swami has to carry a begging bowl to take the food, but Swami *Krishna Ashram* did not bring any vessel for *Dhal* (pulses boiled and served very hot in liquid state with spices and clarified butter). The cook got mad at him and served the hot boiling *Dhal* on the hand of the Swami. The Swami immediately drank the *Dhal* through his lips. The hands of the Swami were scalded, but nothing happened to his lips and mouth. As he came out of the kitchen, his hands became all right. Swami had unbelievable powers of endurance.

Yogi *Bhusunda* was the Master of the Science of *Pranayama*. He could sit in *Samadhi* for any length of time. By practicing the five methods of Concentration, he was able to overcome the effects of the five elements. At the time of the dissolution of the world, when the whole world is burned and scorched by the burning rays he will live in the element of *Akasha*, through *Apas* (water) *Dharana*. When a fierce storm arises breaking the roofs to pieces, he will be in the *Akasha* through *Agni* (element of fire) *Dharana*. When the world is submerged in water, he will float through *Vayu* (air) *Dharana*. Due to his psychic powers, he was able to live for many hundreds of thousands of years in the same body. He was able to see the earth created many times before his eyes and dissolved back into energy.

Tirimolu Nayanar was a great Yogi who lived on Mt. Kailash near Tibet. He had acquired all the eight major *Siddhies* (psychic powers). Once he was wandering in the woods in south India. There he saw the dead body of a cowboy. He saw all his cows surrounding the dead body. It was sunset and the cows did not want to go home without the cowboy, who was lying dead. *Tirimolu Nayanar* pitied the cows. By psychic powers, he entered the dead body of the cowboy and drove all the cows home. Such is the power of the *Siddhas*.

Yogi *Milarepa* obtained transcendental knowledge in the control of the ethereal and spiritual nature of the mind which enabled him to fly through the sky. He could be seen walking and resting and sleeping in the air. At will, he could produce flames of fire and streams of water from his body. He would transform his body into any object desired, thereby convincing people and turning them towards the spiritual path. He was Master of the four stages of Meditation, *Padasth Dhyana, Pindastha Dhyana, Roopastha Dhyana*, and *Roopateet Dhyana*, and was able to project his subtle body into space, as a result of which he could multiply himself and would be present as a presiding Yogi in more than twenty-four holy places at one and the same time.

Chapter 8 GREAT MASTERS MATERIALIZE AT WILL

IT IS THE MIND and the spirit which shape the body. Just as water which is visible to the physical eyes, when heated becomes vapor and invisible to the eyes, and finally disappears in the form of vapor, similarly an Adept is able to transform the physical body made of matter into energy, as a scientist can transform a visible piece of uranium into invisible atomic energy.

Just as invisible vapor materializes into visible water, drops of rain, and drops of dew on flower petals and leaves, similarly an Adept materializes his invisible mental body into a physical body of flesh and bones by his mere wish.

In *Kailashananda* Mission, situated in the Himalayas in India, of which I am the founder and life-time president, live many *Siddhas* (Perfected Yogis) with accomplished psychic powers. They live there invisible to the naked eye, but they materialize at will when they want to. The Mission is situated on *Manikoot* Hills in *Rishikeshi*. It is the most sacred place for spiritual enlightenment. Many Yogis achieved spiritual enlightenment at this place. It is fully charged with spiritual vibrations which help a disciple to develop quickly on the spiritual path. Due to the spiritual significance of this place, many *Siddhas* live at the Mission.

Sometime ago I received a letter from my students at the Mission that one night they were frightened to see a tall person moving in the orchard in the moonlit midnight. The gardener and the watch guard considered him to be a thief who had come to steal fruits, chased him, but were surprised to find that the person disappeared leaving no trace of his presence. I replied that these are the *Siddhas* who look after the well-being of the Mission in my absence, and that they would not do any harm to them, that they were their protectors. I also congratulated them for getting a chance to have *Darshan* (a look) at the *Siddhas*, who are Great Masters controlling and directing the destiny of the world in an invisible way. My students in the Mission were happy to know this, and since that day lost their fear.

In 1957 I was guided to return to India for a short stay. I was also guided to establish *Kailashananda* Mission in the Himalayas to serve the people of India. The Mission has a Sanatorium where people are given treatment. It is situated amid the most scenic Himalayan peaks. It is air conditioned by nature because the Ganges surrounds the hill on which the Mission is situated, practically on three sides. The Mission has springs and streams of water. The streams bring all year around the melted snow from the Himalayan peaks.

The Mission has facilities for seekers of Truth to grow and develop their spiritual talents amid the spiritual environment. Pin-drop silence pervades the Mission.

It is situated deep in the Himalayan woods. In order to purchase the necessities of life, one has to cross the Ganges by ferry, and either walk on foot about a mile, or go by buggy to *Rishikeshi*, about two miles from the Mission. *Rishikeshi* is connected with a shuttle train to the *Haradwar* Railway Station. *Haradwar* is connected with railway lines to Calcutta, Bombay and New Delhi. From beyond *Rishikeshi*, a person has to go either on foot or by buggy to the Mission.

One can bring his car up to the River Ganges, and from there one has to take the ferry to reach the Mission. If one wants to come to the Mission all the way by car from New Delhi, one has to drive from New Delhi to *Haradwar*, and then cross the bridge across the Ganges at *Haradwar*, driving on a road which is used by the Forest Department, in the deep Himalayan woods. On this road one can drive straight into the Mission.

The main idea of creating the Mission was to create a dynamic center where the people of the West could go and stay for some time in the spiritual environment to achieve enlightenment.

The second idea in the creation of the Mission was to prevent the people of India from thinking that I had done nothing for the betterment and guidance of the people of India, my native country. People would think that I am giving my time and guidance to the Western world in preference to the people of India. Now sick and ailing people from every part of India can avail themselves of treatments at the Sanatorium, which is one of the Departments of the Mission. Thus, the people of India would get continuous help at the Mission, which will give them satisfaction and contentment.

An Adept and a Yogi exerts only his thoughts to achieve the guided results, instead of making physical efforts. An Adept makes *Satsankalp* (a firm wish) and the rest is achieved automatically.

I made a firm wish for the materialization of the *Kailashananda* Mission. I knew the type of land and environment I needed for the work.

Next day, a Holy Man walked all the way from his cave where he lived in the Himalayas to see me on the bank of the Ganges, when he heard that I had returned from the United States of America. I knew why he had been guided to be there, and I at once told him my plans.

He told me that he had seen deep in the woods exactly the type of place I needed; that it was quite near, but nobody knew of it, as it was difficult for any human being to penetrate the thick jungle and reach the place which was freely visited by wild animals. He told me that cows and other domestic animals did not dare to go there for fear of being devoured by lions and tigers.

I immediately followed him and managed to reach the place.

As soon as I stood on top of the hill and looked down at the Ganges River and the heavenly panorama, scenic Himalayan peaks and unending plains in front, I approved of the place. It was highly charged with spiritual vibrations.

Immediately I possessed the land psychically without even knowing who the owner of the land was. Next day, hundreds of people were employed to cut down the woods and fence the boundary. Only after the boundary was completed was I told that the land belonged to twelve persons. I called those persons and had the land sold to me through a registered sale deed, simply to find out later that those people had no right to sell the land, and that they were mistaken in their belief that they were the owners of the land. The land had been given to them for cultivation by the Government. They had only the right to use, but not to sell, the land. But since they did not use it, they lost even that right.

To make the whole story short, all things adjusted to my wish, and finally I was recognized as the legal owner of the land. Now, the Mission is a non-profit organization, and is registered under the Indian Societies Registration Act.

This is only one example of how thoughts materialize into things by psychic powers. If I did not use psychic powers, I would need many assistants and secretaries to carry out my work in the United States which I have been doing alone since 1954.

Illustration 5. *Kailashananda Mission Trayambeshwar Temple* at Dusk.

Chapter 9 THE YOGI PRECEPTOR

YOGA IS A SCIENCE of physical, mental and spiritual development, which should be always learned under the guidance of a *Preceptor*, known as a *Guru*. You cannot drive a car by just reading the Driver's Manual. You have to take driving lessons. In Yoga practice you learn to drive your mind, your thoughts, your emotions, and certain internal higher forces; and that can only be achieved with success when you are guided day by day by the *Preceptor*. Books help the intellect, but they do not bring true evolution on the physical, mental and spiritual level. By reading the menu, your hunger cannot be satisfied; you have to eat the food on the table to satisfy your hunger. Similarly, books and other information can only make one more anxious to find a *Preceptor*, but in no event can they be a substitute for a *Preceptor*.

The disciple receives invisible power from his *Preceptor* as he receives instructions from him. This invisible power received from the *Preceptor* is known as the quickening impulse because it quickens spiritual progress. A soul can receive an impulse only from another soul, not from books. You have within you tremendous spiritual forces which are latent, the energies of man which need to be awakened. This awakening cannot be carried out by books. It needs impulse from the *Preceptor*. Just as a magazine of gun powder cannot explode by itself without ignition, similarly, the spiritual forces which lie hidden within you in subtle form cannot be awakened without a stimulus from the spiritual impulse received from the teacher.

Fire exists in firewood, coal and charcoal, but without ignition through a spark from without, it cannot burn. So the divine forces within you will not grow without the impulse from the *Preceptor*. There is butter in the milk, but you can't see it. There is oil in the seed, but you can't see it. Similarly, spiritual forces are within you which you cannot release or perceive unless you make the effort and follow the instructions of the *Preceptor*. You have to be ready before you receive the quickening impulse from your *Preceptor*. The *Preceptor* always keeps an eye on all his disciples and as soon as they are ready he imparts the spiritual impulse to them.

It was a single touch from *Swami Rama Krishna*, Founder of *Rama Krishna* Mission, which carried the spiritual impulse into Swami *Vivekananda*, who came to America. The passing of this quickening impulse transformed Swami *Vivekananda* into a Prophet in a split second.

The very Presence and sight of the teacher subdues the mind of the student and helps him control his mind and achieve deep meditation. In India, a *Preceptor* is generally swarmed by his disciples wherever he goes. Some are followed by hundreds of devotees and visitors when they leave the monastery. The *Preceptor* lives in the awareness of eternal bliss and love of one and all. Disciples and visitors try to come as near to the *Preceptor* as they can. Most people merely come to remain within the aura of the *Preceptor* for a few minutes.

Everyone possesses not only a physical body, but also an emotional body, a body for thoughts, and a spiritual body in which resides his consciousness which is everlasting. The radiating influence of the spiritual vehicle differs according to the holiness and evolution of the *Preceptor*. In the case of the realized saints and perfected yogis, their spiritual aura and its influence can be felt within a radius of 400 to 500 feet. People who come within the range of the influence of the spiritual aura radiating from a *Preceptor* are immensely benefited from the peace and the spiritual powers of the *Preceptor*. The radiation from the spiritual aura helps Adepts in the control of their mind and enables them to continue their yoga practice in their own spiritual lives until they are able to attain the awareness of the inner spiritual consciousness and its bliss which they have experienced being in the company of their *Preceptor*.

During the period of study with the *Preceptor* there is a continuous psychic exchange between the *Preceptor* and the student, which makes it important for a student to understand the necessity of personal instructions and the need of his being in the physical presence of the Master. A *Preceptor* keeps in touch with his students mentally, helping them on their spiritual path, reaching them through his thoughts.

In an Indian monastery, you may be surprised to know that students spend many years living and studying for progress with the *Preceptor*, like children living with their parents till they are mature in their understanding and grown up, when they can be on their own. The *Preceptor* is known as the Divine Father, and the students, the Divine Children. It does not matter that a student may be 60 or 80 years old physically, in the eyes of the *Preceptor* he is like a little baby who does not know much about the world and is guided by his parents. Similarly, the disciple does not have much experience of the spiritual life and he depends upon the *Preceptor* to hold his hand and guide him on the path of spiritual enlightenment. The first father is he who gives birth and looks after the physical development of the child. This relationship terminates with the end of the body of either one of them. The *Preceptor* is the Spiritual Father, who gives birth to the spiritual body within the student, while making him aware of the spiritual forces within him, and this relationship is a relationship in Spirit and not physical, and therefore it is much deeper than the one existing between the parents and their children. The relationship between the *Preceptor* and the student is eternal because the Spirit is eternal. When a person awakens to the awareness of the Spirit that is his next birth; he is born into Spirit Awareness, which can only take place with the help of the Spiritual Father, that is the *Preceptor*.

It is rather impossible to achieve successful meditation and release the mental and spiritual forces within without the physical presence of the *Preceptor*. Until the mind has been thoroughly and patiently trained in concentration in the presence of the *Preceptor*, it is both useless and dangerous to attempt to meditate; useless because the student will not have the faculty of one-pointedness in mind, which is a most important ingredient of successful meditation. It is dangerous to meditate without training from the *Preceptor* because during meditation huge amounts of spiritual and mental forces can get released and if a person is not ready, such forces may easily result in mental disturbances manifesting through bodily disorders on the physical plane of existence.

The *Preceptor* is a person who himself trod the path of spiritual awareness and has seen the Light, and with that background is able to guide you on the same path. A person who has not seen the Light, can never guide you on the path. Therefore, it is no use seeking help from worldly people who are themselves groping in the darkness and looking for a Master and his guidance. Accepting help from persons other than a *Preceptor* is like the blind leading the blind and both falling.

The impulse transmitted by the *Preceptor* to the student, though invisible, contains the energized thought of the teacher and is far more powerful than electricity. Fish maintain mental contact with the eggs they lay in the garbage on the shore of a lake, by seeing them, as a result of which they hatch in due course. If the fish is unable to see those eggs, it loses its mental touch and the eggs will deteriorate, disintegrate and rot without being hatched. Turtles maintain mental contact with the eggs they lay far away in the sand by thinking of the exact location while the parent turtle spends his time in the water. If by chance the turtle lost this contact and forgot the place where the eggs were laid, the eggs would disintegrate and rot and would not hatch. Similarly, the growth and spiritual and mental evolution as well as the awakening of psychic powers in a student depend to a greater extent upon the mental contact maintained by the *Preceptor*. If the disciple loses mental contact with his *Preceptor*, his spiritual growth is not only retarded, but there is every likelihood of his relapsing back into old habits and wrong thinking which become the cause of the disintegration of his spiritual body.

A *Preceptor* helps his disciple in this life and sometimes also in the life beyond. If a student is a worthy and sincere disciple, the teacher may decide to follow him from life to life and from country to country to help him by his physical presence or by his invisible thoughts, towards the achievement of his spiritual goal. Such a disciple after the fall of the body, meets his *Preceptor* on the threshold of the invisible world where he is guided continuously by the *Preceptor*, and when he is born again, according to the *Karmas* of his past life in this world, the *Preceptor* appears in a physical form in this world before him and accepts him as a disciple and guides him on the Path. Sometimes, the *Preceptor*, in the interest of the disciple, may select to guide him through invisible thought.

The *Preceptor* and Great Masters helping their disciples in this world are known as Guardian Angels and Heavenly Fathers. When a person speaks through a microphone, his thoughts express through words, the words express through sound, the sound transforms itself into electricity and travels through the wire, electricity transforms itself into sound, and the sound expresses itself into words, coming out from the loudspeaker. Similarly, a *Preceptor* reaches and expresses to his student through his powerful thoughts. For quicker spiritual evolution of a disciple, it is very important that the disciple be receptive and cooperative in carrying out the instructions for Yoga practice. The *Preceptor* uses positive influence in molding the disciple and guiding him on the spiritual path. A *Preceptor* generally lays down a particular path best suited to the development of the disciple. The disciple should make his best effort to acquire the vast treasures of great qualities possessed by the *Preceptor*. A student in the earlier stages may imbibe the common human foibles of the *Preceptor* rather than the virtues. The *Preceptor*, although he lives and works like a human being and appears to be possessed of the qualities of an ordinary human being, is always steeped in spiritual awareness, and is always immune to the influences to which people devoid of spiritual awareness, are susceptible. Spiritual developments without cultivation of virtues and good qualities does not bring quick results on the spiritual path. A person should feel the Oneness of Life, and the Unity in Diversity. A person who remains unaffected by human suffering, is not ready for spiritual development.

Without sincere effort towards spiritual awareness, life is a waste. True peace of mind and happiness cannot be achieved without spiritual awareness. Real philosophy of life has never been born in a materially prosperous supersaturated society. All that comes out is a state of boredom of the mind, because a man in this world needs far more happiness than what he can receive from cookies, candies, and ice cream. The glittering glamour of cities and the charm of the automobile world is not enough to satisfy the innermost desires of man. Just as it is important to abolish poverty and attain social, economic and political freedom, equally urgent is the freedom of the soul and the abolition of selfishness, hatred, jealousy, fear, anger, and ignorance in the mind of man about his spiritual wisdom. The *Preceptor* aims at bringing to the lives of people in this world a true philosophy of life, whereby they discover the wisdom and spiritual values in material things.

Chapter 10 THE POWER OF MANTRAS

MANTRAS are not a superstitious use of words meant to bring spectacular results. They contain a careful, scientific elaboration of the higher and natural principles underlying the use of words and terms. The careful instructions and the efficient employment of *Mantras* and their correct pronunciation bring unfailing and best psychological results.

Being a Hindu, I am aware of the fact that to an Orthodox Hindu, a *Mantra* may mean a prayer, a sacred and mystic word, hymned and contemplated. But a scientific definition of *Mantra* which the people of the West can understand is that a *Mantra* is a metrical verse having an essential rhythm. The rhythmic virtue is created by a definite succession of sounds as the *Mantra* is repeated over and over again in succession, which tunes in the *Chitta* (Mind-Stuff). This repetition of the *Mantra* automatically creates concentration and meditation, and one-pointedness of thoughts. If a person himself does not repeat the *Mantra*, but hears the *Mantra* repeated by others, even then mind stuff would get synchronized to the *Mantra* and he will be able to achieve the result with which the *Mantra* is pregnant.

Mantras were employed and discovered by the Yogis in their inner research for purely psychological reasons, and they were originally designed and taught with the intention of achieving psychological results. Many people think of translating these *Mantras* into the form of Statements of Truth and Affirmations, and in such cases they lose most of the beneficial effects of the *Mantra* because the original rhythm of the *Mantra* and its power to synchronize the mind is lost in the process of translation.

There is a close relationship between the spoken words of the *Mantra* and the achievement of the results and the fulfillment of the desires, the seed of which is contained in the *Mantra* itself. *Mantras* are specific formulas which have been worked out by the Hindu Yogis in Sanskrit about 6,000 to 7,000 years ago, and they have been taught to disciples in the form of a series of words uttered rhythmically. The effect of these words in the *Mantras* on the body is terrific. It creates a rhythm in the body which is quite remarkable. The repetition of the *Mantra* first arouses a certain specific mental state and then the aroused mental state produces a specific effect on the physical condition. In this way, the repetition of the *Mantra* brings a change in the physical conditions as well as in the conditions of the world by changing the environment according to the wishes of the person.

Mantras are the energized thoughts of the *Preceptor*, which in a condensed and seed form stay in the *Mantra*. Just as science has its various formulas for various results, similarly the Yogis have various *Mantras* which are formulas for creating specific results. Just as the formula of combining oxygen and hydrogen in a certain proportion creates water, similarly the repetition of a specific *Mantra* materializes into specific results, and things start to happen in the physical, material world.

Mantras are very commonly used in India. Generally, cobra bites in India are treated by the use of *Mantras*. The person who heals the cobra bite repeats the *Mantra* continuously for a few minutes and thus he is able to arouse a specific mental condition in the patient which brings a certain change in the function of the glands, which in turn start to secrete most powerful hormones and chemicals into the bloodstream of the patient, that completely neutralize the harmful effect of the poison in the bloodstream injected by the bite of the cobra, and the result is that the person is completely healed.

I know of one person in south India who exposed himself to many bites of a dangerous cobra but nothing happened to him because by the power of *Mantra* he was able to neutralize the poison in his blood with the powerful chemicals he caused the glands to secrete into his bloodstream.

Mantras are taught by the *Preceptor* to students and worthy people who are very sincere and devoted and interested in the well-being of people. A person is administered many vows at the time he is initiated into the *Mantra* by his *Preceptor*. One of the vows generally is that he will not prostitute the *Mantra*, nor accept any monetary compensation, or any other type of favor for his treatments, no matter how much he may be badly in need of money. For treatments through *Mantra*, the healer may not even accept gifts from his patient for food and drink.

Mantras are energized thoughts and as such they are pregnant with results in seed form. Just as a large tree with its fruits and flowers lies hidden in subtle form in a small seed, just as the hundreds of lives a person will have to undergo in the future already lie hidden in the mental body in the seed form of subtle *Karmas*, so results are hidden in the *Mantra* itself. A person who uses the *Mantra*, should look for the result in the *Mantra* rather than outside. When the *Mantra* is repeated, by its hidden power within, it starts to materialize and bring changes in the material world creating psychic phenomena.

Long ago a Yogi, who used to live deep in the Himalayas in a cave for the purpose of doing *Sadhana* (Yoga practice) in a quiet place, gave a *Mantra* to one of the cowboys who lived in a distant village in the mountains. In the mountains, cowboys and people who live in the villages, which are very rare in the Himalayas, always respect the Yogis, and try to give them the best comforts during their *Sadhana*. When this cowboy discovered that the Yogi lived in that cave, he would bring milk and fresh fruits from the trees in the woods every day and quietly leave them at the door of the cave without disturbing the Yogi so that the Yogi would not have to waste his precious time in procuring food when he was hungry. Now the Yogi had more and more time for his *Sadhana* and meditation. He was able to stay in holy communion for a longer length of time because he did not have to worry about his food. Therefore, he was very pleased with the cowboy. Unseen by the Yogi, the cowboy continued to serve him for many years in this way. The Yogi achieved his goal and was pleased with the selfless service he had received from the cowboy and therefore he was on the watch to see when the cowboy would come. The cowboy on seeing the Yogi was very pleased and received the blessings from the Yogi in person. The Yogi gave him a *Mantra* and gave him all the necessary instructions for its use.

The Yogi told him, "This is your personal friend, it is an invisible power which no one can take away from you. This is your spiritual wealth which will serve you when you need help of any kind."

After some time a theft was committed in a wealthy family and the thugs took a huge amount of cash, jewelry and other valuables, and the thugs could not be detected. When the cowboy heard of this incident, he consented to use his *Mantra* to restore the stolen property to the aggrieved family, who were very religious-minded people. When people heard that the cowboy would be restoring the stolen property by the power of the *Mantra*, numerous people from far-off places, officials and dignitaries, came to see the power of the *Mantra*. The cowboy charged a big brass vessel which he used for fetching drinking water from the stream, and immediately with the power of the *Mantra* the vessel started to vibrate and shake as he was holding it tightly with his hands. It seemed as if high voltage electricity had been released in the vessel. Then a strong fellow was asked to hold the jar, and he was told that it would guide him to the place where the stolen property was lying in the jungle. The cowboy pressed the psychic button and the power of the *Mantra* was released, and the container started to move, dragging the fellow who was holding it. First it moved slowly, in a few seconds it gained tremendous speed and dragged the person who was holding it amid the mountains and valleys, and brought him to the spot where all the stolen property was lying in the bush. The result was that by the use of the *Mantra* all the stolen property was recovered. He again released the vessel for the second time, this time to spot out the thieves, who later confessed that they were the true culprits.

In India, *Mantras* are used for physical conditions as well. Just as in the West you will see a medical doctor busy with his patients, in India you will find numerous people waiting at the door of an Adept who restores their health through the power of *Mantras*. Since he does not charge anything for his services in most cases, he does not have an office where people can come and sit, and therefore they have to stand in line on the street at his door and receive the treatment in turn, as I have seen many times, similar to lines of people standing on the street to get a ticket to a Radio City Music Hall movie or people waiting to enter a restaurant on a busy Saturday evening in New York.

Mantras are used for physical as well as for mental, psychological and spiritual results. Primarily *Mantras* work on the mental plane and create a mental state, and from there the results are transmitted into the physical plane. *Mantras* are used for the successful accomplishment of desired objects, to overcome obstacles to prosperity, to win over friends, to overcome enemies, to foresee the future, to achieve immunity from unnatural death, for self-protection from psychic attacks, to achieve promotion in places of honor, to develop individual talents, for the fulfillment of worldly desires, for prosperity and wealth, for relief from danger, for spiritual progress and various other purposes. Each *Mantra* is pregnant with specific results, some *Mantras* are pregnant with results to bring improvement in overall general conditions, physical, mental, as well as spiritual.

The *Mantra* which helps to create a spiritual bond between the disciple and the teacher is known as the Personal *Mantra* or the *Guru Mantra*, which is discussed in detail in the next Chapter.

To achieve the full benefit of a *Mantra*, two things are essential; first, it should be officially received from the *Preceptor*, secondly, it should be awakened and put into action. If you have a watch, but you do not wind it, it will never function. If you have a car and you do not drive it, simply keep it in the garage, it will not serve any purpose. You must have a license to drive the car, and then you should turn the ignition on, then the engine starts and you ride the car. Similarly, first one has to receive the *Mantra* officially from the *Preceptor*. When the *Mantra* is received officially from the Preceptor, with it goes the permission to use it. This permission is accompanied by a transference of psychic impulse. In order to put the *Mantra* into action, it has to be repeated correctly for a specific number of times. In order to put each *Mantra* into action, the number of times that is required to be repeated varies.

By repeating the *Mantra* you earn spiritual wealth. In the same way you can keep adding money to your account in the bank, similarly, you can maintain an account of the *Mantras*. Just as one spends his money, similarly one can spend the *Mantras* he has earned. Just as one can give money away to another person, one can give the benefit of his *Mantra* to another person to relieve him of the maladies in his life. It is very common in India, specially in most Hindu families, that when a person is sick, sometimes even on his deathbed, the *Preceptor* will advise the members of the family to do specific *Mantras* and give their benefits to the sick person to restore his health, to add years to his life. By constant use of the *Mantra*, in due course a person earns credit just as by making regular payments you can earn good credit at the bank. In such cases, a person is able to use any amount of *Mantras* which he has not yet earned. Of course he has to make good in the future by depositing into his spiritual bank the exact amount of *Mantras* which he has borrowed to ward off maladies in his personal life or in the lives of any of his friends and relatives.

Mantra is personified energy wound up in words. As you repeat the words and start chanting the *Mantra*, the sound, vibrations and energy are materialized.

Mantra is your best friend and you should treat it as a person. Electricity, magnetism, force, heat, light, the five elements and their combinations, are all external manifestations of energy which reside in the *Mantra* itself, and therefore, *Mantra* can bring simultaneous changes into any and all of these things. Intelligence, discrimination, psychic powers and will power are all internal manifestations of *Mantra*.

The power of the *Mantra* through the three *Gunas* (good, bad and neutral thoughts and actions) manifests into learning, wisdom, etc. The manifestations of *Mantra* are countless. The energy in the *Mantra* is the same energy which lies dormant in every human being within his psychic centers, known as *Kundalini* . The power within the *Mantra* is the primal force of life that underlies the whole of existence.

The power of the *Mantra* is the energy which exists in the sun, the moon, earth, planets and comets, and makes them move. The power of a *Mantra* is inherent energy such as fragrance in flowers, color in the rainbow, intelligence in the mind, potency in medicines and injections, coolness in ice, flavor in coffee and motion in the air.

The *Mantra* should always be approached for help with an open heart just as you would ask your friend to help you with a sincere heart. For best results one should lay open the innermost secret chambers of his heart, making an unreserved surrender to the *Mantra*. By repeating the *Mantra* successively, the power of the *Mantra* is invoked. Chemical changes take place in your body by repeating the *Mantra*. These physical changes are caused by the state of mind aroused by the repetition of the *Mantra*.

Chapter 11 GURU MANTRAM

AS SOON AS a person is initiated into the technique of *Guru Mantra*, he becomes a member of a new family, i.e., the spiritual family of the *Guru*. When a soul is born in any family, it becomes the member of that family. When a girl is married, she becomes a member of her husband's family. When a disciple is initiated into his *Guru Mantra*, he becomes a member of the spiritual family of the *Guru*, thereby entitling himself to the spiritual heritage of his *Guru*.

The disciple, especially if he is a householder, or a person who lives the life of an ordinary person in the world, is not required to forsake his membership in the family in which he is born, or not to carry out his obligations to his relatives, friends and other people of the world with whom he has been dealing. For a worldly person to be initiated into a *Guru Mantra* means additional responsibilities and obligations which are purely spiritual, while he continues to enjoy, as before, his responsibilities and obligations in the material and physical world.

The *Guru Mantra* is a spiritual tie that makes you a partner of the spiritual family of the *Preceptor*. Just as you sign a contract and become a partner in a corporation or a company, similarly, the *Guru* takes you in as a partner of his spiritual business by giving you the *Guru Mantra*. A person may withdraw himself from a partnership in a company or a corporation, but not from the spiritual partnership with the *Guru*, because the latter is a sacred tie deep in the Spirit, which connects Soul to Soul.

Just as after mixing the water in two glasses, or the air in two rooms, you cannot separate them, similarly, the connecting link between the disciple and the teacher, once established, is never broken.

The *Guru Mantra* makes you a partner in the spiritual wealth of the teacher, and you make him a partner in your material wealth and possessions in exchange for being accepted into the spiritual partnership. A disciple on the spiritual path should know that wealth and possessions, no matter how vast they may be, are commendable if they are used as a means towards higher spiritual and wisdom values in life. It is simply a spiritual and moral obligation on the part of the disciple to share his wealth and prosperity with his teacher, according to his needs. Similarly, the teacher pays attention to the needs and necessities in the life of the disciple. Once a person is initiated into the *Guru Mantra*, he is expected to cooperate fully in all the programs of his *Guru*, according to his means. The disciple should give his cooperation to the plans of the *Guru* in thought as well as action, while the *Guru* always keeps mental contact with his disciples for the best interests of the disciples, no matter where they may be.

The disciple has an obligation to see that the *Guru* is provided suitable boarding and lodging facilities throughout his life. No great Saint initiates disciples in the hope of obtaining support from them, but it is in the interest of the disciples themselves to part with a portion of their wealth to help the *Guru* in his plans, because this will, in itself, give hope and confidence to the disciples that they are sharing what they have as freely as the *Guru* shares his spiritual treasure with them.

A disciple once initiated into the *Guru Mantra* should at least one day each month devote a few hours to the repetition of the *Guru Mantra* and *Satsang*, which includes Yoga practices for spiritual development. On *Guru Purnima* (an auspicious day for the disciple for spiritual progress, which occurs once a year on the full moon) the disciple should think about his *Guru* and the work and plans of the *Guru* should be promoted. Also the disciple should send gifts, money, and such things to his *Guru*, which he can readily use in the development and furthering of his spiritual work.

The *Guru Mantra* is like a ship for a person drowning in the ocean. This world is more vast and dangerous than an ocean, and the people in the world who are far away from the spiritual path, are like drowning persons in the ocean, finding their lives filled with disappointments, miseries, disease and sickness, interrupted with temporary relief and feelings of momentary happiness and joy, prosperity, profits, social position, etc., which never last for long, just as a drowning person cannot keep his head above the surface of the water for long. An ordinary person in the world does not know how to get out of the ocean of the world, and how to be immune to the dangers of this world that are waiting for him in the near future. The *Guru Mantra* is the means to cross the ocean of the world. The *Guru Mantra* is an especially energized thought of the *Guru* placed into your possession for your protection, and when you want, it will manifest before you in invisible form and protect you from the harmful consequences in your life.

The *Guru Mantra* is always for the exclusive use of the disciple to whom it is personally given by his *Guru*, because the number of consonants and vowels in the specific *Mantra* are so arranged by the *Guru* that they make up the astral deficiencies of that person. Astral and spiritual deficiencies are always the main cause of physical and mental handicaps, as well as lack of prosperity. The greatest disease in the world is the disease of birth and death, and the *Guru Mantra* aims to help the disciple to get rid of not only his physical and mental troubles, but also to gain victory over the disease of birth and death by helping him to achieve eternity. Deficiencies in the astral body radiate negative and deficient color vibrations, and these vibrations become the cause of deficiencies in the elements which constitute your body. The color vibrations which are a part of your psychic aura affect your thinking process, and change your outlook.

The deficient vibrations, which are the foundation of physical and mental existence, also affect your power of sense perception, as well as the power of your sense of action. By repetition of the *Guru Mantra*, the disciple is forced automatically to inhale and exhale in a certain rhythm, which creates a certain positive proportion between his ingoing and outgoing breaths, thereby restoring his astral deficiencies. The astral matter is conveyed by the ingoing breath.

The role of the *Guru* is more important than Truth itself, because it is the *Guru* who guides the disciples to find the Truth. It is the *Guru*, and *Guru* alone, who can initiate you into the mysteries of Truth and Nature, and guide you on the road of spiritual progress which he has trodden. The greatness of the *Guru Mantra* and its spiritual power is beyond imagination. The power which created the cycles of earth, that makes the sun, moon, comets and earth rotate in their orbits, is nothing compared to the power generated by the *Guru Mantra*. The *Guru Mantra* will work in your favor in three ways:

1. *Gyana Shakti* (The Power of Knowledge)
2. *Iccha Shakti* (The Power of Will)
3. *Kriya Shakti* (The Power of Action).

Gyana is used by your intellect which makes decisions, and adds to your wisdom and knowledge. When the knowledge of an object has been achieved, then the *Iccha Shakti* comes into existence. *Iccha Shakti* is the strong desire to possess the object of your desire. It is your mind which uses the *Iccha* . As soon as you have a strong desire born in your mind to achieve an object, the *Kriya* is born. *Kriya* is the power of action which manifests through *Prana* (energy in your muscles and nerves) and then there is a physical effort exerted by the power of *Kriya* to possess the object of desire.

The sound emanating from your *Guru Mantra* is connected with the eternal sound, which is the Word of God, which is in you, and in which you are. The eternal sound exists in all matter in the form of unmanifested energy, while in living creatures it exists in the form of energy in manifested form. The energy is manifested in living creatures because they react to their environment, while in matter, it lies dormant. The energy in matter can be made active if it is exploited and awakened. For example, if the energy in uranium is exploited by putting it in a reactor, it can carry a rocket and take a man to the moon, while in the unmanifest form, the energy would never manifest into action. The *Guru Mantra* causes hidden inner energies to manifest. The energy in its original form existed in the form of *Gunas*, i.e.:

1. *Sato Guna*
2. *Rajo Guna*
3. *Tamo Guna*.

The three *Gunas* hold energy in a state of equilibrium in the unmanifest form. By Cosmic Will Power, vibrations start to take place, the equilibrium of energy is disturbed, and the creation of the world begins to take place. The three *Gunas* release three colors which are responsible for the creation, sustenance and dissolution of the world. By the action and reaction of the *Gunas*, the five elements are created. The *Akasha* (ether) manifests first. From ether, air is created, from air the element of fire, from fire the element of water, and from water the element of earth. With the help of these five elements and their combinations, matter in various forms of vegetation comes into existence. Your *Linga Sarira* (physical body) is created out of the five elements.

The power of *Mantra* directs and controls the energy which holds the earth and other planets in their position. It also controls the power which sustains physical and mental health in your life. It also controls the energy which brings old age and decrepitude to the body and when the body becomes unfit for further evolution, it enables you in the next reincarnation to assume a new healthy body to quicken your spiritual evolution. This power of *Mantra* directly stirs your spiritual awareness which resides in your spiritual heart (your inner sanctuary, situated on the right side of the physical heart, its size being equal to the size of your thumb).

The *Guru Mantra* helps to bring full self-illumination to the disciple by removing the veil of ignorance in him. The *Guru Mantra* will transform your body consciousness into Cosmic Consciousness. The *Guru Mantra* can change your wrong and vicious *Samskaras* (*Karmas*), and awaken you to the attainment of knowledge of the Soul. The *Guru Mantra* helps awaken your *Kundalini* and opens the inner eye of intuition. The *Guru Mantra* brings to you direct knowledge of the Soul which the *Guru* himself has experienced. It can bring to you the peace that passeth all understanding because the *Guru* gives the *Mantra* to his disciples with his own spiritual power and *Sattwic Bhawa*.

In ancient days, disciples were put to difficult tests before they were initiated into *Guru Mantra* and into other higher techniques, but at the present, due to circumstances prevailing in the modern age, the standard of discipline prescribed for disciples has been relaxed.

Once, a *Guru* put all his disciples to a test in order to select the best of the group for higher teachings. In order to see the power of sense control, he asked them to keep a teaspoonful of sugar in their mouths without letting it get wet. After a few minutes, the *Guru* asked them to open their mouths and spit out the sugar. In the whole group, only one disciple was able to keep the sugar dry while holding it in his closed mouth for a few minutes, while the sugar in the mouths of the others got wet. The one who spat out the dry sugar from his mouth was accepted for higher teachings, because he had that much control of his senses that he could stop his tongue from tasting the sugar while he was holding it in his mouth. The other disciples did not have firm control of their senses, as a result of which the taste buds on the tongue started to taste the sugar, and the saliva started to flow. The power of taste resides in the mind, and if one can stop it from connecting to the tongue, one would not taste a thing he held in his mouth. The power of taste and other sense perceptions are released from the mind in the form of impulses and they contact the senses and thus establish the process of action and reaction between the mind and the senses. A dead person cannot taste, because he does not have the power to taste in his mind, although he has a tongue.

Once *Guru Gorakhnath* asked his disciples to climb up a tall tree and then throw themselves head downwards on a very sharp trident (a weapon with three sharp-edged points). Only one of his disciples obeyed his order, and as he jumped from the top of the tree, the *Guru* protected him by invisible hand. He was accepted for initiation into the spiritual mysteries, and achieved quick Self Realization. The disciple did not have any attachment to his body. You cannot have your cake and eat it too. Either you will eat it, or you can have it for tomorrow. Similarly, you cannot develop your spiritual awareness while you maintain your physical awareness. People who have too much attachment to their wealth and possessions have great difficulty in achieving spiritual awareness; for this reason it has been mentioned clearly in the Bible, "It is easier for a camel to enter the eye of a needle than for a wealthy person to enter the Gate of Heaven."

Persons who think that they can evolve spiritually and achieve Self Realization without a *Guru*, can hardly succeed in their ambitions. It is very important to have the personal instructions from a teacher; of course with the instruction goes the grace and blessings of the *Preceptor*. A person needs driving lessons to drive a car, a cook needs a teacher under whose supervision he can prepare the food, a lawyer is guided by his senior attorney in court, a doctor works under the guidance of a senior doctor before he becomes a full-fledged doctor, students in science, music and astronomy need teachers. Similarly, to walk the inner spiritual path, it is very important to have a guide (Spiritual *Preceptor*).

A person inherits wealth and property from the parents to whom he is born. Similarly, a person inherits spiritual power from his *Preceptor*. The *Guru Mantra* should never be disclosed to anyone. If possible, it should not be said loudly so that other persons may not hear. If you are instructed by your *Preceptor* to repeat the *Guru Mantra* with the help of a rosary, keep the rosary while using it either in your pocket or covered so that others may not see it while you are using it. The techniques of using the rosary with the *Guru Mantra* should be learned in person from the *Guru* at the time one is initiated into the *Guru Mantra*.

Chapter 12 PRINCIPLES OF PSYCHIC PHENOMENA

CREATING PSYCHIC phenomena with the power of the mind is as simple and easy as eating ice cream when you understand the process to use the higher forces of nature for the purpose of materializing your thoughts into physical conditions or into a material object. The guiding principles in the creation of any psychic phenomena are three:

1. *Akasha* (ethereal substance)
2. *Prana* (subtle energy)
3. Creative Mind

All forms of matter which exist in this world, including the sun, moon, stars, earth, metals, water and gases, have been created from the substance of *Akasha*. The *Akasha* is much thinner than the universal ether known to science. *Akasha* does not have any life or mind in itself, and therefore it is just raw material to be used in the creation of phenomena with the help of *Prana* and your Creative Mind.

Prana is the primal force of energy. It is the sum total of all energy: electrical, ethereal, as well as magnetic. Without the existence of this energy, the sun, moon and earth would not revolve in their orbits. *Prana* is not matter, but it is in matter. *Prana* is not mind, but it makes the mind think. *Prana* is not air, but it makes the air blow. *Prana* is not breath, but it makes the breath go in and out. Yogic techniques let you control this powerful force of *Prana* which flows in and out with your breath and which sets the mind into motion. *Prana* with your incoming breath makes your lungs expand and contract, and the function of the lungs makes the heart contract and expand creating your pulsation, circulation, digestion and assimilation. By the control of *Prana* an Adept can bring suspended animation into the function of his heart or any other vital organ of his body. An Adept, through Yogic techniques, can draw a terrific amount of *Prana* into his system and charge his whole nervous system with it, and then manifest miraculous powers creating psychic phenomena which he would not otherwise be able to manifest.

Creative Mind is the original state of matter. Nothing can manifest in a physical material form in this world if it did not exist before in invisible form, in the mental state in which all plans and desires are first created. Creative Mind lies dormant in every human being. It is by the Yoga techniques that it is put into action. Everything you want to materialize in your life must first be designed in this mental element known as the Creative Mind.

Chapter 13 THOUGHTS ARE THINGS

THERE IS CLOSE association between a material thing and your invisible thoughts. Every thought reminds you of a thing, and every thing connects you with a specific thought. This visible world is but a reflection of the invisible, just as in a painting the objects painted are the counterpart of the mental picture of the painter. Just as you can develop the power of muscles by weight lifting, you can develop the creative faculty of your mind by Yoga techniques taught by the Yogis for the development of psychic powers. By psychic powers you can bring change into a physical condition, as well as bring therapeutic results to your mind and Soul.

The psychic influence which is known as psychologizing includes psychic healing. It consists of using the finer and higher forces of Nature available to all. Just as air is free for all, but still many do not take deep breaths and therefore create conditions of impaired health, similarly the forces of Nature are in abundance around you, and you don't have to pay for them. In order to create psychic phenomena you just have to learn how to use those forces consciously, in the same way as you learn how to take a deep breath so that you can use the air which is all around you.

The psychic powers are purely mental and have nothing to do with the spiritual and religious aspects of your life. The main thing needed for the creation of psychic phenomena is the development of the mental forces and their control, which is purely mental.

Many progressive movements in the West, i.e., Faith Healing, New Thought, Divine Science, Mental Healing, Practical Psychology, and Suggestive Therapeutics, are based on the process of projection and materialization of thoughts into a physical condition.

In many parts of the world, successful businessmen use the process of psychologizing for prosperity and better business by promoting sales of all kinds, through the power of their thoughts only. These businessmen, instead of doing advertising campaigns, do mental broadcasting to attract customers from all over the continent, especially customers who are still uncommitted, as well as those who already like to buy the things which the store wants to sell. Many salesmen have made great progress and had a successful career, simply by the use of psychic powers.

The close connection between your physical condition and your mental state cannot be ignored, because the processes of your body are activities guided by your mind. The curative effect of mind upon body is not a question of mind over matter; it is purely an act of one mind over another mind. Therefore, the difference is not one of kind, but of degree. There is life in every part of your body. Wherever there is life, there is mind, and wherever there is life, there is blood. Everywhere in your body you find blood, life and mind. There would be no life without mind, and no mind without life. The cells in your body would not be able to make blood from the food you eat if they did not have mind. The conscious mind is inferior to your higher mind. All the scientists in the world joined together cannot make a drop of blood from all the food that exists in the world, because they are using their conscious mind, while the cells in your body in the ordinary course of life, make blood out of the food you eat every day, although your conscious mind does not even know the process by which it is done in your own body. All the activities of your body, chemical as well as mechanical, are under the direct control and supervision of your higher mind. It is not your conscious mind which runs your body, digests, assimilates and eliminates your food, makes your heart to beat, your blood to circulate, your lungs to move, and your mind to think. It is your higher mind which does all this work for you. The major part of your mental activities is unknown to you because it lies beyond the reach of your conscious mind. The higher mind does not sleep. It controls and directs the functions of your involuntary organs including the functions of the sympathetic and parasympathetic nervous systems. The higher mind does the healing, repairing, and replacement in your body. The work of the intelligent cells in your every organ is done under the direct control of your higher mind. Your instinctive or higher mind is not confined only to your brain or other greater nervous centers and plexuses in your spine, but it spreads to every part of your body. There is not a single cell, capillary, and nerve where the higher mind does not exist. Therefore the well-being of your physical condition and the healthy function of every part of your body depends entirely upon your higher mind.

When any injury is done to any part of your body, it is this higher mind which does the healing for you. A broken bone is united and made whole and new again by this mind within you, and not by the scissors and the bandage and plaster. If the bandage and plaster could unite the bone, then you would be able to unite the bones in a man who is dead. The bones never unite in a dead person, because the higher mind which does the healing does not exist there any more.

It is this higher mind which unites the broken blade of grass and the broken branch of a tree in a park, without a bandage, plaster and first aid.

The great healing power of Nature is not mechanical or chemical, although it uses both. It is a living force which has mind and intelligence, and makes decisions for or against you. It is your higher mind, also known as the instinctive and subconscious mind. If you know the secrets of your higher mind, you can speed up the process of healing consciously.

Chapter 14 MIND OVER MIND

WHEN YOU LEARN the process of creating psychic phenomena, you simply use the finer forces of Nature, unknown to the masses, but known only to advanced minds. To the psychically advanced minds, there is nothing supernatural about the employment of psychic powers and the effects produced by them, because they know that the power and the effects are purely natural, and they come into existence according to the laws of Nature. By conscious release of the powers of the higher mind, nature is compelled to speed up her process of healing into the body.

Many an Adept and Holy Man in India by using their psychic powers are able to repel the minds of the wild animals, as a result of which the wild animals, such as tigers, lions and wolves, become lovable and friendly, and are completely deprived of their dangerous habits.

For example, there lived in India a Yogi who was known as Tiger Swami, because he always rode on the back of a tiger when he moved into crowded towns. The tiger was not trained like the tigers in the circus. The Yogi, by the power of his higher mind, influenced the mind of the tiger psychically, as a result of which the positive thoughts of peace and love were reproduced in the mind of the tiger, and immediately he stopped attacking and killing people, and became friendly and lovable to them. When the Yogi would go with his tiger, which he used as a horse to carry him from place to place, people would pet him and the children would pull his whiskers, comb his hair, and sometimes the kids would brush his teeth, but he would never harm them, he would just wag his tail like a pet pussy cat.

Such is the terrific result of the higher mind. By means of psychic powers you can transform hardened criminals, juvenile delinquents, and people with disorderly conducts, into lovable citizens and better nationals of the country.

Many Yogis who live in the caves and Himalayan Mountains, deep in the woods, carry around with them a psychic pass-not-ring which is built psychically and held firm by their will. As a result of which, wild animals do not harm them, even bugs, flies and mosquitoes do not bite them. These Adepts know the process of defending themselves by projecting the psychic pass-not-ring around them. This psychic ring can be created around one's house or place of business to protect and defend oneself from harmful thoughts from outside.

Every cell in your body has mind. Your tissues and nerves are made of cells. Cells are everywhere in your body. Each cell is born, reproduces itself, dies and the waste is eliminated, all by your higher mind. When you are able to use your higher mind consciously, you can control the life and death of the cells which constitute your body, as a result of which you become your own creator. The Yoga system of *Kaya Kalpa*, which means a physical and mental regeneration and a new lease on life, is based on this method of restoring healthy physical condition by psychic means.

Every cell in your body has a mind. The cells in your body, by their intelligence, are able to select the various enzymes and mineral salts from your food and use them in specific parts of your body. Each cell performs its duty correctly. The cells seldom commit mistakes. One group of cells picks up the element of calcium from your food and carries it to your bones to be used. Another group of cells is busy picking up the element of phosphorus from your bloodstream and carrying it to your nerves and mind; another group of cells picks up the silica from your blood and carrying it to your skin to make it soft, smooth, velvety and shiny, and so on. If the cells did not have that mind and intelligence which is much higher than your conscious mind, they would not be able to take charge of this complicated function which baffles the minds of the greatest scientists on earth. The cells in your body are able to perform the function of preservation and restoration in your body with the help of this higher mind within them. It is by the power of this mind that some cells build bones for you, others develop your muscle tissues, others make juices, fluids, chemical compounds, hormones, etc. in your body. Some help elimination of the waste and the broken down tissues from your bloodstream, others do the healing of wounds.

Each cell in your body has mind, although the degree of mind differs in each group of cells. The nerve cells are highly specialized and they make a living close-knit telegraphic system throughout your body through which the messages are conveyed to and from your brain. Each nerve cell keeps itself in touch with the activities taking place around it. Another group of cells concentrates only in maintaining the richness of your blood and does not let you get anemic. Cells move in the current of your blood and supply oxygen to the remotest part of your body, and while they return they bring with them the waste products to drop them into the crematory of your lungs where it is all burned in the process of oxygenation. Vital chemicals are created which are again used to maintain your biochemical balance, which is very important for your physical and mental health and long life. Another group of cells works like soldiers always hunting the criminals and the enemies. Whenever bacteria and germs enter your body, these cells immediately destroy them and throw out the waste and the dead cell bodies in the form of skin eruptions, boils and pimples. In infectious diseases the harmful germs are attacked with full strength. It is this higher mind in the cells which helps them to unite a wound which cuts a tissue, a blood vessel, a gland, a muscle, a nerve, or even your bone.

Each cell does its own job in an efficient way. For example, if a person has a deep wound which cuts across the bone, the bone cells would unite the bone from both sides till it becomes one, then the nerve cells would unite the nerves, the flesh cells the flesh, and finally the skin cells would unite the skin. The cells do not unite the nerve with the bone, and the bone with the flesh because they have intelligence and mind. By learning the process of your higher mind you can help the cells in your body to speed up their function of healing by releasing extra strength and healing power which lies dormant within you. If you watch through a magnifying glass, immediately you will notice that as soon as you release the healing powers of the higher mind within you, the process of healing of the wound is speeded up immediately. Thus you see creation in active operation in your body, or in the body of someone else, by the conscious use of the higher powers of your mind.

The cells in your body are organized into a group and community. For example, the people of Manhattan have certain duties towards the Mayor of the City, as well as to the people who inhabit Manhattan Isle. But the same person is also a member of the State of New York, and as such he also has obligations to the governor of New York State. The same person is also a citizen of the United States, and therefore he has his obligations and responsibilities to the government of the United States. The same person is one who inhabits this continent and as such he has rights and obligations towards the people of neighboring countries. The same person is also one of the many hundred millions of people who inhabit the world and as such he has an international obligation towards all human beings who inhabit the earth. Similarly, the cells have their obligations and certain duties to discharge. At the same time, there are obligations to the other cells, so that they do not come in conflict with their work, but rather they work harmoniously for the well-being of the whole body. The cells have their obligations and duties towards the organ with which they are immediately concerned. For example, the heart cells all work together for the better function of the heart; similarly the cells of the lungs, liver, kidneys, etc. At the same time they cooperate with the cells of all other organs in the body. They work for the betterment of the respective organ to which they are immediately attached, and also for the protection of the body as a whole.

The life and mind in the cells is a combination of the life and mind of the billions of cells which compose your whole body and mind. Each cell has its own mind, but then they have a collective mind.

For example, a citizen of the United States is represented by the president of the United States in another country, while the same citizen is represented by his congressman in the White House. At the same time the same citizen is represented in New York State by the governor of New York. In the same way, the cell mind is represented in its own work, it is also represented in the organ mind, and in the brain mind, etc. To make it more clear, the heart cells would give first importance to obeying the orders of the heart mind in comparison to the decision made by their own mind. At the same time, they carry out the orders of the brain mind which is the higher and superior mind because only it can make decisions. The cell mind and the organ mind do not have the power of making decisions because they have an inferior mind, which can be called the negative mind, which can be easily polarized to the brain mind which makes the decisions. Under the condition of polarization, the decisions of the brain mind become the decisions of the organ mind, and finally the decisions of the cell mind, as a result of which the cells perform their function exactly as wished by the brain mind, because the decisions of the brain mind have been accepted by the cells as their own decisions due to the effect of polarization known as psychologizing or psychic influence.

Chapter 15 TAP YOUR SUBCONSCIOUS

THE PARTICLES of the brain are transformed, rearranged, and set into motion and activity by the power of your thoughts, and they change the pattern of your brain mind, and subsequently materialize into the minds of your body cells. The particles of the brain are like the particles of sand, and they send out vibrations, the wavelength of which differs according to the pattern of the thought. A pattern or idea exists in the form of thought waves, which are made of vibrations emanating from the particles of the brain which constitute the brain. These thought patterns can be reproduced efficiently in the mind of animate beings as well as in the mind of inanimate objects, as a result of which corresponding changes take place in your body or in an object as and when you want to bring those specific changes into effect. This will enable you to achieve mastery and control over your cell mind as well as material objects in the world.

When you can raise your thoughts of the conscious mind and make them dip into your higher psychic mind, your thoughts become creative because they derive the power and strength which lies within the jurisdiction of your subconscious. When thoughts become creative, they start to create things rather than staying always as uncreative thoughts. For many people, whose thoughts are not creative, their plans never materialize into reality; their plans in life remain unfulfilled. It is your higher mind which creates the things for you in this world, which you take possession of physically.

In the use of the higher mind for the purpose of creating psychic phenomena, you simply use the higher and finer forces of Nature. When you tap your higher mind in order to achieve what you want, things become so easy that you can hardly believe it. When the powers of the higher mind are tapped, every thought carries with it the powers of your subconscious and it works for you just like your friend would work for you, or an ambassador would represent you and work according to your plans.

For example, I may give you an instance in my personal life of the use of the creation of psychic phenomena. In 1954 I was guided to come to America for the dissemination of the higher teachings, and immediately I made the whole plan, without much physical effort, to put those plans into action. The work of putting those plans into reality I left to my higher mind, which started to work for me right away by rearranging, reorganizing and putting into action the persons and objects which would facilitate my visit to the United States of America and make the whole plan a reality.

Once I pressed the button of the higher mind, the whole psychic machinery went into action, and I only waited for the result. From my past experience I was fully confident that everything would go as I planned, and therefore I did not worry in the least.

It was the first time in my life that I had planned to go abroad. A short time was left for my planned visit to the United States, when I received an invitation from an educational organization in Washington, D. C., inviting me to address a convention at the Morrison Hotel in Chicago. When I was getting ready to leave the *Ashram* where I lived in *Rishikeshi*, Himalayas, a disciple of mine asked me if I had obtained a passport from the government of India.

I replied, "No," because I did not know that a person had to obtain a passport to leave the country. I told him that I thought that just as you can go to the station, buy a ticket and board the train, similarly I would go to the airport, purchase a ticket and board the plane which would carry me to the United States. My disciple replied, "You cannot leave the country unless you have a passport."

I inquired from him where and how to get a passport, and he told me I had to get it from the government of India. Immediately I applied for a passport. All the necessary local inquiries preliminary to the issuing of a passport were unusually expedited due to the psychic thoughts projected long ago from my mind, which kept on working continuously on the persons concerned. To obtain the passport I had to go to *Lucknow*, the only place where passports are issued in the province where I lived. I asked the authorities there to issue me the necessary passport, and they told me it would take more than a month, due to the process which the whole thing had to go through, before I would get the passport. I explained to them my position, that I had to address the convention in Chicago the following week, and naturally I expected the passport much sooner. Most of the people in the secretariat, standing all around me listening to my marvelous plans, even though I did not have a passport, showed tremendous interest in the good work I was doing. They expedited the issuance of the passport. In the ordinary course, it takes many weeks to see the records and inquire if a person has been in any way associated with any organization which is subversive and not law-abiding. If a person is found to have associated with them, he would be denied a passport. My thoughts were working continuously on the whole process, and the papers were forwarded from one person to another, and from one department to another very quickly, and I received the passport the next day.

I had promised to visit Bombay to be the guest of one of my students there before leaving for the United States, although some of my disciples who lived in Calcutta had requested that I come to Calcutta and leave for the United States from there. My host in Bombay had already invited many of his relatives from far off places to be guided into the Yogi techniques of physical and mental regeneration as soon as I arrived in Bombay. People were feeling better so quickly that the message of my arrival in Bombay to help hundreds of people every day, spread like electricity throughout the city. I was busy interviewing people from morning till evening, until the time of my departure for the United States. There was not much time left before leaving for the United States, when one of my disciples asked if I had a visa. I said, "No, I do not." I told him I didn't know what a visa was. He told me that the visa is the permission from the American consulate in Bombay, without which I could not land in the United States of America. Immediately I went to the American consulate and requested a visa. At that time visas were allowed after much scrutiny so that people connected with subversive and illegal organizations would not obtain a visa. In order to verify that I was the right person for the issuance of a visa, I was asked many questions by the American consulate in Bombay. I was asked if I had property. Although I used to have a lot of property in India, since I was a renunciate, I stated that I did not have any property. This might be interpreted as an answer that would not support my claim for a visa, as a person who does not have any property may not come back to India, and thus became a burden on the United States. Also I answered their next question by saying that I did not have any family, as I was a monk, and as such could not marry. Finally I was asked if I intended to come back from the United States. I said I was to speak at the convention, and that finally I intended to come back.

I was also asked how was I going, by sea or plane, and if I had a return ticket in my possession. I said that I would go by air, but at the time I did not have a ticket in my possession. I was asked further if I had money in the bank to buy the ticket. I said, "No, but I will get the money when it is time to buy the ticket," because I knew that the psychic powers were working for me, and that the money would be provided.

Then I was told that if I would bring and show the return ticket by air from the United States, they would issue a visa immediately. I promised to come the next day with the ticket, and returned to my host's house where I was staying. I had hardly entered my room when the telephone rang. My host picked up the phone and told me that some of my students were inquiring if I had returned from the American consulate's office with the necessary visa. I took the phone and told them that the consulate had informed me that I would obtain a visa upon showing them the return air ticket from the United States; therefore I would go to the Office tomorrow to show them the ticket.

The student asked me if I had the ticket. I said, "No, not yet."

Then he said that he would like to drive me in the morning to Thomas Cook & Co., in order to buy a return air ticket for me on Pan American Airways, and then he would like to drive me to the American consulate so that I could show them the ticket and obtain the visa.

Next day, the student drove me to Thomas Cook & Co., and purchased the return ticket for me. Most of the people who heard about the whole matter were very much surprised at how things were happening, but I was not surprised in the least, as everything was expected to happen according to my plans to enable me to come to the United States as already planned long ago. He drove me to the American consulate and they immediately gave me the visa as soon as I showed them the ticket.

When I returned with the ticket to the place of my host, he asked me if I had a dollar exchange permit from the government Bank of India.

I said, "No, I do not. What is a dollar exchange permit?"

He said that unless I had a permit to change Indian rupees into American dollars, the government of India would not let me carry any rupees abroad, nor would the airway company let me board the plane as the dollar exchange permit is a symbol of permission from the government of India to leave the country. In those days the government of India needed the -United States dollars badly and it was not easy to get permission to buy U. S. dollars to spend abroad. People would think themselves fortunate if they would get an exchange permit for 300 U. S. dollars. I went to the bank in Bombay and asked the officer-in-charge to give me an exchange permit, and I was informed that I had to go to the province where I lived in *Rishikeshi* to obtain the exchange permit. I explained that there was not much time left for me to return to *Rishikeshi* to obtain the dollar exchange permit. While all this was going on, I was quite confident that my plans would go according to my wishes, no matter what happened, I would get the dollar exchange permit. On hearing my explanation, the officer of the bank in Bombay gave me a dollar exchange permit for 600 U.S. dollars in exchange for Indian rupees. My host and his friends were surprised that the Bank of India allowed me $600.00 to spend during my 15-day stay in the United States, as they considered it a handsome amount of money to be spending in two weeks time. I was also allowed to spend an additional 14,000 rupees while touring the United Kingdom.

Next day, I took the plane from Bombay as planned for Chicago, and on arrival I addressed the convention at the Morrison Hotel. The delegates of the convention which represented various well-known organizations in the United States, showed keen interest in the material which I had to offer to the West and they extended me invitations to speak in various cities of the United States.

All the things in detail would fill a book in itself, and therefore I would like to cut the whole thing short by saying that everything in the United States has happened according to my plans. I was very well taken care of here by my disciples, who were already waiting for me long before I arrived. My work never suffered for a lack of finances. I always make my plans without having any finances to support me, because I know the money will come when it is needed.

Once it happened that I was staying in a hotel in Washington, and the rent was due to be paid, and I did not have even one dollar with me, but I never worried. I enjoyed a sound sleep in the night in my room in the hotel thinking that something would happen, and money would come early in the morning so that I would be able to pay the bill. In the morning, as I was leaving the hotel, I took the bill from my room to pay it at the desk as I went down, although as I said before, I did not have any money with me. When I came to the desk, I had a big floppy envelope in my mail box. I opened the envelope and found the exact amount of money needed for the payment of the bill, and the bill was paid. The envelope did not contain any name or address of the person who brought that money, because some of my disciples like to give anonymous contributions to help in the dissemination of spiritual knowledge.

A few years ago I was in San Francisco giving lectures. The expenses in arranging the lectures and paying the rents of the lecture halls and publicity were far greater than the contributions I received in response to those lectures. I never care how much I receive in contributions, but I keep on spending and doing the things which will bring fulfillment to my plans. The day had arrived when I had to leave San Francisco for New York, and I knew I had to pay the rent for the whole month to the hotel when I was checking out. I had all my reservations made for traveling and was not worried about the payment of a month's rent to the hotel, because I knew that money would come. When I checked out, the clerk at the desk stamped my bill as paid and gave me about $300.00. I took the money and put it in my wallet and left the hotel. I really needed that money to pay for the fare, taxi, etc. My close disciples always keep my needs in mind and so money was there waiting for me when I needed it.

Thus, no matter how things happen, when you press your psychic button, things do happen according to your plans. Persons will always help you in your plans guided by the psychic powers.

This is only one instance in my life. My whole life is full of innumerable such instances. All my work is mostly done by the use of the higher powers of the mind. If I had to make the physical effort to accomplish my goal to spread the good work, I would hardly succeed in my ambition. What I practice myself, I teach to my disciples, and I enjoy very much sharing this ancient knowledge and wisdom with my friends, disciples and patrons in the United States of America, so that they can likewise use it to promote their ideals and to make their dreams come true.

When you tap your subconscious for amazing results, you really develop new channels in your brain which at present lie dormant and unused within you. In many people, the psychic channels are clogged and those inlets have to be opened to enable persons to use their psychic powers in their everyday life. There is a higher mind which has you in charge, as it has the sun and moon, planets and comets, which move unceasingly. When you are able to tap your subconscious, you succeed in sharing and controlling and using consciously the powers of the higher mind to achieve the objects of your dream. You have desires and wants in your life. At the same time, you also have the store of supply within you, and that is your higher mind. In order to look for the fulfillment of your desires in your life, you have to look to the store of supply within you, rather than look for the answer outside in the world. What you seek and find outside in the world is simply an effect. The cause is within. When you create the cause, it will always materialize into a physical phenomena which you can acquire physically and take possession of, to satisfy your needs in life.

Why you cannot solve many of your problems is because you are not able to tap your subconscious and take your problem deep within your higher mind which has infinite knowledge and power, and which directs and controls your conscious mind. The awareness of your body and your conscious mind cannot help you much in your life because it is limited in power and manifestation. When you are awake you cannot fly with your gross body because your consciousness of the gross body makes it too difficult for you to fly in the air. But during dream, you rise above the gross body consciousness and you can fly. Your conscious mind can make only petty decisions, The larger decisions in life can be made only by the higher mind.

If you take a piece of cloth and you tie a lump of sugar in one of the corners and put the whole cloth inside a cup of water, except the corner of the cloth which holds the lump of sugar, you will find that the sugar is hardly affected by the water. Then again, if you let the whole handkerchief including the end with the sugar go inside the water in the cup, you will very soon find that the lump of sugar melts and disappears and becomes a part of the water, making the water sweet. Similarly, as long as you keep your problem outside the higher mind, it never melts and never gets solved. Every day you find that the problem is as acute, serious and as large as it ever was. But when you dip your problem deep into your higher mind, it immediately disappears like the lump of sugar into the water, and your problem is solved. Because you immediately receive the answer to your problem and you discover that you were strong enough to solve the problem rather than the problem being stronger than you. If you use only your conscious mind, you find that your problem is bigger than you, but when you use your higher mind, you find that you are bigger than the problem, and naturally you don't have any difficulty in getting through the problem.

Chapter 16 PSYCHIC PERCEPTION AND ASTRAL SENSES

EVERYTHING PHYSICAL and material in this world is simply a counterpart of the things which exist in the form of invisible thoughts. Things are only a reflection and counterpart of the invisible thoughts. Physical senses are simply a counterpart of your astral senses. Advanced scientists have also realized that the real power to see is not in the eyes, but in a brain center in the head. Similarly, the power of the other senses lies deep in the brain centers, which are the seat of the astral senses. The real perception takes place there rather than in the physical senses. It is these astral senses which have the power to perceive, taste, smell, see, and feel sensations of hot and cold, etc. When the astral senses leave the body at the time of death, the eyes cease to see, the ears stop hearing, the nose does not smell, and the tongue does not taste, the skin does not feel the sensation of heat and cold—though the physical senses are still there. In the absence of the astral senses, the physical senses are incapable of discharging their duties.

It is not the loudspeaker which speaks, but it is the person whose voice is carried through the loudspeaker that is important. If the person who speaks through the microphone does not exist, the loudspeaker itself cannot speak for him. Similarly, when the astral senses cease to function, the physical senses are dead as a stone. Even if you touch the eyeball of a dead person, it does not react, because the astral senses which makes a person perceive the world through the senses, have departed.

The astral senses are a part of your higher mind, which in itself is the part of the higher universal mind which fills all space. When you use your astral senses consciously, you become the center of universal dynamic psychic power.

The astral senses when used consciously can help you penetrate the various layers of consciousness, like a diver who penetrates the layers of water in the ocean and brings out pearls. Similarly, the astral senses penetrate the layers of consciousness and bring the knowledge and wisdom which lie beyond the reach of the conscious mind, and make the mysteries of Nature an open book to you.

This higher mind is everlasting and eternal. It does not die with the fall of your body; it never becomes extinct, because it is everlasting, and continues to function even after you are dead. The astral senses are part of this eternal mind, which speaks to an understanding ear, which is always ready to counsel those who are intuitive. By using the astral senses you can exchange your views with those of your dear and most loved ones who have departed from this physical world. It is this eternal mind which sees, thinks and tastes, through the astral senses. You can reach it by inner perception through your astral senses. The Adepts and the Yogis always rely on the use of their astral senses. John the Baptist, while using his astral senses was asked, "Who are you?" and he answered, "I am a voice crying out in the wilderness."

When your body falls, your eternal mind and astral senses survive. The eternal mind expresses its thoughts by vibrations of color. The more a person has evolved into the higher powers of the mind, the more he is able to consciously use those powers. A person awakened to the astral senses has not to clatter his tongue against the upper palate to express his thoughts in the form of words, because he can send his thoughts with the rapidity of the speed of sound in the form of vibrations of color. A person awakened to the use of the astral senses can translate the music of the spheres into language and thus be in communion with the higher forces of Nature, because the music of the spheres is the language of Nature. Only those awakened to the use of the astral senses can understand the mysteries of Nature.

The power of the conscious mind and your physical senses is very limited, and they can only understand the words which pop out of your mouth when you start to clatter your tongue. Spoken words are the broken expression of your thoughts. The astral senses use the language of silence. They hear in silence and they speak in silence. Silence is their language.

A rose tree in the winter seems to be covered by snow; all the flowers fade and the petals are scattered by storms on the surface of the earth, but still the tree is not dead and gone. When the next spring comes, you see the first branches coming out of the same root and bringing new flowers in the orchard. Similarly, the eternal mind does not die when the body falls.

The whole Bible, especially the New Testament, is full of numerous instances of Christ using the astral senses and bringing the knowledge of astral perception to the people of the world. It is by the use of the astral senses that Christ entered the mansions which do not exist in this world, but exist only in the astral. It is this eternal mind which shapes the destiny of the whole world. It is this eternal mind which created the world and is still directing it towards its goal. The world as you see it now is not in its ideal pattern. It is still in the melting pot and is being shaped towards its goal by the higher invisible forces.

See the work of eternal mind in the formation of crystals. The whole world is nothing but the formation of a crystal, crystallized into definite shape by the indwelling mind. Mt. Everest and other great mountains in the world are nothing but the results of this crystal formation by the power of eternal mind. The whole earth is nothing but a broken down crystal formed long ago. It is very important for the people of the world to know, to use, and to share this power of the higher mind within, which can take you directly to the store of your inner supply, where you can obtain the fulfillment of all your desires in life.

When you have approached your inner supply, you never fall short of anything you need in life. You will always have miraculous results in your life no matter what you do.

Sometime ago, one person asked one of my disciples, "Why is it Yogi Gupta gets unfailing results no matter what he does, in his service career, in his career as a businessman, in his career as an attorney at law in one of the most prominent high courts in India, and also as a Spiritual *Preceptor*? I don't know of any other person who can match him in this world in his diversified accomplishments." My disciple answered, "When one controls and shares the powers of the eternal mind that knows everything, such a person can never be wrong because eternal mind can only be right."

Eternal mind, which has the astral senses as its instrument, is older than the human race. It existed millions of years before the human race came into existence. As such, its knowledge and wisdom can hardly be perceived through physical senses and the conscious mind.

At the time of my being ordained into the Order of Monk, my teacher told me, "Do not care for the opinion of the public or for the advice of your disciples. Do not ask for advice and guidance from anyone in the world. Follow the commands of the eternal mind and you will always be right."

My *Guru* told me that the people of the world have their opinions and advice based upon their conscious mind which is limited and therefore not infallible, and when you rely upon the voice of your eternal mind you can be confident that the advice is always right; no matter what you do in your life and whatever your plans are in life, you will always stand on the Rock of Gibraltar, unshaken and unmoved.

Chapter 17 THOUGHT FORMS AND ASTRAL PICTURES

IT IS YOUR THOUGHTS which exist in the form of vibration that in due course materialize into physical objects and your actions. Every action, physical or mental in your life, is preceded by a specific thought in your mind, and that specific thought in your mind is preceded by specific astral pictures or astral images. The astral image may be your own, or it may be a projection from someone else, absorbed into your mind, and thus the astral images of someone else become astral images of your own, and as such exert influence and determine your thinking as well as your physical actions.

The majority of murders and lewd crimes are committed by innocent persons who are weak in their psychic defense and therefore cannot resist the astral images and thought forms of hardened criminals. It is these innocent and weak people who become instruments of these negative astral pictures, and have an irresistible urge to do wrong things. When a person is in the clutches of negative thoughts, he can commit suicide, murder, theft and any heinous crime. The nature of the crime is determined by the nature of the astral pictures which have entered his mind.

When you go to the movies, the pictures which you see on the screen are determined by the film which is projected far away from you, high on the balcony through a projector. Similarly, the actions of a person in this world are determined by the astral images which are far from being perceived and detected by the physical eyes. The play on the screen is only an effect, its cause being the images on the film. Similarly, the actions of a criminal are only the effect, the cause of those crimes being the astral images in his mind. A criminal can be corrected in his way of life by correcting the external images in his psychic mind. The science of the creation of psychic phenomena is drawing the interest of numerous people across the world, because people have realized that this is time that they must use their psychic powers and protect and defend themselves in the interest of their country. The students of today in the psychic field are sure to become the prophets and leaders of tomorrow, because they are falling in with the tide. When you do something which is sorely needed by the people, you become successful. When you do something which is not needed, you can become a failure.

Ford started to manufacture the car when the world was ready to use them, and he became the most successful auto manufacturer in the world. Many people are starting new businesses for the manufacture of cars, but they cannot become as successful as Ford. An expert swimmer in the ocean falls in with the tide, and thus he has a way back to the beach or into the ocean with absolutely no effort, because he simply knows how to swim with the tide. On the other hand, a novice may swim against the tide simply to find that no matter how much he swims against the tide to go deep into the ocean, he is thrown back on the beach by the tide. No one in the world has been able to fight the forces of Nature. The power of Nature is very strong, and those who challenge it are doomed to destruction.

This is the time when the whole world is ready for the use of the forces of the higher mind in the creation of psychic phenomena and as such, the people who come into this field at the very start will become the leaders and prophets of the world in the near future. It is this need of the people of the world which inspires the teachers and the prophets, and as a result of their inner inspiration, they come to the world to disseminate the knowledge, wisdom and truth of the eternal mind, to the people of the world who sorely need it to enable them to make their lives more peaceful, happier and better.

The psychic forces affect not only human beings, who are the only ones who can consciously create psychic phenomena, but also affect everything animate as well as inanimate. In due course, even vegetation and insects develop a psychic immunity to harmful forces. Every, insect, germ, no matter how harmful it may be, has been created by the forces of Nature, because its presence in this world is needed, and as such no forces of the conscious mind or human effort can cause their extinction in this world. By unconsciously developing psychic immunity, even bacteria and germs can stand the effect of poisonous drugs. Long ago DDT spray would kill germs and bugs in the hospitals, but now they have achieved immunity to these insecticides. Similarly, the various chemicals and sprays now cannot kill the harmful plants and weeds in farms because they have achieved immunity to these insecticides.

The time has come when the people of the world must achieve immunity from the psychic attacks from outside and the negative thoughts from other persons so that they can better evolve in their lives and help the evolution of the world itself on the right path. It is the dissemination of this higher occult knowledge which sends forth the great teachers from country to country, from one part of the world to the other, initiating the people into these mysteries of Truth to help them achieve this psychic immunity, so that they become better nationals, better citizens, and better persons of the world, to enable the world to become better and better on its path of evolution towards a better world. The A and H Bombs cannot provide enough security to a person to give him strength and peace of mind, because the real security comes by achieving psychic immunity. Any amount of physical protection by arms and bombs cannot stop the astral images which can penetrate deep into the mind of a person, and thereby control his actions.

Your thoughts are a living force as your thoughts enter the mind of someone else. Similarly, the thoughts of others enter your mind. Thoughts create waves in the mind-stuff like the waves of the ocean, and thus they inject a thought into another person's mind in the form of thought forms and astral pictures which subsequently materialize into physical actions and create physical changes. Thought forms shoot from the mind like a bullet from a rifle, generally unconsciously.

The thought forms which are generally released unconsciously actually set up an astral picture in the ethereal substance which fills space, and around that astral picture the atoms, electrons and protons begin to unite in order to materialize the results with which the astral image is pregnant. The astral image carries with it intelligence, will power and life, and thus is able to discriminate between the electrons, protons and atoms of various wavelengths, and is able to draw to itself those electrons and protons which vibrate at a specific wavelength and push away the others which are not wanted, and thus helping in the creation of a thing or thought in the astral in the form of colors invisible to the physical eyes. These thought forms of specific colors get injected into the psychic aura of the person and finally they materialize into his physical actions because it is the psychic body which feeds the physical body.

Just as you need regular training to become a good rifleman, driving lessons in order to drive, and swimming lessons in order to swim, similarly, one has to learn the process of the creation of psychic phenomena and shooting the thought forms to make them materialize into physical things and create psychic phenomena. The personal instructions should be taken under the guidance of a teacher who is an expert along these lines.

Astral pictures are but a thought made visible, and the thought can be combated by a similar force, thus enabling you to defend yourself against the harmful and negative thoughts which may materialize into a physical condition in your body if they are not countered.

First a person gets various allergies and colds psychically, simply to find that the cold and virus have affected him physically. If you can defend yourself from these viruses, allergies, and sicknesses psychically, there will be nothing wrong with you physically, because you have eliminated the root, and therefore the tree and fruits will never bloom. The invisible thought form is the root of the sickness, and its fruit is its manifestation into the physical form.

For example, first a person gets cancer in the form of astral images, then the cancer comes into the bloodstream and finally it appears on a part of the body. A person having cancer in any part of the body will find that he does not have a single drop of blood in his body which does not contain the contamination of cancer.

Thoughts never die, and therefore they are much more formidable if they are negative. Germs die, but thoughts do not die and as such, negative thoughts can do harm to more people than germs. Just as antibiotics and serums when injected into your blood try to protect you against the contagion of germs and bacteria, similarly, the psychic immunity is the greatest antibiotic, which protects you against psychic attacks and thereby ensures your physical health. It has been universally recognized that mental diseases are contagious, but so far science has not developed any drug or pill to combat the contagious thoughts, and they float in space from city to city attacking the people with poor psychic defenses, forcing them to do wrong and creating certain physical conditions in their bodies, including bodily sicknesses. If people are helped to achieve psychic immunity against harmful astral pictures, I am sure that within a short time there will be nobody in the mental institutions.

Since thoughts never die, once they leave your mind, they live through eternity and keep on working either for you or against you. Either they bring good luck and create good physical conditions for you in your body, or they create mishaps, bad luck for you in the world, and at the same time physical sicknesses, one after the other, affecting your physical and mental health. You must realize that you are living in a world where only the fittest can survive. Those who ignore the operation of the higher psychic forces are taking the greatest risks of their lives, because no one in this world can stop the functions of the forces of Nature. If you do not control the forces of Nature, they will control you and disappoint you if they are unfavorable, or help you if they are in your favor.

It is psychically weak persons who suffer tremendously. If you place a candle burning on the outside of your window, the storm will put it out because it is weak. But if the house is on fire, the same storm will give tremendous speed and strength to the flames and they can devour and engulf the whole city. Thus it is a hard truth that Nature destroys the weak and helps the strong. The time has come when the people who are weak and cannot defend themselves against negative psychic influences will be the losers. On the other hand, those who learn how to use the higher and powerful forces of Nature and the mind, become the leaders and guides of the world.

By the use of your psychic forces you can materialize, objectify and actualize in physical life, things, powers, events, happenings, conditions, circumstances, and everything and anything that can be wished by you. The creation of psychic phenomena has to be learned just like one learns to shoot a rifle. You may say, "Well, all right, tell me how to create this psychic phenomena." Well, you cannot learn to shoot simply by reading a book or description. You cannot learn to drive a car by reading a driver's manual. It is much more important to have the personal instruction of a teacher when you learn how to drive your thoughts on the psychic and astral plane.

Chapter 18 FAME AND FORTUNE BY PSYCHIC MEANS

THOUGHTS ARE THINGS in the invisible form. When thoughts become creative, they polarize and influence the inferior minds of objects and things, and bring change in the existing phenomena by drawing those objects and things to you, or by drawing you to those objects and things.

Thoughts do not have drawing force and creative power unless they arise from your higher mind. The thoughts of an average person arise in the conscious mind, which is very limited in its power of expression and creation, as a result of which these thoughts and plans seldom materialize into physical form. When thoughts arise in the higher mind, an additional quantity of *Prana* is infused consciously into such thoughts, as a result of which, the thought shoots from the mind towards its target like a bullet shooting from a rifle, hitting its target.

Thoughts in the conscious mind are weak and poor, and are expressed through words. When thought expresses through words, much of its power is lost. Thoughts from the higher mind need not be expressed through words. Creative thoughts from the higher mind emanate in silence in the form of thought vibrations, and proceed towards the persons and objects for whom they are meant.

Long ago in Calcutta, there lived a person who wanted to be a publisher. He did not have any previous experience in publishing or editing. He was unknown to the public and did not have any experience writing. Financially, he was completely broke. He had an idea of publishing his own magazine that was to become a reality. He used psychic powers in order to achieve fame and fortune and become a successful publisher of the magazine. As he used the psychic powers, the creative thoughts started to proceed from his higher mind, reached the people and results started to materialize. Shortly, he received a letter from one of his friends who volunteered to guarantee the printing bill of his proposed magazine for the first month. That is how the work got started. He continued to use his psychic powers, as a result of which he got enough subscribers from the persons to whom he sent sample copies. Now he had enough to pay the bill for the first printing, and also to guarantee the second and third printings. In a few month's time he had a very large list of subscribers and every month he sold more space in his magazine to advertising clients, who paid him handsome money. Very soon he had a fat account in the bank and success after success followed in his life and business. His business friends would remark that he always falls on the jackpot. Anyone, making his thoughts creative, can bring fame and fortune into his life. When one wants to use psychic powers for fame and fortune, it is never too late.

Until thoughts become creative and positive, it is difficult to achieve sound results, because weak and poor thoughts attract similar thoughts. A person whose thoughts are negative and dominated by fear, anxiety, a feeling of insecurity, an inferiority complex, hatred, jealousy, etc., will always attract similar thoughts towards himself, thus making things more negative, which in the long run becomes the main cause of their failure in life. Like attracts like. A person who is positive and whose thoughts are creative will attract like persons and objects towards him, or he will be attracted to such persons and objects. On the other hand, a person with negative thoughts will pick up only negative thoughts, ignoring positive thoughts around him.

There was a woman in New York whose husband was getting away from her. He would generally ignore her and would seldom pay proper attention to her. He would stay away from home till very late at night. Sometimes he would return early in the morning. One day the wife told him that she had a right to know where he stays at night. At this, the husband became angry and threatened her life. The woman was terrorized and lost consciousness. Since that day, she never asked him what he does and where he goes.

She came to study the process of the creation of psychic phenomena, and when she learned the techniques and the working process, she started to use them on her husband. Very soon results started to materialize in her life. She would reach her husband through her thoughts, and her thoughts would be reproduced as his thoughts, as a result of which he started to think, speak, and act for her. After a few days, he lost interest in the outside attractions, and did go anymore away from his home leaving his wife alone. One day he came to his wife and made a sincere confession, asked for forgiveness, and told her that he had completely broken off all his outside affairs. Since that time he became a good, honest, sincere and devoted husband.

Many people unconsciously drive friends away from themselves. A person may need a love friend, for instance, in his life, or a spouse may need a sincere partner in married life; but on numerous occasions uncontrolled negative thoughts drive away the love friend or partner. There is no use blaming the partner for being unloving and not paying enough attention, because the fault lies with the person himself as his uncontrolled wrong thoughts of suspicion, doubt etc., repel the friends away.

A woman tried to get a divorce from her husband because he was an alcoholic and nervous. After the divorce, she married another person, only to find out after sometime that he too, was an alcoholic and nervous. She again worked hard to get a divorce. When she married the third time, she was surprised to notice that the husband happened to be an alcoholic and a very nervous person. Then she started to doubt herself, that maybe there was something wrong with her that she picks up the wrong partner. She consulted a psychiatrist and many specialists in the matter who advised her that she was to blame for attracting the wrong partner to herself, who was an alcoholic and nervous. The best advice for her was that she first change herself so that she would be able to reach persons who are positive and strong and do not have any vices and wrong habits. She started to study and develop the use of the powers of the higher mind, as a result of which she succeeded in attracting to herself, and finally marrying, the person whom she had had in her mind since long ago as her most cherished ideal.

No matter what the nature of business of a person is, no matter what the objective of a person is, when your thoughts become creative you don't lose time in making your dreams come true. I will tell you an interesting case of a person in Bombay. He was a financial tragedy and physical wreck. He had many major operations performed on him removing many parts and vital organs from his body. Due to ulcers, part of his intestines was removed, and practically three-fourths of his stomach, as a result of which he was tremendously handicapped in life. He had tried to become successful in his life but all his efforts were completely fruitless. He was introduced to me through one of my students who has achieved fame and success through the creation of psychic phenomena. He was initiated into the mysteries of psychic teaching and the results were outstanding. He was a writer by profession. As a result of his developed psychic powers, the stories started to write themselves for him, and from all over Bombay business started to flow to his studio. He became one of the topmost original motion picture and film story writers, of international fame. He had a large advertising client list for his magazine and a big account in the bank. He lived like a lord, rolling in wealth, fame and fortune.

The timeless wisdom of psychic powers is as good in modern times as it was thousands of years ago. The use and development of psychic powers is neither a religion nor creed; it is scientific and practical. It teaches people the use of the higher and finer forces of Nature, which are available for use everywhere.

Another interesting case where fame and fortune came by psychic means was a young boy, a very handsome and smart looking person, who had all the qualities of an actor. He was quite fit for the screen, but still he could not succeed in his ambitions. Whenever he would be called for an interview, he would drive people away by means of his uncontrolled and harmful thoughts emanating from his higher mind, as a result of which his applications were always rejected and in his interviews he was never selected. He was guided to learn the process of creation of psychic phenomena and psychologization. He successfully studied and used these powers. This time it was not he who asked for the job. He was invited by a film company to come for an interview. Next day, when he went for the interview. Everything was set psychically, and immediately he was selected and asked to do a screen test the same afternoon. The directors were very much impressed during the filming. One of them remarked that he was really marvelous and wonderful. The other director remarked, "He does not look like he is acting, he looks like he is the character." He made the greatest hit on the very day of his interview. A contract was signed between him and the director. That was the beginning of great success in his life as an actor. He became a leading star.

If you have tried everything in your life to gain success, fame and fortune, and your dreams have not come true, try the process of psychologization, i.e., reaching the minds of persons and objects through your thoughts and drawing them to you for the fulfillment of your dreams. If you have tried everything from Christian Science to castor oil, and nothing has worked in your life to make your dreams come true, try this method of psychologization. I am sure you will never feel sorry you did.

Chapter 19 PSYCHIC INFLUENCE TO WIN FRIENDS

ORIENTALS ARE past masters in psychologizing. In India, since time immemorial, Hindus have had the opportunity to learn the process of psychologization while quite young and living with their parents and teachers.

Psychologization is quite contrary to hypnotism, mesmerism or black magic. Just like day is different from night, and darkness from light, similarly, the use of psychic influence is different from hypnosis. Psychic influence is the use of the higher and finer forces of Nature in reaching the minds of objects and persons in a perfectly natural way. Universal healing and prayer for world peace are all based on the use of the finer forces of Nature, known as psychologization. In hypnosis, the will of the subjects is overpowered, as a result of which they become weaker and are unable to exert their own will. On the other hand, in psychologization a person is helped to make his will supernormally strong and creative, as a result of which he is able to create the things which do not exist in his life. In hypnosis, a person can be made to believe or see something which is not true. For example, the subject may be made to smell or taste an object which does not exist. On the other hand, in the process of psychologization the object is created by the use of the finer and higher forces of Nature with the help of the strong will, of an Adept or a person who is fully trained in the process of psychologization.

In the process of psychologization, thoughts in the form of vibrations are injected into another person's will, as a result of which he starts to act in a natural way according to the wishes of the person whose thoughts have been reproduced into his will.

In the process of psychologization the thoughts of a person, in a natural way become a part of the will of the person in whom they are injected through the susceptibility of his imagination. The desires and wishes of one person by psychic means are reproduced into the other person's will and imagination, and as a result of which the latter starts to think, act and speak for the person whose thoughts have been reproduced into his mind. Just as the cuckoo makes other birds hatch its egg by making them believe that it is theirs, so the thoughts of one person are accepted by another person as his own.

Your thought forms are alive and they have distinct form. Thoughts manifest a certain astral color and they have a vibratory motion. The form and color of your thoughts depend upon the variety of thoughts. Thoughts of hatred, jealousy, and depression have negative colors, while thoughts of love, joy, wisdom, etc., have positive colors.

To an average person, thoughts are not visible as a physical entity, but on close scrutiny to the bare eye, thoughts may seem cloudy in appearance, bearing the color belonging to them. Thoughts are like a vapor. The degree of density of the vapor constituting the thought varies with the nature of thoughts, and is just as real as the air around you, or the vapor of steam or gases. Many times in hospitals at the time of death, a person's thoughts together with his soul are seen leaving the dead body in the form of mist and vapor. When your thought comes in contact with the mind-stuff of the other person, it imposes upon it its distinct character and rate of psychic vibrations, and thus sets up thought waves in his mind-stuff, as a result of which your thoughts become his thoughts and he starts to think and speak for you and do things for you.

Thoughts are transmitted across space like waves of electricity, light and heat. For the Hindus in India it is as easy to understand and practice psychic influence, as it is easy for a Westerner to understand and use radio, microphone and wireless telegraphy, whose waves travel through space like thought waves. It is very common in India for the Yogis and Adepts to transmit thoughts to their disciples and followers, and also to receive thoughts from afar from people who are able to tune in with them.

Psychic influence can be successfully used in winning friends and also during personal interviews. During a personal interview, in the process of psychologization, the thoughts of one person move in astral form towards the other like a torpedo proceeding to hit its target.

One person was called for an interview for the post of supervisor in a company. The person asked for a minimum salary which was equal to that of a director of the company. While he was being interviewed for the post of supervisor, he presented his case on the psychic level, in addition to showing his diploma and qualifications to the panel of directors. His psychic presentation hit the panel of directors on the mental plane like a torpedo, and they decided to hire him for the position of director which could be created in the near future, because he was a person with special talents and qualifications. In the meantime, he would be asked to discharge the duties of a personnel assistant to managing agents.

In this way, this person was invited to interview for the post of supervisor, but got himself appointed as a director. You are not created for the job, the job is created for you. If you want a job or position which is not available, or which does not exist in the world, it will be created especially for you when you use your psychic powers. The above said person created a position of director for himself. When you know the process of psychologization, you can change events and happenings in your life to fit into your dreams, rather than adjusting yourself to fit in to existing circumstances and surroundings of the world. A person with psychic powers never has to compromise with circumstances in life. The circumstances change themselves to fit into his life.

You, too, do not have to live a life of adjustment and compromise. Be the master of your destiny. Control the finer forces of Nature. Learn to express your wishes through your higher mind.

Make your thoughts creative and change your environment, and make things happen as you want them to in your life. Draw the type of persons and friends to your life that you wish.

Recently scientists have been making an effort to translate thoughts as they travel through space so that they may be able to read thoughts before they transform themselves into phenomena. For example, if a person has a thought of anger, jealousy and hatred and one can read the thought before the thought manifests into action, he will be able to evade the consequences of such action. For instance, if your friend is mad at you due to some misunderstanding, by reading such thoughts you can leave the room before he punches you in the face, and thus you are able to avoid the consequences.

Every action is preceded by a thought, be it a thought of love, jealousy, anger, hatred, joy or happiness. Thoughts, sooner or later, materialize into action. In other words every action is an invisible thought before it materializes.

Many have become topmost salesmen handling the transactions of big firms by knowing the secrets of psychic influence in personal interviews, as well as psychic influence in winning friends while making personal contacts with customers and other desirable persons in business and society. It is during these business and social meetings that they present their case on a psychic level and transactions are made, as a result of which they become topmost salesmen, while most of their sales are done psychically.

Many people of marriageable age have successfully used psychic influence in personal interviews while selecting their love mates and also to attract to themselves the type of friends they want.

A leading insurance man used to sell his policies psychically from his apartment by reaching customers psychically all over the country who were prone to buy insurance policies, and also those who were still uncommitted. When he would go into the office, he would find the customers there ready to finalize the transaction. As a matter of fact, the insurance policies were sold psychically. The physical meeting between the salesman and the customer was only a result of the commitments made psychically, and the salesman did not have to make a lot of effort to satisfy the customer about the potential of the policy when he came to his office. In order to achieve the best results, you should present your ideas during an interview, on the psychic level.

During the interview, one should not use compulsion, because it is a force from without which can turn a friend into an enemy. For successful results one should use impulsion, as a result of which your thought gets lodged in the mind of the other person, and a natural impulse is created in him, which can transform an enemy into a friend. The details of impulsion and compulsion should be learned under the personal guidance of a teacher. Thoughts presented psychically work in silence. Your thoughts are unspoken words, and are more powerful than the spoken word. Thoughts are the voice of silence and a soundless sound which fills all space, which is more powerful than the loudest sounds which exist in the world. Just as men of action (scientists) concentrate in laboratories and find the secrets of planets and comets, and send rockets to the moon and Venus, so Yogis (men of contemplation) concentrate on inner psychic centers, since time immemorial, and are able to reach psychically far off constellations and millions and billions of solar systems about which practically nothing is known by science. The science of astrology is based on knowledge acquired psychically.

Chapter 20 MIRACLES OF PSYCHIC S.O.S.

TEACHING THE USE of the psychic wavelength has always been one of the duties of spiritual teachers. Throughout the ages, the psychic wavelength has been used successfully by most religious teachers and prophets. Psychic healing is one of the results of the use of the psychic wavelength. The great teachers of all religions have developed great followings having tremendous faith in them by creating phenomenal changes by the use of the psychic wavelength.

Through the psychic wavelength one is able to attract persons, things, circumstances, conditions, events and happenings, and is also able to change them successfully according to his wish. Either you are drawn to them, or they are drawn to you, whichever happens to be in the line of least resistance. If you reach a person for help by psychic wavelength, either the person will be drawn to you immediately, or you will be drawn to that person. The one which happens to be in the line of least resistance moves towards the other. In many cases, the movement takes place on both sides, till they meet each other.

By learning the law of the psychic S.O.S. one can benefit himself, as well as his friends. A psychic S.O.S. is when you make a mental demand and a psychic call for help. Such a call may be made either to a specific person, or to the people as a whole.

By psychic S.O.S. you are able to reach a person no matter how far away he is. When you make a mental call, it will be received by people who are vibrating at the same wavelength and they will respond to your mental call. For example, an S.O.S. sent by a sinking ship will be received by other ships on the ocean which are equipped with the instuments of the same wavelength, and they will come to help the ship in distress. On the other hand ships that are not equipped with the instruments of the same wavelength will not receive the message and will not come to help the ship in distress. Similarly, when you send a mental call for help, only those will be reached and attracted who are in a position to give you the type of help you need in your life.

Once a person was writing a book; he needed certain references and information before he could complete his book. He tried his best, but could not get that information. Then he sent a psychic S.O.S., and immediately the response came. He had an irresistible urge to visit his neighbor. While he was waiting in the living room for his friend, he idly picked up one of the books from the shelf, which he was guided by psychic wavelength to pick up. When he opened it, there right before his eyes were the references which he had been looking for to complete his book. Thus he found the missing link which enabled him to complete the book. The book became one of the best sellers of the day, and brought him success.

When you need help and are tired of reaching people by phone, by post, through telegram, radio, television, magazines, etc., try the psychic S.O.S.; the results will be amazing and faster. Help will come to you, or you will be drawn to the place and person where you can get the help.

There is nothing supernatural in the sending and receiving of a mental call. It is supernormal, because a normal person is not able to send a mental call. When you call a person on the phone, your call travels through the telephone wires, but in the psychic S.O.S. you use the astral tube which is formed across space full of astral matter. The astral tube is formed by your creative thoughts and psychic powers, and thus it becomes the medium of your contact with the person who receives the mental call. The astral tube can penetrate walls of steel and stone, because it can penetrate the atoms, electrons and protons which constitute a piece of stone or a plate of steel. When you call a friend on the phone, he may be busy in the other room and may not be able to attend to the call, but when you send a mental call, no matter where the person is, the call will be received and the response will come. All other means of communication may fail, however, you can always rely on a psychic S.O.S., which is based on the forces of Nature, and Nature never fails. Nature reaches all human beings in this world; it maintains and creates life in plants, animals and human beings, but it has no wires of communication. It reaches out through invisible forces of Nature.

A business man in New Delhi had a wonderful plan to start a new business, but he did not have the money. Previously he had tried many financiers who promised to back him, but they did not fulfill their pledge and therefore his plans never materialized. He was disappointed and had practically no hope that he would find a financier who could enable him to realize his dreams. Finally, he learned the process of sending a psychic S.O.S. In response to his mental call, there was a financier who was looking for a person with a wonderful plan for starting a new business to make a large fortune. Due to the psychic S.O.S., the financier was drawn to him, rather than he trying to find the financier. His plans were financed very well and he made the biggest success of his life. He made a big fortune and his dreams became a reality. The financier got his share of the fortune as well.

In the use of the psychic S.O.S., natural law and order is called into operation and manifestation and results are produced in a natural way in the world. There is nothing miraculous about the results of the psychic S.O.S. Every object has mind that can be reached psychically. The mental call is similar to a call sent through a telegram or radiophone.

Psychic calls by salesmen and businessmen, merchants and storekeepers can bring a lot of customers to their shops, and give them a real big business. Mental calls from a storekeeper or a businessman are received across the country by the persons who are prone to purchase those objects. They are also received by people who are still uncommitted in their decisions whether to purchase. All these people are drawn psychically to the store and they buy the goods. Mental calls can be successfully used by all professional men, writers, actors, physicians, and artists. Also by men and women who want a love friend or those who are seeking a love mate or helpmate. They can successfully send their mental calls by a psychic S.O.S. Persons who are seeking a job, real estate, or a specific type of house to buy, can send mental calls successfully as well.

A hard-hitting publicity campaign is able to reach only a very limited number of persons. For example, you advertise your business in a magazine or newspaper, but a very small proportion of the people who live in the whole country read that specific magazine and that specific advertisement. A huge number of persons who are anxious to buy the object of your advertisement do not read the magazine in which you have advertised your product, and as such, they are not able to buy your product. When you send the mental call, you reach only those people who can use your product in their business, and in their life. Also those people who are uncommitted and have not decided what specific product to use in their business, become naturally committed to your product as a result of the mental call. Your call with the help of their imagination and will power materializes into reality and very soon you find them all sending orders to you for the purchase of the product in question. You have to learn the working process of psychic broadcasting which enables one to send a mental call.

The disciples on the Path are guided by Masters by mental calls. The disciple, far away from his teacher, when he is ready, receives a mental call from the teacher and is able to find the teacher meant for him deep in the Himalayas, in the wilderness. If it were not for the mental call, I would not have found my teacher, who lived in a Himalayan valley, in a thick forest.

Chapter 21 YOUR PSYCHIC INCOME

THE THOUGHTS of today are things of tomorrow. Psychic debits and credits of today are the debits and credits of tomorrow in your business. Just as you can cultivate virtues and eradicate evils by use of the mental forces taught and practiced by the Yogis, known as Yamas and Niyamas, similarly you can eliminate your debits and create credits in your business. In other words, you can prevent loss and bring success and profits into your life and business.

Many people know that they have not achieved the amount of success and prosperity in their lives which they would really like to achieve. Although they may not admit their shortcomings to others, still in their heart of hearts, they know that they would like to achieve certain things which would bring them perfection, prosperity and success.

Prosperity and income should be earned psychically. Once you have a good psychic income, then you simply wait for the psychic income to materialize into physical, material income. A businessman may have a million dollars to his credit in his account in the bank. At the same time he may be in debt psychically for two million dollars, as a result of which very soon he will find that the debt materializes into reality due to some unforeseen things happening and all the credit is gone and he finds his books one million in the red. On the other hand, a person who knows the law of psychic income, does not feel sorry to see in his books a million dollars in the red, because he can create psychic income worth two million, which will pay off the one million in the red, leaving still to his credit one million in the black. Credits and debits should be worked on the psychic level. In order to bring prosperity and more income, a person should increase his psychic income—the income and dollars would automatically increase. Once you learn the control of the forces of mind and are able to use the finer forces of Nature through your mind, you can increase your psychic income. By the same process psychically you can pay all your debts and bills.

There is a close relation between physical actions and mental states and mental conditions. Physical conditions, for example, such as ulcers, diabetes, etc., are created due to certain mental states. Similarly, income in business is increased or decreased due to the psychic forces operating for or against the person. Everything physical and material is only a reflection of a specific mental state.

If you stand up and look upward towards the sky for a few seconds you will find the feelings of devotion and reverence rising in your mind. If you look sideways, in a few seconds you will find a feeling of restlessness, doubt and suspicion arising in your mind. If you look downwards, in a few seconds you will find that you are in a mental state of reverie or half-asleep, and if you fix your eyes to one side, and a little downward at the same time, feelings of jealousy and worry will start to rise in your mind, because every physical movement and expression is a manifestation of a specific mental state.

When I was studying with my teacher, he taught me how I could know how wise or stupid a person was, also what was cooking in anyone's mind. He told me, "Copy the expression of his face on your face and wait a few seconds to see what thoughts and feelings start to rise in your mind, and then you will know exactly what is cooking in the mind of the other person."

Once my teacher went to the city and I followed him there. It was a day of festival for the pilgrims; a huge crowd of people surrounded him to have his *Darshan* and blessings. In the hot summer day he was standing under a tree and I was standing by his side. Countless people were huddling together to approach him, to ask him questions about the most important things in their life. Some wanted to know about their businesses, another wanted to know about his wife's recovery from sickness, another wanted to know if a son would be born to him, yet another wanted to know if he would sell his present business and start a new one, and so on.

It was difficult to hear the questions of all the persons and then answer them individually. Although my *Guru* could know their thoughts psychically. Sometimes he would just watch their physical expressions and thereby know their mental states. He watched the faces of the people, one by one, and knew their mental states and the questions they had in their minds, as a result of which he gave them only answers without letting them ask their questions.

Yogis have developed Yogic postures. When you sit in a posture for a few minutes it creates within you a specific mental state, because the physical state is closely connected with the mental state of the person. These Yoga postures are very important, especially for the beginners to change their mental states and prepare them for higher mental and spiritual powers. By controlling and changing your mental conditions through Yoga postures you can work out and solve your physical problems and conditions on a psychic and mental level.

Increasing psychic income is very handy for professionals, artists, singers, swimmers, and people who want to be champion in any field.

Your mind is the most valuable thing in your possession. It would cost more than twenty billion dollars to prepare a sensitive instrument which could function like a mind; still it would not be able to register and broadcast feelings of love and other higher emotions of devotion, reverence, compassion, sympathy, etc. An average person uses less than 1% of his mental capacity. By using the mind to a larger extent or full capacity, a person can increase his income many, many times.

The process of using the finer forces of Nature through your higher mind for psychic income should be learned under the guidance of the teacher. During the study and control of mental and psychic forces, it is important to maintain mental contact with the teacher. In the beginning it is very important to be in the presence of the teacher in order to help establish the mental contact. Later on this mental contact is maintained without physically being in the presence of the teacher. Whatever is done, physically and consciously, later on is passed over to your psychic and higher mind, which takes charge and continues to perform those actions without the knowledge of your conscious mind. The physical presence before the teacher helps create a beaten track to be used by the psychic mind in maintaining the contact mentally with the *Guru*.

Chapter 22 PSYCHIC TELEGRAM

MAN IS A PSYCHIC being and he creates his phenomena and environment around him whether he wants to create such phenomena or not. A psychic message can be directed to a specific person like a telegram to a specific office, transmitted through a particular wire. The psychic telegram can also be broadcast over the infinite area of space as is done by radiophone messages, which are transmitted to radio stations established across the world, equipped with instruments of the same wavelength.

When a telegram is directed to a particular person in a particular city, it is picked up by a specific telegraph office over a specific wire which is tuned into the wavelength of the station transmitting the message. When a psychic telegram is sent to a specific person, it is picked up by only that person and that person alone, and all other persons are by-passed.

When a telegram is broadcast wirelessly, the message is picked up by numerous stations across the world with the instruments of the same wavelength with which the transmitting station is equipped. A psychic telegram sent to the people as a whole in the world, is picked up by millions of people, and all those who vibrate at the same wavelength will respond.

For example, if you have a specific piece of land in Florida and you want to sell it to a specific person, you send a mental telegram to that person and it will be received by the person, no matter where he is in the whole world. As a result of which, he will be guided by invisible forces to find you and reach you to make a proposal for the purchase of the land. If you are interested in the sale of said specific piece of land in Florida to the highest bidder rather than to a specific person, then in such cases you have to send a psychic telegram to the people as a whole, like a wireless message, as a result of which people across the country who are looking for land in Florida will receive your mental telegram. Also, the people who are uncommitted and have not made up their minds whether to purchase land in Florida or California, they too would receive your psychic telegram and all of them will be invisibly guided to your office, or place of business, or residence, as the case may be, for the finalization of the purchase. Sometimes you may be attracted to meet these people in places away from your office, where you happen to be, on a business trip, on a pleasure trip, etc. This will prepare the environment for the sale of the land in question to the prospective buyers. Similarly, the mental telegram can be sent by people who want to sell cars, merchandise, refrigerators, etc.

Psychic telegram can be sent successfully by businessmen to all debtors who have purchased goods on credit, requesting them to release the money promptly. Such psychic telegrams will be picked up only by those customers who owe you money, whether they still live at their old addresses, or at any other place in the world. They will receive an impulsive urge from within to remit the money to you at the earliest. The psychic telegram to debtors for the release of money will not be picked up by those customers who do not owe you money, nor by those customers who would rather like to return your goods rather than releasing the money.

Mental telegram is very useful in everyday living, because it provides you twenty-four hour service, rain or shine. Space and time do not affect your mental telegrams. The service takes place immediately as soon as the psychic telegram is transmitted, because psychic forces are not affected by time and space. I myself live in New York, while I direct and control all the activities of the Mission in the Himalayas in India by mental contact and psychic telegrams.

Psychic telegrams are based on the principles of the law of mental attraction. It is as good and reliable as the law of electricity and gravity. No one is an exception to the law of mental attraction, whether you are familiar with it or not, whether you believe in it or not. It works and it works either for you or against you.

By consciously operating the law of mental attraction in his favor, a businessman is able to attract wealthy, profitable customers to his store, who make prompt payments. On the other hand, a businessman who does not understand the law of mental attraction, falls victim to the unfavorable results of the law of mental attraction, as a result of which he may attract customers who are not honest, and do not make prompt payments and always ask for goods on credit, but may never show up again once they purchase the goods.

Due to the law of mental attraction many people unconsciously attract, gloomy, depressed, hopeless, cheerless, discouraged and weak persons as friends. Such a person must learn to operate the law of mental attraction to bring to him cheerful, happy and loving friends. Otherwise he will always attract gloomy persons no matter whether he goes to Toronto or Timbuktu. By changing the psychic wavelength, the same person can attract and draw to himself friends who are cheerful, hopeful, encouraging and loving. There are plenty of good loving friends, as well as depressed and gloomy persons. You will get only what you are able to tune into by your psychic wavelength.

When a person has mental power on the reverse, it works against him just like when you have a car in reverse it takes you backward rather than forward. When a person consciously changes his power from reverse to drive, it works for him and he is able to reach and attract nice, good, friendly and sociable people toward him who are positive in their thinking.

This world has everything you want in your life, good friends, fame, fortune and prosperity, just around the corner. You are getting wrong things and wrong persons in your life simply because you are asking for the wrong thing. Of course, you are asking for this mentally and unconsciously, thereby making the law of mental attraction work against you and bringing you the wrong persons and wrong things, which give you additional worries in your life.

For example, if you need a heavy winter coat, but when you go to Macy's store or Gimbel's store, you ask the salesman for a hat rather than a coat, he will give you what you asked for, and when you come back home you will still be shivering in the winter, because you don't have a coat. Why did the salesman not give you the coat which you needed so badly in the winter? Simply because you did not ask for a coat. You asked for the wrong thing which you did not need, and you got it. Similarly, when you learn to operate the law of mental attraction, you are able to send the right psychic wavelength to be picked up by the right persons and naturally, you get the right persons and things in your life.

When you master the law of mental attraction, you are consciously able to supplant your unconscious, vague and ill-defined thought waves by positive and specific wavelengths of thought, thereby reaching a completely different type of people. When your radio in your apartment is tuned in on a specific wavelength you hear a specific program, broadcast from a specific station. By changing the wavelength, you are able to switch from one program to another. On one station is broadcasted rock 'n roll, but it is late at night, you want to sleep and so you want to hear some soft music and lullaby songs. The only thing you have to do is dial the radio and change the wavelength and you will have the soft music instead of the jarring rock 'n roll. If you find depressed and gloomy persons attracted to you, or you find that nice, loving, cheerful and good friends are being driven away from you, what you have to do is just change your psychic wavelength by working the law of mental attraction. The result will be that you will attract the people you want.

First you have to acquire enough working knowledge of the process of the law of mental attraction under the guidance of the teacher. Once you have made the route for the operation of the psychic wavelength by your conscious mind, to be used later on by your higher mind, then you can do it yourself and can make things take unexpected and amazing turns for you in your life. You can make things, happenings, and events take place in your life as you want them to be. There are higher forces of Nature available for your use all around you; all you have to do is to get yourself trained in the use of the higher forces. Only then will they work for you, otherwise, the higher forces will use you according to their own sweet will.

If you have a car and you don't know how to drive, it is useless to you although it stays in your garage. But once you are able to drive your car, you are able to use it and then you have the power behind you. You move at the speed of 40-60 miles an hour, rather than slowly walking on foot. By learning to operate the car and shifting gears from reverse to drive, you acquire the knowledge of the car, and from knowledge comes the control of the car and by controlling you achieve power. The power of the car becomes your power. Similarly, when you learn the process of the law of mental attraction, you get the knowledge of the psychic wavelength; by acquiring the knowledge of the psychic wavelength you acquire its control, and then you have the power. The power of the law of mental attraction becomes your power, which you can use consciously at your will to acquire the results you wish in your life.

Chapter 23 ETHERIC RECORDS

ETHERIC RECORDS are your thoughts recorded in the ethereal substance, which fills all space. It is this etheric substance which is the cause and source of all matter. Etheric substance is finer than waves of light and electricity. It is known by science as pure space. It is finer than the ether known to science. According to science, the whole of space is full of universal ether. This ethereal substance is the universal medium uniting all bodies, all persons and all molecules in matter which are in objects, as well as the various planets and solar systems.

The ethereal substance is a transmitter of motion and energy. The ethereal substance does not create any friction, as a result of which the planets, sun, moon, stars, and comets pass through the ethereal substance. Similarly, waves of light and heat penetrate and pass through the ethereal substance at a terrific speed without any friction being created. The ethereal substance is unaffected by time and space. From etheric substance all things in this world animate as well as inanimate have been created, and everything returns back to this substance upon the dissolution of the world. Animate and inanimate objects, solids and liquids, electricity, and gases, are all the various states of existence of this etheric substance.

The truth about the etheric substance was discovered by the Yogis during meditation and inner contemplation more than 6,000 years ago. In this etheric substance exists the Akashic Records (etheric records) of everything that has happened in the past. Every event and happening is imprinted and photographed on this etheric substance. As in a movie camera, everything is photographed, similarly all the happenings and the events of the past millions of years before the earth was created, have been photographed in this etheric record, and those records are everlasting and indestructible. Whenever pictures taken on film, are projected on the screen, you can see the whole events of the past. The characters you see on the screen, i.e., Shakespeare, Bernard Shaw, etc., may have been dead since long ago, but still you see them active on the screen. Similarly, the happenings and events of millions of years of the past become an open book to you when you can tune in to these etheric records. Etheric records are unalterable. Every single event, scene, or thought, that has ever occurred in this world is recorded in the etheric records. The innumerable times the world was created and dissolved, everything that happened in the world in its various evolutions and dissolutions has been photographed in the etheric records.

The etheric records represent the memory of universal substance which fills space, just as your brain cells represent your memory. By reaching these records, one is able to reach, hear and be one with people of the past and great prophets and saints like Jesus Christ, Mahatma Gandhi, Abraham Lincoln, the Lord Buddha, Saint Germain and others.

When you develop your psychic powers and gain access to these records you can read them like the pages of a book; you can hear them like the sounds reproduced by the phonograph records. The sound of a singer is recorded on the record, you bring that record home and play it on your record player; every time you play it, you hear the sound reproduced. Similarly, when you are able to contact these etheric records, every time you tune in you see the voice of the Great Masters reproduced for you, and the events of the past projected on the screen.

When you see a book in your hand, or a storm in the sky millions of miles away, you see it by means of the vibrations in the ethereal substance which are known as rays of light, which passes from the object seen by you to your eyes. Said vibrations travel at a speed of about 190,000 miles per second. The psychic projection into the astral is above space and time, unlike the projection of the vibrations of light, heat and electricity. It takes about eight minutes for light to travel from the sun to you. It takes about fifty years for the light from the Polar Star to come to you. When you see the Polar Star through an observatory, you see it only as it was fifty years ago. In the meantime if the Polar Star has completely dissolved, still you will be able to see it. It takes many thousands of years for the light to travel from other solar systems and stars. If you see other solar systems through a very powerful observatory, you see them as they were a thousand years ago. If any of them have disappeared in the meantime, you will still be able to see them.

On the other hand, when you project your thoughts psychically and tune in with the etheric records you lose no time and you reach anywhere and everywhere in space, which connects the various celestial bodies and solar systems. It will take the same time for you to reach mentally a person who is ten miles away from you, as it will take for you to reach a person one hundred million miles away from you. Scientists have come to know that there are other universes far away from the universe in which life exists, and it takes more than a million years for the light from these universes to travel across space and reach our telescopes. But by astral projection you lose no time in reaching these universes from which it takes a million years for the light to travel. In the Akashic records your perception is continuous, you do not lose even a millionth part of a second in seeing the events and happenings of the past as they were photographed at the time of occurrence.

Etheric records are the infinite brain in the Cosmos. They have a material base, an indwelling mind and intelligence. The ethereal plane, which contains these records, is not a layer of substrata in the sand, but a rate of vibration.

When you dig the earth you find the various layers of substrata in the sand, one different from the other. In order to reach the astral plane, one does not have to penetrate the layers of substrata, one has only to penetrate the layers of consciousness. The layers of consciousness are penetrated simply by changing your wavelength. The astral is everywhere, inside and outside you, as well as filling all space. You are only aware of those things to which you are tuned in by your wavelength. Your wavelength is determined by the rate of vibration of your mind. The rate of vibration of the mind is determined by the intensity of the radiation from the brain particles which are similar to those of sand. Most of the vital nervous centers and glands, especially the pineal and pituitary glands, are full of particles like those in sand, which radiate vibration; this radiation determines your wavelength, and consequently your plane of awareness at a specific time.

Yogis have developed the methods and techniques by which they are able to change the wavelength of their minds, and thereby they are able to change the plane of consciousness at their sweet will. This enables them to travel from one plane of conciousness to another. The knowledge of the astral plane and the mysteries of Nature become an open book to a person who can change the wavelength of his mind, and thereby tune in to various planes of conciousness. Such a person is able to visualize the events of the past photographed in the etheric records and hear the sounds recorded in the ethereal substance reproduced to him.

Just as you have physical senses, similarly you have astral senses. When you make astral journeys, you take with you these astral senses, which help your perception of the etheric records. In order to reach the etheric records, one does not have to leave his home and travel by plane or train, you can stay wherever you are, only change the wavelength of your awareness and penetrate the astral phenomena.

Thoughts travel from one point of space to another on the astral plane, immediately and without losing any time, as a result of which you are present in all of space at one and the same time. Naturally, everything is seen at one time in the astral. Etheric substance is finer than the waves of electricity, and therefore thoughts penetrate through solid objects like X-rays penetrating into your bones producing an image on a plate. The ether penetrates through stone walls, through plates of a steel box or vault, or inside a closed book. The mental projection makes all opaque become transparent. Your thoughts in etheric substance penetrate through the molecules, electrons, protons and atoms which fill space. For example, if there is a letter inside a locked vault, one can project his thought through ethereal substance into the vault when it is locked, and thereby know the contents of the letter which has never been opened and still lies inside the vault. On this valuable knowledge is based the miraculous powers manifested by the Yogis. These are the perfected powers of the mind known as *Siddhies*. Such is the dynamic power of your thought. You have to learn to use these powers by learning the various techniques and processes under the personal guidance of a teacher. Once you know the working process, you are able to accomplish and use the dynamic powers of your thought and mind, which will make the mysteries of Nature an open book to you.

Chapter 24 YOUR PSYCHIC ALARM CLOCK

YOU ARE WELL acquainted with the fact that when the alarm is set on your clock to wake you up at a specific time early in the morning, it goes into operation exactly at that time. Yogis discovered in their inner research during contemplation, that similarly, an alarm can be set in the psychic mind for a specific thing to happen at a specific time.

My *Guru* used to maintain mental contact with a large number of people across the world. When I finished my studies with him, he treated me as his close friend, and always allowed me to help him in his work. Senior disciples always help their *Guru* in his work. My *Guru* told me to take charge of the junior followers across the world, establish mental contact with them, keep them psychically on the right path and prevent them from falling into dangers and conditions which could distract them from their goal in life. Just as a shepherd keeps his sheep on the proper path, similarly people are mentally directed to stay on the Path by their *Guru* for their psychic and spiritual development.

As desired by my *Guru*, I had to treat many people who lived in Europe, America, and other foreign countries. 8:00 p.m. in India is 8:00 a.m. in the United States. If I had to give a psychic treatment to anyone in America, I used psychic alarm clock, as a result of which the treatment was released exactly at the time when it was meant to be released. By the use of the psychic alarm, the person receiving the treatment is benefited when the treatment is released and not before that. The most convenient time for me in India was to give treatment at 6:00 p.m. due to the daily schedule of my work in India. At 6:00 p.m., the time I was giving treatments in India, it is 6:00 a.m. in the United States, and people are still in bed at that hour, and the treatments are most effective when the person is awake. In such cases I would use the psychic alarm clock, as a result of which the treatment was held in the psychic mind of the person till eight o'clock in the morning, when automatically the alarm would go into operation and the treatment would be released and the desired changes would take place in his body. When the healing forces are held in the psychic mind due to the use of psychic alarm clock, the brain cells and the brain mind of the subject are charged with the healing forces while he sleeps. At the appointed time the psychic alarm fuse goes into operation, when the healing forces are released into his body and the subject receives instantaneous relief at that appointed hour.

One of the numerous cases in which I gave psychic treatment was that of a lady in Pennsylvania, who had a stiffness in her spine and had great difficulty in discharging her everyday work. I treated her psychically around six o'clock in the evening in India, and by the use of the psychic alarm clock, the benefits of the treatment were held in her brain mind until it was eight o'clock in the morning in the United States. At the appointed hour, the benefits were released and she wrote me that she found herself in very good spirits and could hardly believe that her spine had become so flexible that she could bend and twist it without difficulty. She wrote that she could not believe it at first till she twisted her back many times to all sides.

Your psychic alarm clock is like a time bomb which goes off at the appointed hour. As the psychic mind is above time and space, it will go into action at the appointed hour like a burglar alarm in a bank, which will go into action as soon as the robbers start to open the safe. This operation is also similar to that of the fire alarm which goes into action as soon as fire breaks out in a building.

Many people who do not learn the process of operating their psychic alarm clock generally set the psychic alarm clock unconsciously. Mostly, the alarm set unconsciously happens to be an alarm which goes into action at the wrong time. For example, one of my students would always have profuse bleeding and nervous exhaustion from piles exactly on the hour when he had a very important business appointment, in his office, with a customer coming from a foreign country, as a result of which he would never be able to make his deals successful.

Another case was of a girl who would unconsciously let the psychic alarm clock go into action when she had a date with her boyfriend, as a result of which the boyfriend would feel upset and nervous while he was in her company. The same thing would be repeated when any of her boyfriends would come to visit her. She was herself confused to see that she, being an attractive and charming girl, was not attracting boys, while the less attractive girls had attracted better boyfriends. Finally, she came to know that the main reason why the boyfriends were repelled and sent away from her was as a result of the psychic alarm clock going into action.

Another interesting case I would like to bring to your notice is of an old uncle in Canada, who unconsciously set the psychic alarm clock for his own death at an appointed hour. He was not even conscious of the fact that he had a feeling of dying as a result of the psychic alarm clock which he had set. He wrote to his nephew to come to see him at the appointed hour because that was the time when he was going to die. The nephew had not seen him for over a decade and he thought that maybe it was the proper time to go and see him, although he did not believe that the uncle would die at the appointed hour. The old man took the nephew inside his apartment when he arrived. He explained to him what things he wanted to give him and to his other relatives. He took him to the basement and gave him minute details for the disposal of the articles accumulated there, according to his wishes. Then he drove him to the graveyard and showed him the pit where he was to be buried, and also showed him the coffin and other arrangements made for him by the undertaker upon his advice. He then drove back and prepared coffee and served it in the living room, and while drinking it he told the nephew that all his chinaware and silverware should be given immediately to the nephew's wife.

The nephew looked at the uncle's face and remarked, "But uncle, how will you prepare your coffee?"

The uncle replied, "But I have told you, I am going to die, and that is why I called you," and after these words the uncle fell dead. He kept the appointment with the nephew as well as with death.

My *Guru* always used the psychic alarm clock. If anything would happen or a dangerous situation would arise for close followers, the alarm would go into action and the *Guru* would immediately know it before his followers were affected.

Once, my *Guru* was giving spiritual instructions to a group of people when the psychic alarm clock went into operation. He immediately that knew one of his close followers, who was in the banking and financing business, was reaching a danger point. *Guru* asked the people in the meeting to be excused for a few minutes. During the period he was excused, he appeared at the house of the banker and ordered the banker and his family to get out of the house at once, leaving all the contents inside. They had all rushed out of the house, when it collapsed. Had it not been for the operation of the psychic alarm clock set by the *Guru*, these people would have lost their lives.

In another case, one of the followers of my *Guru* was going on a pilgrimage in the deep forest of the Himalayas. It was after the rains and the whole area was covered with wild trees and grass. There was hardly a place not covered with greenery. Being a tropical country, especially after the rains, all manner of poisonous snakes and scorpions, etc., had come out from under the earth due to the excessive heat during the rainy season. During those periods they move freely in the wilderness of the forest. While the student was proceeding into the valley, he was only a few feet away from a deadly cobra, who had seen him approaching. The cobra was furious for being interrupted in its stroll and was angrily flickering its tongue with its hood high above the ground ready to plunge upon the student and put an end to his life as well as the pilgrimage. As the danger point was reached, the psychic alarm clock went into operation and the *Guru* came to know of the danger to his student. Immediately, the student was knocked backward by an invisible shock.

When the student opened his eyes, he heard the voice of the *Guru* telling him, "Don't you see the cobra waiting to bite you on the path on which you were proceeding?" The *Guru* told him, "Go back about ten yards and turn to your left. You will see a foot path, follow it."

The student followed the advice and reached the goal of his pilgrimage without any incident.

Training and practice in establishing psychic contact with their students for psychic healing, as well as in the use of the psychic alarm clock for keeping their followers away from danger, has been one of the important duties of a family Yogi. Just as in the West many families have a family doctor, similarly in India, especially among Hindus, each family has a family Yogi, who gives them physical, mental, emotional, as well as spiritual guidance.

The psychic contact is unaffected by the element of time and space. It is established instantaneously no matter how far away the subject may be at a specific time. The distant psychic contact can be established with one specific person or with millions of people at one and the same time. When an Adept wants to establish contact with numerous minds at one and the same time, he shoots his mental images, which have life and mind, into space, and from there millions of people are influenced by those thought images, which without losing any time, reproduce themselves into the brain minds of people and they start to think, speak and act according to the thoughts projected from the brain mind of the Adept. While doing psychic healing, the psychic contact can be established with one single person during the treatment period. When the healing forces are made available to all the people of the world, then such forces are projected into space where they continue to live independently of the person who projected them. The healing forces in space maintain a magnetic contact with the person who projected them. Any person in the world who needs psychic healing can receive help from the healing forces released into space as soon as he is able to tune in to them consciously or unconsciously. The Adepts and the Yogis silently release such forces during their contemplation in their caves and thereby establish a pool of healing forces in space available for the well-being of all the people. The pool of healing forces in space is similar to the pool of blood in blood banks from where people who are anemic, or short of blood due to an accident, can get blood to save their lives.

During the use of the psychic alarm clock in establishing distant psychic contact, a rapport or an astral tube is established as a medium through which the healer is able to reach his subject. You may think that the psychic contact and use of psychic alarm clock may interfere with the thoughts of some other person and that it may not be proper to interfere with someone's internal affairs of the mind. When you do good to someone it is not at all necessary that you receive his permission. When the sun shines and the rain falls, the consent of the people of the world is never taken. When you use psychic forces, there can be absolutely no question of interfering with the thoughts of other persons provided you do not use them for a selfish and ulterior motive. Anything that the law of the land permits you to acquire and do, can be done and acquired psychically. Any action which would be an offense according to the law of the land, if done physically, should not be done psychically, because psychic phenomena are governed by a similar ethical code and no one can escape from its results.

In the interest of mankind, all the great prophets and teachers like Christ, Mahatma Gandhi, Buddha, etc., have used these powers. When you want to establish psychic contact for the purpose of psychic healing, it is very important that you keep your mind clean of distracting thoughts, and that your psychic channels be prevented from being clogged. The healer must keep his psychic battery fully charged with energy. For a Yogi, the human body is a living battery of energy, and as such it should always be kept charged. If the battery in your car is discharged, the car will never function. Similarly, if your psychic centers are not kept charged, the psychic healing will not be effective. Those people who are not able to generate psychic powers within themselves, should get their batteries charged by the healer so that they can enjoy good physical and mental health. In the long run, I advise people to become self-sufficient and be able to charge their own batteries and heal themselves. In the meantime, a person can always ask for help from a psychic healer.

Chapter 25 ASTRAL TELESCOPE

ADEPTS AND Yogis during their inner research in search of Truth automatically develop psychic powers and power of the mind. The search for Truth lies beyond the reach of the mind. In their effort to for spiritual mastery, Yogis are able to master the mind and achieve psychic powers known as *Siddhies*, without any specific effort to acquire them. Once you have achieved psychic powers, you will be able to use them at your wish. Many times you may not even know that you are using them, but you will still be using them, because the effort needed for their use is so little. When you breathe, you hardly know that you are breathing. Similarly, when you blink your eyes, you hardly notice that you are blinking. Likewise, once you have acquired psychic powers, you use them with the slightest effort.

I will tell you an interesting case to show you how easy it is to use the psychic powers once you learn the process and the technique. A few months ago, one of my disciples in New York made an appointment to discuss something personal. Generally, disciples make an appointment for spiritual guidance. At the appointed time the lady disciple came and told me that she was very badly in need of financial help. She told me that she must get a loan of $5,000-$6,000 right away.

I told her, "I am a *Preceptor*, I can give you spiritual guidance. I am not a financial advisor, therefore you should go to some financial advisor for that type of guidance."

She knew the thoughts of a Yogi can help in everything, and therefore she asked me to whom she should go to for such help.

I replied, "It is better that you go to your friends who may help you." She again asked, "Which of my friends should I ask for help?"

By chance I happened to know some of her friends who used to accompany her to various functions and parties held by my disciples in New York, and accordingly I named the friend whom she should go to. During my talk with her, the astral telescope was automatically established between me and her friend whom I named to her. My thoughts projected through the astral telescope and were reproduced into the mind of her friend. When she returned home from my studio, she found the telephone ringing. She picked up the phone and found her friend telling her over the phone that if she needed any financial help he would be glad to lend her money for as long as she wanted it, without any interest. She answered in the affirmative and got the loan the next day.

When you learn the process of establishing astral telescope and you have enough practice behind you, the work becomes very easy and smooth. Through regular practice, establishing astral telescope becomes as easy as eating candy.

Every human being is a psychic being who creates his phenomena and practices telepathy unconsciously. If the world were not full of so many gross forces as exist today, it would be much easier for the people to practice telepathy consciously. During the establishment of astral telescope, the mind functions on the astral plane and uses the astral senses, and astral perception takes place. An average person in this world has astral senses which are dormant. In order to awaken and make the astral senses active, one must make a conscious effort and learn the process taught and practiced by the Yogis for the last 7,000 years. The physical is a counterpart of the mental and astral, as such, whatever you perceive through the astral senses manifests at once in the physical. During a dream you see your close friend keeping company with you and very soon you find that your whole body reacts to such a perception. In dream, if you happen to eat candy, the saliva will start to flow in your mouth while you sleep. This is an example of the astral influence upon the physical. Yogis discovered long ago that the whole earth is controlled and directed by invisible astral influences from outer space. Outer space influences are also known as astrological influences. The science of astrology is based on this research and people have realized that the sun, moon, various planets, Venus, Saturn, Mars, etc., surround the earth on all sides, and have tremendous influence upon the destiny of this world, as well as mankind.

In psychic perception you are able to penetrate the veil of the astral plane and see clear astral images in thought form. The astral images are the cause of the physical objects which do exist or existed in the physical plane. Everything in this world in physical and material form, can be perceived psychically in its psychic form. The world to be in the next hundred years can be perceived psychically in thought form, as well as the world as it was a few centuries ago. Things are created and destroyed in this world, but they continue to survive their destruction and stay alive in thought form.

It is quite natural for a human being to be psychic. The more interruptions and worldly distractions there are in life, the more difficult it is to manifest psychic power consciously. Unconsciously, at one time or another, occasional flashes of psychic perception take place in all human beings. The thoughts, feelings and secrets of dead persons should always be respected, because their revelation hurts them with the same intensity as it would hurt them if they were alive amidst you. Psychic perception brings instantaneous changes into your psychic body, known as your aura, which surrounds your body. The changes in your aura bring change into the physical and chemical conditions of your body. An astral perception may bring the beautiful rose color to your aura, which can materialize into an emotion and feeling of pure affection, and this feeling may create a physical action expressing affection. Another astral perception may bring to your aura a rich blue color, thereby creating the feeling of devotion. Another perception may bring negative colors such as a hard dull brown creating selfishness, deep scarlet creating anger, lurid red awakening the feeling of sensuality, livid gray creating fear and a feeling of insecurity, a black cloudy color creating a feeling of hatred and malice, etc. Similarly, astral perception can bring into your aura positive colors of green, yellow, orange, and saffron, creating within you the feelings of wisdom, guidance, generosity, spiritual knowledge, etc.

Astral images are made of thought forms. Astral images are like movie films, which do not contain real characters but they represent the real characters. In a movie, the people you see on the screen may have been dead since long ago, but still you see them in the form of images which are not real, but represent the real characters who lived amidst you. Similarly, astral perception is not limited to things amidst you. Psychically you can also perceive things which were amidst you. The real things and persons are the counterpart of astral images and astral perceptions. For astral perception, no one is advised to try short cuts, because they are dangerous. A person can evolve scientifically on psychic lines only under the true guidance of a perfected teacher.

Chapter 26 WHEN YOUR THOUGHTS BECOME THINGS

THOUGHTS AND THINGS are correlated. Every thought reminds you of a thing. Similarly, every thing reminds you of a thought. Always there is an action and reaction between things and thoughts. Things react to your thoughts, and thoughts react to things. Thoughts bring change into a thing, so does a thing bring change in the form of thoughts. According to the modern sciences of psychology, physiology and metaphysics, it has been proven that thoughts do transform, rearrange and set into motion and activity the material particles in our brains, thereby creating a specific mental state. The mental state produces a similar effect on the minds of your cells, organs and physical body. The influence of thoughts on objects of the world is as effective as the one on the mind of your cells which constitute your glands, nerves, bones, skin, flesh, etc. The psychic treatment can be given to the objects, conditions, circumstances, environment, etc., exactly in the same way as you give psychic treatment for physical conditions in your own body, or in the body of another person.

When your thoughts become creative psychically they will bring results in your life which at first will appear to you to be just unbelievable, startling, miraculous and supernatural. But really there is nothing miraculous and supernatural in the results which come purely by the use of the higher forces of Nature, known as psychic powers. Every move of the process which transforms your thoughts into things is made in accordance with natural law and the order of Nature. The psychic law is natural and it works 100% along natural lines. You must know that the psychic laws work for you only when you set them into operation and activity; otherwise nothing will happen to bring desired results into your life. If science did not set into operation the law of electricity, you would not be able to use electricity for lighting, in your refrigerator, heater, air conditioning, etc. Once you have controlled electricity, then you just have to press the button to make electricity available for the desired use for your good living. Similarly, as soon as you control the psychic forces of Nature, all you have to do to make them function for your well-being and good living, is to press the button psychically and they go into action instantaneously, while you wait for the immediate and instantaneous results. As soon as you plug in your radio, you only wait for a second to hear the program. Similarly, you press the psychic button and just wait to get instantaneous results. Just as electricity and thought waves materialize into music and sound on your radio, similarly when you press the psychic button your thoughts become creative and they materialize into physical and material conditions, circumstances, environment and happenings in your life.

People who have not mastered the process of psychic creation and whose thoughts are not creative, think that things would have happened anyway in their lives. They are not able to understand that they happen due to the forces of the higher mind. The wrong belief that something would have happened in their lives anyway, makes people more and more negative and lazy, and they start to accept good and bad things as they come to them and do not make any effort to improve their condition in life by supplanting negative and harmful thought projections with positive and creative thoughts. As soon as you start replacing the negative and uncreative thoughts with the creative and well-defined ones, immediately you find that the undesirable persons, objects, happenings, and environment in your life start to disappear and instead, good objects, positive conditions and happenings, and environments start to appear, and thus your whole life is changed in a short time.

This change could never be achieved by physical efforts and the use of the conscious mind. When you can make your thoughts creative, you can do wonders in your life, because you can really create things for yourself.

When your thoughts become creative, they have drawing power behind them which can pull or push persons, objects or things to you or from you. The creative thoughts make the framework around and about which start to materialize conditions, events, things, environments and happenings, which you desire to become a reality in your life. Around and about the indwelling creative mind forms a crystal around your thoughts and the phenomena is created as desired by you. When your thoughts become creative they set into operation and activity the higher forces and powers of the mind, and the law of mental attraction goes into action, drawing persons and objects to you. The law of mental attraction, once set into operation, proceeds like a big piece of machinery or like some powerful physical process and creates instantaneous results in your life. When thoughts become creative, their magnetic power starts to attract and draw, pull and push in numerous ways, the things, persons and conditions necessary to materialize your thoughts into reality.

Thoughts transform themselves into things making unexpected things happen. New persons and things will come into your life. You will make contacts with new persons. Automatically, new and higher ideals will start to spring into your thoughts, and new conditions and circumstances will form around and about you. You will be able to get rid of unfavorable conditions and circumstances which must make room for the better ones.

Sometimes you may find that things and objects do not come to you, but due to the operation of the law of psychic attraction, you find yourself amidst a new environment exactly as you always wanted in your life. There are really no lifeless nor mindless things in Nature. Every atom has life and energy, as I have already mentioned about crystal formation. The lower minds in objects are negative and inferior, and can easily be polarized and transformed by you. You need not be disappointed in your life that you could not make your dreams come true and your ideals a reality. Make your thoughts creative and transform them into reality. Your thoughts become things when they are creative, not otherwise; and thoughts become creative when they have the drawing force behind them.

The drawing force behind thoughts is developed by the techniques and process practiced and taught by the Yogis since time immemorial, and should be learned under the personal guidance of a perfected instructor.

Chapter 27 PHYSICAL DISEASES AND MENTAL PROCESS

TELEPATHY, thought transference, and practical psychology, all are based on influencing the indwelling mind in animate and inanimate objects. The brain waves emanating from your mind stir the mind and life in other persons and objects and thereby bring physical and material change.

Your feelings, emotions and the state of your mind are reflected in your physical condition. Your condition of health or disease depends greatly upon your mental state. When you are in the company of good persons and cheerful surroundings, you will find that your body functions better. When you go picnicking in the woods, or sun bathing on the beach, you will find that you can eat a lot more than what you eat in your house on account of better appetite. The dishes which you like mentally can make your mouth water. On the other hand, unpleasant scenery can make you feel sick to your stomach.

A friend of mine, while he was dining, by chance happened to swallow a fly with his food, as a result of which he got sick to his stomach and vomited all the food. Many years have passed since this happened, but those impressions of the past are still as fresh in his mind as they were at the time of the incident. Even now, if he sees a fly sitting on his food, he will start to vomit. As long as these thought patterns stay in your mind, they keep on creating physical conditions in your body no matter where you are and what you do.

Another interesting case is of a girl who suffered, since birth, with a chronic disease of shooting pains in her stomach followed by coughing and vomiting. She was treated by experts for more than twenty years without the slightest improvement in her condition. She was in love with a boy, and finally the date was set for the wedding. The bride arrived in the church at the appointed hour for the wedding, where all her friends and relatives were waiting. The bridegroom did not turn up. He was reached on the phone by the father of the bride, and he told the father that he had come to know on the day of the wedding that the bride suffers from a chronic disease, and therefore he had no intention of marrying her. The bride was informed accordingly-that her boyfriend would marry her only when she was cured of the malady. Without any further treatment, the bride was cured, and more than fifteen years have passed since their marriage, and during that time she has not suffered from a single attack of pain or vomiting. The cause of her sickness was in her mind. The temptation to marry was too strong, and unconsciously, the thought patterns of sickness in her mind were replaced by those of health and positivity, as a result of which she unconsciously created a condition of good health.

Depressing and negative thoughts force the glands to secrete poisons into the blood, which not only obstructs the normal functions of the body, but also can retard the functions of circulation, digestion, assimilation, elimination, etc. In many patients at the Sanatorium of which I am the Director in India, I discovered that the main cause of their excessive smoking and drinking was their negative and depressed thoughts. Every year millions of people are made ill, and thousands and millions get well, due to a change in the state of their minds. When you are angry, the saliva in your mouth can become poisonous due to the influence of anger. I know of numerous persons in whom diabetes and similar chronic diseases have been created as a result of mental shocks and mental disturbances. Mental states can create devastating diseases like cancer, epilepsy, insanity, paralysis, hepatitis, etc.

Mental impressions can create or remove functional diseases. Negative and depressing emotions generate in the system injurious and harmful components which are extremely poisonous. Happy emotions make the glands secrete chemical components into the blood which have great nutritive value. Poisonous chemicals can neutralize all the nutritive elements in your blood circulation and can throw the balance of your body chemistry off. Positive emotions can create healthy secretions of tremendous nutritive value, and thereby neutralize the poisonous chemicals in your body and restore a healthy biochemical balance in your blood. By controlling the mental forces consciously, you can speed up or slow down the functions of your body. When a person is nervous or emotionally upset, he naturally starts to breathe short and sometimes finds it very difficult to breathe because the function of the respiratory organ is affected, like any of the other organs, by mental processes. Your mental state exerts tremendous control over your nervous, vasomotor, circulatory and other systems.

A friend of mine in Calcutta who had lived for a long time in China, in Formosa, told me that in his village when anybody committed theft he was asked by the head of the family to swallow rice. If the person could not swallow the rice, he was pronounced to be the thief, and liable for punishment. The person who committed the theft naturally created negative mental impressions in his mind, as a result of which, under fear, his saliva completely dried up in his mouth. In the absence of saliva he could not swallow the rice. Many people would return the stolen objects when the theft was discovered by this process. Mental conditions have tremendous influence upon your nervous system and thereby they can cause functional derangements of the liver and other vital organs. Similarly, they can restore vital organs to their normal function.

Mental patterns precede the physical conditions. By using your mental processes consciously, you can bring health and happiness to your body. The forces of the mind are like the gear shift on your car. When you shift it to drive, the car goes forward; when you have it on reverse, it goes backward.

Similarly, when you keep your mental forces on the direction of your health, you acquire radiant health, but if these forces go on reverse, sickness overtakes the body.

The influence of mental patterns upon the physical condition is not a question of mind over matter, but a question of mind over mind. By influencing your physical condition you are able to influence the mind in those parts and organs of your body. It is your mental patterns which control the activities of your involuntary organs and your autonomic nervous system through the sympathetic nervous system.

One person had ulcers in his stomach. When he was mentally worried or insulted by anyone, his intestines would start to secrete a cupful of acids which would eat up the inner membrane in the stomach and intestines and blood would start to gush from the wounds. The harmful chemical components and acids have great effect upon your physical condition. It is these acids which help you digest meat, poultry, fish, etc. Under harmful mental impressions, when too much of these acids are poured into the stomach and intestines, they start to digest your own meat, as a result of which you may have bleeding ulcers and wounds. Cancer is also one of the numerous diseases caused by mental patterns. First the cancer appears in the mind in your thoughts in the form of vibrations, then it appears in the bloodstream, and finally it manifests as a malignant growth on any part of the body. A person having a malignant growth on his body will find cancer in every drop of his blood. A person whose blood tests show cancer will always have cancer in his thoughts in the form of vibrations. Science can discover cancer when it is in the blood, but I do not know of any method by which science can detect the cancer when it is still in the thoughts of the patient and not in his blood.

Your thoughts, feelings and emotions are as real as houses, cars and buses. I know many patients at my Sanatorium in the Himalayas who had skin eruptions preceded by mental strain. Yogis have discovered the science of mental and psychic patterns by which they are able to prevent the sickness in the thoughts before it reaches the body and interferes with normal bodily functions.

A wrong mental pattern can not only cause disease, but it can also cause actual death. Once I was visiting my parents during summer vacation. In those days the British ruled India, and in the colleges we used to get at least two months of summer vacation, and three weeks of Christmas vacation. In those days, the kings and maharajahs occupied big estates and paid only a part of the receipts to the government. My father had inherited a large estate and was known as a landlord. He was the landlord of five villages all together. Each village is like a county in the state of New York. He had all the pomp and show of the ruling class. He descended from the *Gupta* Dynasty. Long before the British ruled India, it was ruled by the *Gupta* Dynasty. The period when the *Gupta* Dynasty ruled India is known as the Golden Age of India. When I reached the railway station to visit my parents, I was welcomed by the officers of the estate belonging to my parents, and a big decorated chariot with eight wheels and thousands of bells hanging around it. The conveyance (chariot) was sent to bring us home from the railway station.

That same evening upon my arrival, I heard in the village that there lived a ghost in a banyan tree about a mile away from the main settlement. The ghost was supposed to have attacked many people passing by on the road near the tree, making them sick and creating conditions from which it took a long time for them to recover.

I heard that there was one brave person who said to the villagers that there was no such ghost in the tree, and who would be the first to go there and face the facts. A handsome reward was promised if he succeeded in going there at midnight. As the clock struck twelve midnight, he was ready to leave for the tree. Some of the villagers asked what proof they would have that he had been to the tree since none of them wanted to accompany him for fear of losing their lives in case the ghost decided to attack. The person was given a wooden peg and a hammer.

He was told to hammer the peg in the root of the banyan tree before he returned, as proof of his visiting the designated place haunted by the ghost. It was wintertime. The brave man wrapped himself in a woolen shawl and rushed to the spot with the peg and hammer It was a dark, stormy night and he rushed to the tree, looked around and started to drive the peg into the root of the tree by hitting it hard with the hammer. While he was driving the peg into the root, he heard some rustling sounds in the leaves and he became suspicious about the ghost. While he continued hammering the peg, he was looking not at the peg, but around him thinking that maybe the ghost could appear. He quickly turned his back and rushed, leaving the hammer near the peg which he had driven into the root, due to the fear that the ghost could come and overtake him soon if he stayed any longer. He had hardly gotten a few feet away from the root when he fell down, lost consciousness and died.

The villagers were waiting anxiously for his return till morning, but when he did not return, they insisted that he must have been attacked by the ghost. None of them wanted to go alone to learn the fate of the brave man. When it was five o'clock in the morning, about a dozen of the villagers got together with a lantern, to see what had happened to the man. They found him lying under the banyan tree. When they tried to pull him out, they could not. Many people started to pull him unsuccessfully. Very soon, with the light of the lantern, they saw his whole body was wrapped up in the shawl, and one end of the shawl was driven deep into the earth with the peg which he was hammering in the darkness. Thus they found out the reason why they could not pull the body, which was wrapped in the woolen shawl. They also found that due to the same reason the brave man could not return. The mental patterns of fear were created in his mind and they were so strong that death took possession of him instantaneously. Most poisonous chemical compounds were created and entered into his bloodstream, as a result of dreadful patterns of fear in his mind, that the ghost had overtaken him, and death was the result.

Many progressive authorities in the West and modern science, have advanced to the point where they are able to corroborate the findings of the Yogis that your emotions and mental patterns are reflected and materialized in your physical conditions, thereby creating in you a state of health or disease.

Chapter 28 IMPULSIVE URGE FOR WRONGDOING

ON NUMEROUS occasions one gets the urge from within to do a specific thing without an obvious reason. Such things happen in the life of the average person. On occasion, you will find yourself attracted towards a certain person; on another occasion you may find yourself uninterested in some other person. This urge to do or not to do is very strong and reasoning is too weak to affect it. This urge is known as an impulsive urge. An impulsive urge to do the wrong thing is destructive. It is generally found in criminals, juvenile delinquents, alcoholics, and others who have become accustomed to doing the wrong thing, although they would prefer not to, if they were not forced by the strong urge from within.

The impulsive urge is created by influence from outside, as well as by association with persons and objects. As a person associates with different persons and objects, the urge within him changes. When you enter the gate of church on Sunday morning you feel an urge within yourself for devotion, reverence to Truth, and a strong religious urge. On another occasion, when you are in the company of a boyfriend, you find a different type of urge arising from within you than when you are in the company of your father or uncle. The urge within you in the company of your girlfriend will be different than the one you may have while you are in the company of your sister or mother. You will have a different urge when you are in the company of the minister of your church or your *Preceptor* in comparison to the urge you may have while in the company of a hardened criminal or an alcoholic.

When a person is under the grip of an impulsive urge for wrongdoing, he is so uncomfortable and restless that he can commit the most heinous crime a person can conceive of, even committing suicide. An urge to shoot someone, to divorce, to harm others and yourself, are some of the urges that arise due to inner impulses.

I know one person who had an irresistible urge to go out and spend money on unnecessary things, while she should have stayed home and attended to her more important household work. On another occasion, the same lady would have the urge to stay home alone when it would have been more appropriate to accompany her husband to Europe on vacation, and other places on weekends.

Urges for wrongdoing are so strong that you may find yourself too weak to resist them. There was one very prominent widow, who had absolutely no intention to remarry. At social meetings and parties, being a business woman, she would get a strong urge to marry. Under the influence of such an urge, she would find herself doing unusual things. Sometime ago, another lady had a strong influence from an impulsive urge of fear that the water level of the ocean would rise on the California coast, as a result of which, she thought the house which she owned on the coast would be submerged in water in due course. She disposed of the property very cheaply and suffered a heavy loss. You will find many persons who have an impulsive urge to buy when prices are high, while they have an impulsive urge to sell when prices are too cheap, as a result of which they suffer tremendous losses to their business, and can hardly become successful in their lives.

If you can control and master these internal forces scientifically, you can become completely immune to undesirable impulses and urges. The effect of urges for wrongdoing upon health is terrific. It can ruin your health, physical as well as mental, and can transform you into a nervous wreck if you don't stop them quickly. Many persons find it difficult to resist the temptation of food, which they have been prohibited to eat by their family doctor due to serious physical conditions. Still they find themselves too weak to resist the inner desire and they do eat the food causing pain and suffering and aggravation of their condition.

Two small children had an impulsive urge for hearing the sirens of fire engines in their neighborhood, and therefore they set their house on fire when their parents were gone. The neighbors set off the fire alarm and the fire engines came. When the children were questioned by the police they told the reason why they had set their house on fire.

Another child killed a small girl as he felt a strong, irresistible urge to do so. The neighbors found the boy kneeling near the dead girl on the roadside. They asked him what he was doing.

He replied, "I am praying for this girl." They asked him who killed her and he said, "I did. I killed her because I had a strong urge for killing."

The boy had no grudge against the girl, still he killed her, being under the influence of a strong urge for wrongdoing. Most of the crimes done by juveniles and others are due to the fact that they are under the influence of an impulsive urge for committing a specific crime.

It is very important for you to protect yourself from the influence of impulsive urges for wrongdoing, so that you only can do things that are positive and good. Nature has provided you with a defensive weapon against such urges provided you care to use it consciously. An average person unconsciously tries to defend himself against the influence of such urges, because Nature wants to protect people from harmful and negative influences, but he may not be able to defend himself because he is not trained to do so.

In many countries, the number of mental hospitals and the patients who live in them are increasing by leaps and bounds. Most of the people in mental hospitals have been affected by these outside influences and they themselves become an instrument of spreading the contagion of mental sickness.

Since mental diseases are contagious, the thoughts of people who live in mental hospitals carry with them the contagion, and normal, healthy people are affected by it and become mentally sick.

Some people are exceptionally strong in defending themselves from such impulsive urges for wrongdoing. Hindus by nature are awakened to the knowledge and training in the use of this power of self-defense almost instinctively, and therefore they are practically immune from harmful external influences. At present, very few Westerners are trained in these techniques. I am sure very soon the West will be thoroughly equipped to cope with these harmful influences which create impulsive urges for doing wrong things, a condition of mental sickness, a state of indecision and mental confusion. By training yourself in the processes of your mind, you can replace urges for wrongdoing with positive urges for right action and right thinking.

Great teachers, *Preceptors*, ministers and leaders always do things guided by strong impulsive urges for right action. I, being a personal friend of Mahatma Gandhi, can say that all his actions were backed by right impulsive urges. If Mr. Gandhi had to go on a fast, he would set the date and time of starting his fast, as well as the date and time of discontinuing his fast, as guided by this strong urge from within, which he used to call "the voice of Truth." When Mahatma Gandhi would make any political decision, it would come as a result of his inner voice. Once, Mahatma Gandhi observed a very long fast which extended to many weeks. The determination to fast was made on hearing the inner voice and the date and hour of the fast was set. The inner urge within him was just like hearing a voice from afar and yet quite near. It was as unmistakable to him as a human voice, definitely speaking to him and it was irresistible. Mahatma Gandhi was not dreaming at that time because he heard the voice within giving him directions. He was calm and serene. The decision was made and joy filled his body, mind and soul. He felt refreshed and immediately noted down all the directions received from within. Not even the unanimous verdict of the whole world against Mahatma Gandhi could shake him from the belief of what he heard from within. The inner voice was more real than his own physical existence. It never failed him in his life. This power is within every one of you, but like anything else in this world, it requires training and preparation to enable you to use these forces for constructive purposes in your life.

Anger, worry, hatred, jealousy, etc., are a few of the negative impulses which have the most weakening mental effects known to men of this earth. Such impulses can render even the most positive individuals negative in their lives. Once you develop immunity to all such intents and purposes to and from any harmful psychic impulses, you will be able to prevent the most potent impulses by your mind, will power, and conscious as well as unconscious efforts. Once you have trained yourself and cultivated a proper mental attitude towards such impulses, you will be able to establish an unconscious habit of resisting and repelling these impulses whenever, wherever and however they may arise within your mind. This will also create within you a high degree of psychic positivity which will render the manifestation of your psychic influence very efficient and powerful. The various techniques for preventing impulsive urges for wrongdoing should be learned under the personal guidance of a teacher.

The techniques for a beginner to develop power for resisting and neutralizing impulsive urges for wrongdoing have been given in the latter part of the book (*Chapter 39* "Two-Month Course In Psychic Phenomena").

Chapter 29 PROTECTIVE AURA AGAINST PSYCHIC ATTACKS

HARMFUL INFLUENCES penetrate the psychic aura of a person and then they are reproduced in his mind. Once someone's harmful thoughts coming from outside are reproduced in the mind, then the person starts to think, speak and act accordingly. The best thing is to prevent these thoughts from entering your mind, and this can be achieved by strengthening your aura, which is your only defense.

Rhythmic breathings, *Nadi* purifier breathing, *Nadi* stimulator breathing and *Nadi* vibrator breathing, are some of the techniques which will enable you to create a strong psychic aura of thought, mingled with the forces of life, mind and *Prana*. They will serve as a protection against psychic attacks from outside. This aura will act as an armor through which psychic arrows cannot penetrate. By Yogis the strong auric defense is known as "the ring-pass-not." You create a psychic ring-pass-not around your body and carry it wherever you go. The psychic ring can be created around your office or place of residence to protect you from external harmful influences.

It is the persons with weaker psychic defenses who are very susceptible to psychic attacks from outside, due to their weak resistance, just as a person with weak physical resistance will be the first to be affected by colds, viruses, allergies, germs and bacteria. Due to this reason, a person who is negative, depressed, nervous and alcoholic, will be more susceptible to attract to himself people of the same species, and he will be susceptible to be attracted to people with the same habits and vices.

Since time immemorial, psychic protection, psychic healing and psychic influence have been a part of the duties of the

Yogis. Each Hindu family in India is guided, trained and helped with these psychic methods by the Yogi *Preceptor* of the family. The various Yogic techniques taught and practiced by the Yogis bring not only physical but chemical, mechanical, mental and psychic changes as well. The various Yogic breathings create similar mental and psychic changes within you. By lowering or raising the mental vibration, a change is created in the mental and psychic state. The change in the rhythm of the breathing taught by the Yogis is able to lower or heighten the rate of vibrations of your mind. In other words, the breathing rhythm controls your psychic and mental state at a specific time.

The power which you use for self protection can also be used for psychic healing when you start to use it in influencing the mind in the cells and organs of your body in making them do what you want them to do for healthy living. Matter and energy are the two poles of the same substance, because there is life in mind, in everything. Each cell and part of your body has life and mind and the atoms which constitute matter have mind and life—in every electron and proton. When you are able to send these psychic forces to the mind of your organs and cell minds, they will start to respond. The use of psychic influence for psychic healing awakens within you the sixth sense, making you more sensitive to the functions of the mind, unknown to a person not awakened to the functions of the inner psychic powers.

For a person doing psychic healing, it is very important that he learn self protection, otherwise he can unconsciously create self destruction. Before a person starts doing the work of psychic influence, he must clean the psychic channels within his body, which are known as the *Nadies*. *Nadies* are the astral tubes through which the psychic forces move. In an average person these channels are clogged due to their mental attitudes and external unfavorable influences. The techniques for cleaning psychic channels are given in *Chapter 39* "Two-Month Course In Psychic Phenomena."

Channels which are choked with the debris hamper the free flow of psychic forces within them. If the Great Lakes are full of sand, ships can't move through them. First the sand has to be removed and the water made deep, then only can the ships sail. Similarly, the first step is to clean the channels before you press the button and release the psychic forces. Otherwise, these forces can dismantle the sensitive astral tubes and bring mental and moral degeneration. Higher psychic forces should only be released when the channels are open, in order to prevent physical and mental disturbances. When the inner astral tubes are cleaned of their debris, you will be able to draw healing psychic forces from outside. At the same time, you will be able to use them freely while creating psychic phenomena, and you will be only an instrument or a medium.

On the other hand, if the astral tubes are not cleaned, you can drain all your reserve forces in the process of healing and neutralizing the condition of your subject and patient, but you will not be able to charge yourself and draw within you an equal amount of strength, *Prana* and healing forces from the outside. Such ignorance and deficiency can ruin your career and health.

Long ago a king fell seriously ill in Agra in India. The only son of the king came to the bed of his sick father and made seven rounds around the bed of the sick father, holding a cup of water in his hand. When he completed the seventh round, he wished that the sickness of his father should come to him in exchange for his father's health. While wishing his father health, he drank the water of the cup, supposedly taking the sickness of the father upon himself through the water. Unconsciously, the healing forces were released from the son and the king recovered. The young prince, being ignorant in the process of psychic phenomena, could not recharge himself as his psychic channels were choked. As a result, he fell ill and died.

Unless a person is thoroughly trained in the process of psychic influence, I would personally not advise him to try psychic healing, because it would be detrimental to his own health and life. Until a person is able to charge himself, he should go to an expert teacher who can charge him with psychic forces till he himself becomes expert in charging his astral tubes, known as *Nadies*, with the psychic forces and *Prana*, which does the real healing. It would be wise to give treatment to others only when you are strong enough, not otherwise. By cleaning the psychic channels, the required amount of *Prana* and will power is made available for the purpose of treatment.

The knack of generating *Prana* and psychic forces is like the generation of electricity. Once these healing psychic forces are created, they are stored in the inner psychic centers, just as electricity, after being generated, is stored in powerhouses. Your psychic centers within, are your inner powerhouses charged with the healing forces from where the healing power is released when you treat yourself or to somebody who is near you, or treating someone who is in a foreign country. Psychic forces should never be released for the purpose of a healing treatment unless you are trained in the process of generating them.

A person fully charged with the psychic forces radiates strength, positivity and healing towards all who come near him. Nervous people are benefited simply by being within the psychic aura of their teacher. When a person is within twenty to thirty feet of an average *Preceptor*, he is within the spiritual aura of the *Preceptor*.

Healing forces from a person who has less *Prana* can be transmitted to a person who has more *Prana*, provided he is trained in the working process. Just as the flow of water can be reversed towards higher land by constructing artificial dams in the river, the *Prana* and its flow can be diverted from one part of the body to the other, as well as from one person to another.

You can freely use your psychic forces to protect yourself against the use of psychic influences in an unscrupulous manner by other persons who desire to influence and affect you psychically. Once you learn the creation and use of the protective psychic forces, you will be able to unconsciously erect a psychic barrier against psychic harmful influences from outside. An average person has around him a psychic aura which is constituted of psychic ethereal forces of a very low degree of intensity. Such psychic defense can give protection only against very weak external attacks. But when the psychic attacks are strong, this low degree of intensity cannot resist them and the immunity is overcome and one becomes subject to such external psychic attacks.

At present there is tremendous need of instructions and knowledge along these lines in Western countries. I have personally seen that a great number of persons are subject to deliberate harmful psychic attacks, and it is very important that this knowledge be made available to the people as a whole to enable them to defend themselves against external psychic attacks.

The psychic attacks have a destructive effect upon one's mental and psychic forces in comparison to a physical attack. A psychic attack in the long run affects the condition of the body because there is a close connection between the brain mind and the cell mind in your body. The connection between said minds is instinctive. As soon as you are able to erect a dynamic psychic ring around you of such terrific intensity that no undesirable thought influence will be able to penetrate it, you can be confident that you can render ineffective the strongest psychic attacks.

The knack for strengthening your psychic defense has been given in more detail in *Chapter 39* "Two-Month Course In Psychic Phenomena."

Chapter 30 MENTAL PROJECTION AND PSYCHIC PROPULSION

THE STRENGTH of psychic projection depends on the propelling power behind your thoughts. It is this psychic propulsion which pushes your thought without your knowledge. The greater the propelling power behind your thought, the stronger your thoughts are.

An airplane takes off from the airport and then moves into the air with the propelling power of the propeller. The stronger the power of the propeller, the greater the speed of the plane. A jet has a very strong propeller and can move in the sky at the speed of sound, while an ordinary cargo plane has a very weak propeller and moves at a speed of 100-200 miles an hour. People who have weak psychic propellers, have thoughts that move slowly and do not materialize as desired. On the other hand, persons who are well trained in the creation of psychic phenomena and as a result of which have developed their psychic propulsion, have a very strong mental projection and are able to create psychic phenomena with perfect accuracy and confidence.

What you do on the street before others is not as important as what you think in your room with all the doors closed when you are alone. Your actions on the street may be noticed by a few hundred people at most, but your thoughts from a closed room in which you are alone, contact millions of people across the world. Every person contacted by the thoughts reacts. Therefore, it is very important to know what thoughts are going out from your brain. It is these outgoing thoughts which can create a better, healthier and happier world for the people who inhabit this earth, or which can make things and conditions worse for the people as a whole. Your action of firing a rifle towards a crowd is less harmful than making a negative and harmful thought arise in your mind. The bullet from your rifle may not hit the target or may only affect one or two persons in the crowd, but harmful thoughts will never miss hitting anyone and everyone who happens to be in their way as they move across space indefinitely till they come back to you. Unlike the bullet from your rifle, your thoughts can harm persons whom you never expected to get harmed. The wrong and harmful thoughts can do equal harm to your foes as well as to your friends. The members of your own family, your own neighbors and relatives may unconsciously contact your harmful and negative thoughts and suffer from them.

For example, the wrong thoughts of a person can hurt his own children and spouse in the apartment in which he lives, because there is a likelihood that they will be the first to come in contact with your thoughts as they leave your mind on their journey across the world, and as such, great harm is done to the persons one loves. Thoughts are contagious and so, will affect others accordingly.

Yogis are very careful in the process of thoughts. Many great teachers spend most of their lives sitting in caves in the deep Himalayas radiating and broadcasting thoughts of world peace, health, happiness, joy and Divine blessings to all the people of the world. If it were not for this mental and psychic broadcasting of the great saints and teachers, the world would be by this time in great turmoil. It is true that the Great Masters and the spiritually-developed Adepts of the world control its destiny, and not those who rule it.

Creation of psychic phenomena should not be confused with hypnosis. Hypnosis is a destructive course, while the creation of psychic phenomena is a constructive approach. Under hypnosis, a person can be made to believe in the existence of something which really does not exist. On the other hand, by the power of psychic forces something can be created and produced materially which never existed before. Hypnosis also makes the will of the subject weaker and weaker, which creates a destructive effect in his life. It is people with weak wills, especially teenagers and women with weak will power who are easily susceptible to hypnosis. The creation of psychic phenomena needs a stronger and greater will and as such, people who yield to hypnosis are not fit for the creation of psychic phenomena. It is the will power which propels your thought and creates the mental projection. Once thoughts are projected by the force of psychic propulsion, they move like a torpedo towards its target. Psychic propulsion and mental projection are followed by the imagination. Once imagination is provided the desired direction, will power will follow that path. Once the will follows the imagination, the next step is that those people start to will, think, act and speak accordingly.

An Adept who is trained in the creation of psychic phenomena, controls mental projection and psychic propulsion. For example, a person is affected in the duodenum by negative thoughts and thoughts of worry and strain in his mind. An Adept can control the thought process and its influence on the nervous or autonomic system, which produces ulcers by stimulating the glands to secrete acids which eat up the inner membrane. In the civilized world, ulcers are considered a proof of efficiency and hard work among executives. It is known to science that the primary cause of ulcers is a mental condition. When people can stop the mental projection and control the psychic propulsion, not only can millions of people prevent ulcers in their bodies, but in the same way prevent numerous negative physical conditions and create healthy and positive conditions. Mental projection is in the form of secret brain waves, which have a language of their own.

Psychic propulsion is the result of the propelling impulse of the will by means of which the thought is released and projected into the outer world from your mind. With the help of the propelling impulse, the thought is discharged towards the mind of some specific person or towards the mind of the masses of people. Sometimes a thought is projected into space with the sole purpose of creating an impression upon the ethereal substance by reproducing itself into space. From space, the thought reflects towards the minds of people and reproduces itself in their minds, as a result of which they start to think and act accordingly.

Mental projection is a process which takes place by the action of the will of the projector. In many cases, the projection is seen to take place even when the projector apparently has no such intent. This is the reason why many people manifest mental influence upon others and upon themselves without even having the knowledge of doing so.

There is a strong element of will in any thought which is held firmly in consciousness by attention. Greater attention and concentration automatically generate will power. Every strong thought has a strong element of will which helps to project the thought in space. A person who is trained in mental projection and psychic propulsion does not depend upon the inherent power of will. He consciously generates will power by distinct and deliberate effort. Once the will power has been generated, the mental thought pattern is projected by releasing the forces of will and *Prana* to push it as a propeller. Releasing the propelling forces to project your thought is purely a mental act and can be done by developing inner awareness.

The power to operate on these inner forces of mental projection and psychic propulsion is developed by practicing the technique detailed in *Chapter 39* "Two-Month Course In Psychic Phenomena."

Chapter 31 THIS CAN BE THE MOST SUCCESSFUL YEAR IN YOUR LIFE

MAN IS A SEVENFOLD being. You express yourself through various vehicles: the vehicle of thought, the vehicle of mind, the vehicle of emotion, the vehicle of body, and the vehicle of Spirit which houses the soul, etc. Just as a person can travel by bicycle, motor-cycle, boat, helicopter, plane, jet and rocket, the expression of a person through each vehicle creates a specific result which varies in degree.

The expression through the lower vehicles is mechanical, but in order to express himself through higher vehicles, a person must exert himself. The power of expression through higher vehicles comes through perseverance and making continuous efforts to develop inner awareness, which awakens the psychic powers. When thoughts are expressed through the higher vehicles, immediately they start to materialize into objects and things and create phenomena. When the expression of thoughts is through words, through physical actions or other lower vehicles of expression, it does not create good results of materialization. For example, if a person wants a million dollars and he expresses himself through words, and does make every effort physically to earn a million dollars, he would hardly succeed because the conscious mind and the material and gross vehicles of expression have very limited power as far as materialization is concerned. When you can express your thoughts through the higher vehicles of mind without speaking a word or expressing physical effort, you will easily create phenomena to help you acquire a million dollars. When your thoughts express through the higher vehicles of mind, your will is as strong as the Will of God. Things in this world have been created and are being created by the Will of God (the Supreme Mind and Intelligence governing the world), and when your thoughts and will are as powerful as the Will of God. you are able to create things yourself as God does. The Will of God is nothing but thoughts expressed through the world brain, not in words and physical actions but through higher vehicles of consciousness. Such thoughts are backed by will, and thereby create chemical changes into phenomena to help materialize the objects in question.

Your mind is like a very precious engine and the load which it can carry depends upon the amount of power that is released in it. Your mind is like an engine of unlimited capacity. Unsuccessful persons in the world are like big engines but with little power, and therefore cannot succeed in large projects in their lives, simply because they are not able to release the greater amount of mental forces. A person who is unable to increase the flow of higher forces into his mind becomes frustrated and depressed when he is confronted with the bigger problems of life and cannot get over them. When the project and plans demand extra efforts, resources, money and help, the unsuccessful people are unable to use the higher vehicles of mind which can automatically bring extra help, and the result is their nerves are affected by frustrations and obstacles in their lives.

On the other hand, persons who can consciously release the forces of their mind on the higher level, never leave things half done in their lives. If they find more money, more resources and more help are needed for the fulfillment of the plan, they just use the higher vehicles of mind and the results are right there. This is the secret of a successful life.

An average person hardly uses even 5% of the power of the mind; the rest is seldom used. The more and more a person is used to using the mind and its power on the higher level, the more successful he becomes in his life. When you can express yourself through the higher vehicles of mind, there is nothing in this world where success will not be waiting for you: in singing, business, sales, art, painting, teaching, acting—anything you want, you succeed right away. A successful salesman, by the use of the higher vehicles of mind, used to sell his goods by mental projection and psychic propulsion, and when he would come to the office, would find the customers waiting for him.

Many people have the power and will within them and can easily use the mind on its higher plane to make their dreams come true if they just make a little effort. Many people are failures in their lives simply because the power of the mind is on reverse rather than on drive, as a result of which they start to sell when it is time to buy, and start to buy when it is time to sell, and as such they are a failure.

If you want to make this year the most successful year in your life, you must learn to release the maximum amount of mental forces through the higher vehicles of your mind, which are of unlimited capacity. When you wish, desire and act through your conscious and lower mind, the results are very meager. While releasing the power of the mind, you should always be sure that the forces are on drive, rather than on reverse. It is very important to be sure that the mental forces are on drive before you take any steps in a new project. Before you step on the gas, you have to make sure that the gear shift is on drive and not in reverse.

Those who possess and release big mental forces but cannot change the gear from reverse to drive become the greatest failures of the world. All things remaining the same, if they would simply have changed the gear from reverse to drive, they would be destined to be among the most successful people of the time. The greatest failure of today can become the most successful person of tomorrow in this world by reversing the flow of forces of mind from negative to positive.

There is a strong action and reaction, and a strong correlation and connection between things and thoughts, and as a result of direction from thoughts, things are made to move and act. Each thought has color, and each color has a thought. When you express through the higher vehicles of the mind, the thoughts express in the form of color. In the higher vehicles of expression of the mind, life and matter are subservient to the spiritual forces, and they stay in a form where life cannot be differentiated from matter.

For example, a thought of a triangle (which means a space surrounded by three sides) when projected from the higher vehicles of mind creates triangular things in the physical and material form. The thought of a triangle is backed by will, as a result of which it is able to draw atoms, electrons and protons, and colors and elements in their subtle form necessary to materialize the specific objects in the form of a triangle.

If you go to the beach, you will find particles of sand have been arranged in a specific pattern. If you see snow falling on your window or the open lawn, you will find after the snowfall everything has a specific design. Everything in this world has a specific shape and form which is determined by thoughts. Why are apples always round, and bananas long? Who made the design and gave them the form? By the use of your conscious mind and the lower vehicles of mind, you cannot make a banana round and the apple long, but you can do so by expressing your thoughts using the higher vehicles of mind.

Thoughts can bring rarefication of matter. The more powerful the thoughts, the more creative they are, the more they bring the rarefication of matter. Thoughts are creative when they manifest through the higher vehicles of mind, which use the astral senses instead of the physical. In the process of rarefication, the chemical changes start to take place in matter. The eyeglasses you wear are nothing but pieces of ordinary stone rarefied by chemical process. When a stone is rarefied it becomes transparent, and you can see better through it than through your bare eyes. Science has discovered that if a stone is rarefied even more, it will become inflammable.

Just as science can transform matter into energy and life (electronic brains and computer brains, etc.) similarly an Adept can materialize his thought vibrations into material and physical things. An Adept always relies upon the forces of his mind and thought for the creation of the psychic phenomena. A Yogi is seldom attached to the objects and possessions of the world because they can always be created by the power of the mind, no matter where he is, by using the spiritual forces, which are the expression of thought through the highest vehicles of mind. Expression of your thought through the highest vehicle controls both matter as well as life, and as such, any change can be brought about in things which are animate, as well as inanimate.

The process of using the higher vehicles of the mind should always be learned under the personal supervision of the teacher, because each individual is different, and only the expert teacher knows your ability and background, and can guide you on the path ahead, specifically suited to you and train you in the use of the higher vehicles of mind as soon as you become ready.

Chapter 32 SECRET OF YOUR PROGRESS

THE SECRET of your individual progress in this world, physically, mentally, as well as spiritually, lies in giving. To give does not mean only charity of money, clothes, food and other tangible things. Good mental disposition towards others and forgiveness towards others are better types of giving than charity of money. By giving a good mental disposition and forgiveness to others, you don't lose anything, but you gain manifold. On the other hand, when you give objects in charity, you really lose the object of giving. This is one of the great secrets of my progress, and it can bring progress and happiness to you in your life.

Charity is rather incomplete without charity of disposition, understanding and human feeling. Charity is self-sacrifice on different levels of one's being, without the pride of self sacrifice. When a person gives charity in order to show society his importance or wealth, it is guided by inferior motives and takes away the very spirit of charity. Charity in its true sense should be without any motive and desire. The highest type of charity is *Jnana-Yajna* (imparting of the knowledge of soul and spiritual instruction). As a missionary, my foremost mission in life is to share my knowledge and wisdom with the people of the world, to bring in their lives spiritual enlightenment. Spiritual instructions are more essential in the life of the people, to bring them happiness and the peace that passeth all understanding, than bread needed by a starving person. There are millions of people in this world who are materially prosperous and physically over-nourished, with their souls still starving for the secret of Truth. Food is needed for the body, but more important is spiritual food for the starving souls. Man cannot live by bread and bread alone; he lives by the love of God. No one can have inner satisfaction without being initiated into spiritual knowledge and wisdom, which serves as food for the Spirit. Just as the stomach needs good food, so the mind needs good ideas to chew, and the soul needs spiritual enlightenment as its food. Giving spiritual food to the millions of starving souls is much higher than giving bread to starving people. It is good to give bread and charity to people so that they may have healthy bodies. The body is a means towards an end. The body should not be used as an end in itself. The usefulness of the body lies in its service as an important vehicle for the evolution of mind and soul which is housed within it.

Life without philosophy brings no happiness because it is ridden with fear, insecurity and hatred. True philosophy of life does not come from a materially supersatiated prosperous society. Philosophy of life brings peace and happiness to people, which they cannot get from ice cream, soda, candies, and the glitter and glamour of the automobile world. True philosophy is the realization of the Divinity of the Universe, the immortality of the soul, and the unity of creation with the Absolute Consciousness. We all breathe the common air, which is the breath of life. There is no difference between your breath and my breath. My breath becomes yours, and yours become mine, so everyone in this world breathes the breath of the Great Cosmic Being, whose joy we share in our lives.

Philosophy of life is not a dream. It is not self-negation. It is not limited humanism. One can have all the prosperity and wealth of the world, and still develop a true philosophy of life which can only bring more peace, happiness and joy of good living to his life.

The highest Truth has manifested on various planes, and so one must realize this fact of manifestation. Body and matter have been created not as an end in themselves, but as a base to provide evolution of the mental and spiritual faculties in them. The reading of books is intellectual gymnastics and can only make a person a walking encyclopedia. It does not bring him realization of the Truth, and experience of the inner peace that passeth all understanding. Philosophy must be practical; it must be a vital experience, and living possession. It must express through every action in your life. Life itself should be philosophy. True philosophy of life is one of the greatest secrets of happiness. In order to express the higher philosophy of life in your worldly actions, you must be able to control and master the physical, vital, mental and intellectual vehicles of your consciousness in order to achieve self perfection, self illumination and self evolution.

Raja Yoga is the most suitable method to initiate the people into the secrets of true philosophy of life. I have guided and trained numerous people into the secrets of *Raja Yoga* (initiation into the mysteries of spiritual knowledge) and have found from my personal experience that it is the easiest way for the people of the modern world. *Raja Yoga* has eight limbs, i.e., subdivisions: *Yama, Niyama, Asana, Pranayama, Pratyahara, Dhyana, Dharana, Samadhi.* The detailed instructions on *Raja Yoga* should be studied under the personal guidance of a *Preceptor*, for the reasons explained in the foregoing chapters.

Progress in life does not come without the realization of the fact that there is something above human perception which controls and directs all that is invisible, even your own pulsation, circulation, respiration, digestion and assimilation. The present unrest throughout the world, anxieties, crippling diseases like polio, cancer, epilepsy, heart failure, the horrors of nuclear devastation, remind us again and again of a higher goal to be achieved in this world, which is the love of one and all. Our purpose in this life and in this world is not to become an instrument of destruction and devastation, but to realize, experience and bring unity in diversity, which comes by the realization of the Oneness in

All. The restlessness of man and the miseries that fill the phenomena remind us of our higher goal in this life, which only can provide absolute security, perfect peace and true happiness.

It is this strong inner urge for the dissemination of spiritual knowledge and initiating people into the mysteries of Truth to help them realize unity in diversity, that guided me to renounce the world and enter the Order of Missionary, dedicating my life to *Jnana Yajna*, the highest charity a person can do in his life.

A course of serious penance, self discipline and ascetic life in the Himalayas endowed me with the courage and strength to see the new vision and to live in this world like an ordinary person, yet unaffected by the phenomena of the world. For the dissemination of this knowledge I have founded *Kailashananda* Mission in a lovely part of the Himalayas in India, where people will be trained into the realization of the Truth and Spirit, so that they can radiate the message of peace, selfless service, and love of one and all.

The pains of mankind, the dangers of war, i.e., the Korean War, Japanese War, German War, atomic war, etc., in which people have no alternative but to live underground challenging the call of Spirit for freedom and movement upward, all remind us of our higher goal in life. Mankind by his own lack of true philosophy creates wars and pain, killing one's own friends, countrymen and people in various parts of the world. If you would realize the unity in diversity, there would be more love, friendliness and unity, which would help all achieve a better understanding, and facilitate the achievement of our goal, which is mental and spiritual enlightenment. The most urgent need of today is to make man realize and attain the worthier end of life and to awaken man to his errors and follies. Man must be rescued from the forces of his lower nature, which creates wars and sufferings in this world, to the consciousness of his true relation to the Universe. This is the work of arousing religious consciousness and the awareness of the Divinity of man. This is the time when the world is ready for a spiritual renaissance. The time has come when people are looking for nobler things in their lives, which lie beyond any ideology, belief, religion or creed.

Among the charity of objects, i.e., money, land, food, clothes or property, the best charity is the one which is anonymous, where the identity of the donor is never disclosed. Anonymous charity is still very popular among Hindus. I have seen many Hindus who place silver and gold coins inside the fruits which they distribute to the Holy Men and the poor, specially on the occasions of religious festivals. It is not an uncommon sight in India to see the poor and incapacitated persons sitting in a line on the road to receive gifts from the devotees who come to bathe in the Holy Ganges, or to attend prayers in the Temples and Holy Shrines. In the crowded streets sometimes these persons do not even have a chance to know who gave them the anonymous gift in their lap. The benefits of anonymous gifts are very great.

Chapter 33 EMOTION, THOUGHT AND MENTAL PROCESS

Yogis DISCOVERED in their inner research the inner process which creates thought and emotions, as well as the process of their effect on the body and mind. The rhythm of breathing controls and directs the movement of thought and determines the state of mind of a person at a specific time. The rhythm of breathing is like the reins of horses pulling a carriage. Thought and emotions are like the horses of the carriage, and the human body can be compared to a carriage, which is drawn by the function of mind and thoughts.

Nature changes the rhythm of breathing from time to time which brings change in the mental state. In inner research Yogis are able to perceive the whole phenomena in the same way you see physical and material things through your eyes. The rhythm of breath directs the special beat, also known as the special pulse rate in the brain under the skull. The pulsation rate of the brain in an average person is not more than twelve beats per minute, while the pulse rate in other parts of the body including the heart varies between 80-100 beats per minute, and sometimes even more. The special beat of the brain controls and directs the function of the involuntary organs and glands throughout the sympathetic and parasympathetic nervous systems.

By controlling this rhythm, a Yoga student is able to change his state of mind and emotions just as you can control the speed of the horses pulling the carriage by pulling or relaxing the reins. Desired changes can be brought into the autonomic nervous system and the endocrine glands which secrete enzymes and hormones in your blood. The autonomic nervous system is conditioned by the state of your mental and emotional bodies. The involuntary organs, including those of pulsation, respiration, digestion, assimilation and elimination, as well as the endocrine glands, work in conjunction with the autonomic nervous system which controls and directs them.

The rhythm of breathing controls the state of mind, and the state of mind controls the body chemistry. Any change in the body chemistry produces a subsequent change in the rate of vibration of the mind, and in this way a circle is created. Under emotional upset, the mind is disturbed and thoughts are affected to such an extent that reason is replaced by feelings and emotions. Under emotional conditions a person knows the right thing to do, but still he does not have any control over the situation.

One of my students happened to be suffering from diabetes for a long time. He was required by the doctor not to eat muffins and other items containing too much sugar. Although he knew what was harmful for him to eat, still he could not stop his hand from opening the refrigerator and eating the muffins and cookies all day. Different types of emotions make people do different things in their lives, and they are unable to get away from the wrong habits no matter how much they try to reason them out. The root of your emotions is in your mental body, which consists of a bundle of thoughts which are made of vibrations and astral matter. The mental body is also known as the astral body. Unless you go deep and tap your astral and mental body, it is not possible to root out the cause of emotions from your life.

The astral and mental body is that part of the human organism which survives the death of the physical body. At the time of death, life, emotions, thoughts, feelings, and yearning for unfulfilled desires, are all transferred to your astral body and very soon you awaken to your new life in the astral body, when life in the physical body has come to an end.

Psychoanalysis and various other advanced methods used in the psychic field make an effort to discover the cause of emotional upset, but they cannot go beyond the time of birth. In many cases the cause of fears and phobias and emotional disturbances lies in the far distant past, many hundred years ago, when the person lived in a different country. When the cause of emotional disturbance lies in a past life, it is difficult to remove it by psychoanalysis or similar methods. In many cases the injury is received in the astral body not in this life, but in lives before. Since the astral body survives the fall of body, it carries with it its astral injuries and emotional problems into the new body where it migrates. Until the problems of the astral body are solved, it continues to affect likewise the nervous system, especially the nervous centers and the various plexuses and vital glands in the new body where it has migrated. As a result of which, conditions of fear, apprehension, phobia, feelings of insecurity and various types of allergies are created. Such conditions are followed by nervous exhaustion and fatigue. It is these impulses in the astral body from past lives which makes the duckling know how to swim as soon as it comes out of the egg. Most people having one or the other types of allergies have the root of the allergies in their astral bodies from past lives, as a result of which they find it difficult to get rid of them.

I had one student in Washington, D. C., who was allergic to closed windows. The first time I came to know about her problem was when she joined one of my breathing and relaxation classes in Washington, D. C. During relaxation she was lying on the floor on the rug with the other students in the class. Noise from the street cars was coming into the class, therefore I closed the window. As soon as the window was closed, she became allergic about the closed window and restless. She could not speak but indicated by her hand that I immediately open the window. I opened the window at her request. It was over an hour before she completely recovered and told me that she was allergic to closed windows since she was born. She continued to practice Yoga under my supervision for many weeks. In about two months she became completely immune to the said allergy. To prove her immunity she closed herself in a room with all windows closed and nothing happened to her. By erasing the cause of her allergy from the astral, she was able to get rid of it.

Another interesting case I remember very well was of another student who lived in New Delhi. He was allergic to his wife. He came to overcome his emotional difficulties and allergies at the Sanatorium in the Himalayas where I happened to be the Director-in-Charge. Because of his fear of the allergy, he could never enter his wife's bedroom when she was alone. Nor would his wife enter his bedroom when he was alone for fear that her husband was allergic to her. Both of them slept in different bedrooms. He would not become allergic and hysterical in the company of his wife when there were other persons present. He was extra careful to leave his wife before the friends departed, because if the friends left first, he would be the only person with his wife, and would get allergic. His allergy problem was in the astral body, from a past life. By removing the cause, he was able to overcome his condition. Now they have only one bedroom.

A few days ago, a business man came to see me in my studio in Manhattan. One of his difficulties was that he was allergic to riding in elevators, and also to climbing staircases leading to higher floors. As soon as he entered my studio, I found him shaky, pale and, nervous.

I asked him, "What is the matter?"

He replied, "'This is the ninth floor, which is too high for me because I'm allergic to going to higher floors."

The cause of his allergy, lay more than 200 years ago in a past life when he lived in Mongolia. His astral body had migrated many times during the past 200 years, but it still carried its injury in the astral body. Since he died in Mongolia, his injury could not be erased from the astral body, as a result of which it was affecting his mental as well as physical state. While he lived in Mongolia he was dragged to the top of a very high hill by his enemies. They made him stand on the top of the hill and threw him down on the hard rocks below causing instantaneous death. This was the reason behind his fear of climbing staircases and taking an elevator to upper floors.

Similarly, I have seen people suffering from various allergies of fear of imminent danger, death, insecurity, etc. Also I have seen persons allergic to certain types of foods, climate, colors, persons, etc. It is very important to control emotions which are negative and harmful. If harmful emotions are not held in check, they may ruin your nervous system, and completely wreck your physical and mental health. Harmful emotions saturate your bloodstream with poisonous chemicals and the cells start to die and disintegrate due to the effect of the poisonous chemicals which feed them. By controlling even the one emotion of anger, a person can easily stretch his lifespan 20-30 years. Harmful emotions neutralize the enzymes and nutritive chemicals in the blood, as a result of which a person starts to lose his memory, and also the thought process is slowed down. Due to reduced strength of the brain, a person loses his power of observation.

The functions of the lungs, heart and nerves are affected by emotional disturbances. Under emotional upset, the mind sends harmful nerve impulses bringing complex changes to the body and creating contractions in the muscles and blood vessels, i.e., clenching of fists or teeth, etc. In many cases, emotional upset can completely stop the mental process and create moods of depression, insomnia and nervous exhaustion.

The astral body has color, force, will, intelligence and astral senses. It is made of tenuous astral matter like ether which is invisible to the physical eyes. A person continues to live in the astral body as soon as the physical body falls. Various nervous centers in the physical body are simply a counterpart of the astral centers, i.e., navel, tip of the nose, third eye, pituitary and pineal glands. A person should not concentrate too much on the vital nervous centers because it awakens the function of the astral centers which are closely coordinated. Concentration on the nervous centers should be done after the body has been purified by simple Yoga techniques. Awakening the astral centers releases tremendous astral and mental powers into the body. The astral centers are also known as *chakras* or lotuses.

Chapter 34 REVELATION OF ASTRAL JOURNEYS

THE KNOWLEDGE of psychic phenomena is as old as Christianity itself. The Bible is full of experiences gotten during astral journeys made by Christ and other prophets. All Prophets, Great Masters and Yogis make astral journeys. During astral journeys, the mind is enabled to connect itself with the astral sense of perception, which is known as the inner eye.

The astral body consists of five senses of action, five senses of perception, determinative faculty, intelligence, and mind. Mind is in a position to connect itself with any one of these astral senses which gives it the power to perceive without the use of physical senses. In astral journeys, mind connects itself with the third eye through color vibrations and then projects its awareness into space through the third eye. In astral journeys, the physical senses are not used. The perception of the astral journeys takes place through the astral tube which is created in space. The astral tube is made of the ethereal substance in space. The will power and intelligence which project with the thoughts help manufacture the invisible astral tube. If an Adept wants to perceive the sun, moon, Venus, Mars, or any other distant solar system, he is able to perceive it very clearly in the astral journey. The sun, which is much larger than the earth, is perceived during the astral journey as clearly as you can perceive a mustard seed in your palm through your physical eyes. In astral perception, an Adept gets knowledge not only of the physical aspects, but also of the mental and subtle forces which work behind the physical, including the life, mind and intelligence which guides and controls them.

For example, an Adept makes an astral journey for the perception of a comet. He not only perceives the physical aspect of the comet, but also the subtle forces of Mind and Nature which create, direct and sustain the function of the comet. When a comet is created, there are certain forces in mind and intelligence which draw together the ethereal substance, electrons and protons of a specific wave length which will bring about the formation of a comet. A scientist during physical perception can know only of its physical aspect, but does not perceive the invisible forces which are the cause of the phenomena.

All planets and comets, including the sun, moon, Venus, and Mars, are populated by astral and mental bodies which exert, from there, influence on the earth. Astral bodies are held in the orbit of a planet by the law of gravitation. As they become more and more rarefied, they become lighter and are able to escape from the law of gravity which pulls them towards that planet. When the astral body stays with a planet, it keeps on revolving with the planet as human beings do on this earth. As soon as an astral body is released from a planet, it joins another planet which is the fittest place for it to stay. It waits for further rarefication which would enable it to escape the law of gravity of a specific planet and move still higher in space.

While a person is alive, he stays within the orbit of this earth and keeps on revolving with it. Due to the law of gravity, the earth does not let him go out of its orbit. When the physical body falls, the astral is released and is free to be automatically in the orbit of another planet in this solar system or a solar system far off, according to the rarefication of his astral body. If the astral body has not been rarefied and purified, and is still full of negative emotions and selfish motives, it cannot escape the law of gravity due to its weight, and it stays earthbound, waiting for an opportunity when the astral body can migrate to this earth again in another physical body.

Astral journeys are made consciously. They are not a trance or hypnosis. In order to make astral journey, a person should be thoroughly trained in various types of Yoga under the guidance of an expert teacher. During training for astral journey, one has to develop, step by step, the eight limbs of *Raja Yoga*. All the mysteries of Nature and Truth are revealed to man in astral journeys. It is in astral journey that you can know the reason for your being on this planet, the goal of your life, as well as your true nature and your position in the vastness of space. Man is truly a being of space. He comes from space, and returns to space. Man's stay on this earth is hardly a millionth part of his eternal life; he lives in the vastness of space. Man comes on the earth for the specific mission of bringing about more rarefication and purification of his astral and mental faculties to enable him for his further journeys in space. The matter out of which the human body is made is only a base for the evolution of mind and Spirit within, not an end in itself. Those who do not know their goal in life and the mission which they have to perform on this earth, commit the greatest blunder in their lives because unless the goal is achieved, the whole life on this earth is a waste.

About 7,000 years ago, the new world was revealed to Yogis during their astral journeys, the same new astral world became known to the West during early Christianity when Christ, John the Baptist, and others were able to penetrate the astral phenomena by making astral journeys. You must not be satisfied with the limited life you spend in this world. You must discard the illusion and ignorance that makes you believe that your life in this world is limited by time and space, disease and disappointments. You must make astral journeys to see for yourself the causal world from which the earth you inhabit has been created, as well as the sun, moon and other planets which orbit around the earth. At the end of the cycle, the earth, sun, moon, Venus, and everything else is dissolved back into the causal world.

The whole of Christian teachings is founded upon knowledge received through astral journeys and only upon such knowledge can it endure. It was not until the resurrection of Christ, which was the demonstration of conquest over death and realization of Truth that the astral body survives the fall of the physical body, that prosperity, power, glory, and leadership came to the Christian world. Before the resurrection of Christ and the astral journeys he made, his followers were poor people who did not have the strength to stand by the side of their Master.

7,000 years ago, through astral journeys, Yogis perceived true knowledge of earth, sun, moon and millions of other solar systems. This knowledge was imparted by Yogis to their disciples. With astral perception you will have the full vision of the earth on which you live. You will perceive earth like a lotus flower and various continents as its petals and you will find it equally rounded like a ball on its sides. Also you will perceive the exact length, width and other minor details of each continent, including rivers, mountains, persons and races inhabiting them and the religions which they follow. You would perceive that India (*Bharat Varsha*) is the only land on which souls inclined to *Karma Yoga* are born.

India is *Karma Bhumi*, that is the land where people live to create *Karmas*, the fruits they will reap in their future reincarnations. United States is the *Bhog Bhumi*, that is the land where people enjoy the fruits of their *Karmas* in the form of luxuries and easy life. Once a person enjoys his fruit, then he must again create the seed of *Karma* to enable him to enjoy the fruits of luxury and material possessions again. If new *Karmas* are not created, then the *Bhoga* (enjoyment of worldly things) comes to an end, and one has to start again from the very beginning. Fruits cannot come without a tree, and a tree does not come without a seed. *Karmas* from life are the seeds to bring fruits in future reincarnations.

Souls which have unsatisfied desires for wealth and material prosperity and have earned that prosperity in their past lives by good *Karmas*, will be born in prosperous countries like the United States of America, and later in their life they turn out to be persons like Henry Ford, the founder of the Ford Automobile Industry, and persons of that category. On the other hand, souls which have yearned for spiritual enlightenment only, ignoring reinvolvement in material life, will be born in India. Such souls may reincarnate in the form of persons like Mahatma Gandhi, Lord Buddha, and King Harsha Verdhan. Harsha Verdhan ruled India long before the British people came there. He was very religious. One of the laws in his government was that every year the whole treasury must be emptied and its contents given away as charity. On the appointed day, the treasury was thrown open and the poor and needy would come and help themselves. Each continent on this earth has been created for a different group of souls to help them fulfill *Karmas* of their past lives on this earth.

The regions beyond this earth you will perceive are the abodes of the spiritually developed and Yoga Adepts. The sun is named after a highly developed soul which is the presiding deity of this body. The sun is centrally situated between the higher celestial regions and the earth. In your inner perception you will find that the distance between the sun and the earth is 25 *Koti Yoganas*. The sun gives light and life to creatures and seeds. You will find the earth and celestial regions connected by the ethereal region known as *Akasha* which intervenes between them, and in the middle of the two is stationed the Divine Sun, the Lord of Light, which extends its heat and light on all sides. Also you will perceive in your psychic projection that the Divine Sun by its northern, southern, slow, quick and tolerable courses, duly rises and sets, creating night and day of long and short and equal duration in various *Rashies*. The *Rashies* are the various astrological constellations. When the sun goes to

Mesha Rashi and *Tula Rashi*, then days and nights become of equal duration. When the sun journeys in the five other *Rashies* (signs of the Zodiac) beginning with *Vrisha Rashi*, then the days have a longer duration and the nights become shorter by one hour every month. When however, the sun is in the five other signs of the Zodiac beginning with *Vrishchika*, then the course of day and night is reversed. The nights become longer in duration. In other words, so long as the course of the sun is southernly, (*Dakshinayana*), the days are shorter than the night, and when the course of the sun is northerly, (*Uttarayana*), the nights are shorter than the days.

You will perceive the mental, astral and spiritual aspect of this body, besides its physical aspect as it is known to science. In your inner perception you will realize that the Sun is a celestial body, like one of the Heavenly Fathers, using the whole planet of the sun as its chariot. The Sun is attended by *Rishies* (spiritually evolved souls) which are known by the name of *Valakhilyas*. The bodies of the *Valakhilyas* are in dimension equal to the space of your thumb. The body in which the Sun and its 60,000 attendants known as *Valakhilyas* live, is purely mental body. The great celestial bodies by their will create the planets and comets on which they live and from where they radiate their thoughts across vast space. These comets, planets, sun, all are made of the ethereal substance which is held firm in the shape of a solid physical body by the power of the will of the celestial beings. A comet is dissolved back into energy at the sweet will of the celestial being which owns it. Exactly in the same way as it was created by the will of that celestial. You will also find in your inner perception that the *Valakhilyas*, who attend the Celestial Being Sun, are always humming sacred *Mantras* praising spiritual development of the Divine Sun as it moves on its chariot across vast space. They all adore the Divine Sun as being identical with the Great Soul or God manifesting in that body. You will also have the clear understanding in your perception of how the year, month, and days are created. As the sun travels through the ethereal regions, it creates seasons and the year. The Indian calendar is based on this knowledge perceived by the Yogis 7,000 years ago.

Also you will perceive that at a distance of 100,000 *Yoganas* above the sun is the moon. In two fortnights, the moon enjoys one year of the sun; in two days and a quarter, one month of the sun; and in one day, one fortnight of the sun. When the phase of the moon is in the course of rising, it makes the Day of the Celestials, and when it gradually wanes it makes the Day of the *Manes* (the *Pitries* on the moon). *Pitries* are the souls who inhabited this earth in the past. Having made the day and night of the Celestials and *Manes* respectively, by the dark and bright fortnight, the Divine Moon enjoys one planet in thirty seconds. You will also perceive the wisdom and spiritual values of the Moon, that the Moon is full of food and nectar, and provides life to animals and healing power to herbs. The Moon itself is a creature. If scientists were able to reach the moon, they would find it a monstrous place unfit for human habitation, because they would discover only physical and material values on the moon, while unable to perceive its wisdom and spiritual values. Thus the Divine Consciousness of sixteen phases manifesting as the moon, possessed of mind, material body and bliss, upholds the existence of the celestials, *Manes*, human being, elements, beasts, birds, reptiles, vegetation, etc. Thus Divine Consciousness of the Moon pervades all.

At a distance of 200,000 *Yoganas* above the moon, you will perceive in your astral projection the planets being set to the Wheel of Time by the Supreme Power. The number of these planets seen as stars is twenty-eight, and they are known as *Abhijit*. The Wheel of Time is an invisible wheel. All the planets of life within the orbit of this wheel die and get old as time moves. Beings and planets beyond the

Wheel of Time are not affected by the element of time at all.

Then again, 200,000 *Yoganas* above the starry region is the planet Venus. In your astral projection, you will perceive that when it enjoys a planet at its front, it enjoys one at its back. Venus is also like the sun, gifted with quick, slow and equal motions. The planet Venus is always favorable to mankind and the creatures on earth. It is with the advent of this planet that the earth gets rain.

The planet Mercury has the same position and course as the planet Venus. You will perceive that Mercury is 200,000 *Yoganas* above Venus. The planet Mercury is the son of the Divine Moon. At times when Mercury goes far off from the sun, it engenders violent storms, scarcity of water, clouds and drought.

Above the planet Mercury you will perceive Mars who is 200,000 *Yoganas* away. In three *Packhas* (fortnights) it enjoys the signs of the Zodiac, if it does not have an oblique course of movement. The planet Mars, you will perceive, is generally an inauspicious and ominous planet.

At a distance of 200,000 *Yoganas* from the planet Mars is the planet Jupiter, and if it does not have an oblique course, it journeys for a *Parivatsara* in *Rashi*. It radiates good influence for spiritually developed persons.

200,000 *Yoganas* above the planet Jupiter is the planet Saturn which stays in every *Rashi* for thirty months, and in thirty years it goes around the twelve *Rashies* (signs of the Zodiac). This planet brings miseries on persons concerned.

At a distance of 1,100,000 *Yoganas* to the north of the planet Saturn, the Rashis are seen distributing peace to all. They are always journeying around the central station, i.e., the Cosmic Brain, also known as Cosmic Consciousness, or the Creator.

At a distance of thirteen *Yoganas* from the planet Saturn lies the illustrious sphere of the Great Master known as *Vishnu* which transcends every region. In that excellent region there dwells that great devotee of *Vishnu* whose name is *Dhruva*. Long ago *Vishnu* was incarnated in India as one of the Great Masters. *Dhruva* was born in India to a king named *Uttanpad*. This auspicious devotee, *Dhruva*, is known as the North Star or Polar Star. *Dhruva* (Polar Star) is circled by many other celestials, i.e. *Agni* (Fire), *Indra*, etc., all simultaneously occupying the stars known after their own names. Just as *Dhruva* occupies the star known after its own name, *Dhruva* (Polar Star). Similarly other celestials occupy planets named after them. These beings, after whom these planets have been named, live for *Kalpa* (the cycle of earth). Due to spiritual greatness, *Dhruva* exists as a pillar to support the astral spheres that constantly move in their course in the heavens in accordance with the course of the Wheel of Time, also known as the Wheel of *Kala* or Death. Just as a horse tied to a post fixed in the center of a grain-threshing floor goes round and round, similarly, fixed on the inside and outside of the circle of time, stars and planets exist supporting themselves on the North Star and propelled by the wind, move in every direction until the end of *Kala* (end of the cycle).

In your inner perceptions you will have full knowledge and realization of the billions and trillions of solar systems, their wisdom and spiritual values and the process by which they are created, preserved and dissolved, and the role they play in vast space. This will help you realize your own position in the sphere full of worlds occupied by visible as well as invisible beings.

Chapter 35 YOUR GUARDIAN ANGEL

IT IS THE Invisible Beings which control and direct the action of the visible world. It was the Invisible Cosmic Being which created matter and the earth we inhabit. The Invisible Beings have an active life. The real activity starts after the fall of the body. The life in space through which an astral body has to undergo after death is a very active life. Those who are highly developed mentally and spiritually, occupy responsible positions as our heavenly fathers and guardian angels. They share their responsibilities regarding Nature in molding the destiny of the earth and also the people who inhabit it.

They are direct agents of Nature, and Nature works through them. It is with the help of these heavenly fathers and guardian angels that billions and trillions of solar systems have been created. It is at the command of these heavenly fathers that comets and planets appear and disappear in vast space. Psychic phenomena changes at the mere wish of these celestial beings.

One of the functions of the developed beings in space is to help all the people of the world who deserve it and are ready to receive help. When undeveloped souls leave this earth they are like blind persons in daylight. They are not able to share the beauty of Nature. Souls which are evolved mentally and spiritually, receive first attention from the heavenly fathers. In many cases, the earthbound souls have their guardian angel to guide them in their astral journey and prepare them for returning to this earth until they evolve fully in mind and Spirit. In astral life, distance and time do not exist. Time and distance are relative terms which govern this earth. The guardian angels are people of this world who have evolved and perfected themselves by rarefication and purification of their mind and soul. Through thoughts, they read the mind of man and fathom the deep oceans. The guardian angels watch the world progressing and evolving.

One of the duties of the guardian angels is the dissemination of spiritual knowledge to souls in the life beyond, as well as while they live on earth. Some persons receive part-time guidance from the guardian angels, while others have a full-time personal guardian angel. The personal guardian angel may not leave a person until he has fully evolved mentally and spiritually to enable him to make the astral journey where he can share the responsibilities of the Universe. In such cases, the guardian angel incarnates in this world to meet a soul as soon as it is born, and keeps on guiding it on this earth for the duration of his whole life. Sometimes the guardian angel is in the form of a *Preceptor* in this world. If the soul has not been able to achieve its goal in this earth, the guardian angel will again meet the soul on the threshold of the invisible world at the time of death. It continues to guide the soul till it has achieved its goal. Thus the personal angels devote themselves to the embodied souls, sustaining them along the rough path of life in this earth from birth to death, as well as through their successive lives.

In order to receive the guidance of a personal angel and *Preceptor*, an embodied soul must be ready to follow instructions, and also ready to receive them. Readiness comes by achieving purity of heart and mind. Long ago there lived an embodied soul in India in a Hindu family. The embodied soul was born as a son to a very wealthy person. When he was fully grown up, he took on all the responsibility of the business. His personal guardian angel materialized on the earth and started to guide him in his worldly life as his *Preceptor*. In India, every Hindu family has a *Preceptor*. When the person was about forty years old, the personal angel in the form of the *Preceptor* initiated him into the mysteries of *Raja Yoga* and spiritual knowledge after accepting him as his disciple.

The *Preceptor* has to look after many other disciples, and therefore he used to visit this wealthy disciple once every four or five years. On the next trip, the personal angel reminded the disciple of the goal which he was to achieve on this earth. The *Preceptor* asked if he would like to follow him for further guidance. The disciple replied that he would follow him after ten years, in the meantime he would like to get married. After ten years, the teacher returned and reminded him of his promise. The disciple said that he would very much appreciate if he would excuse him until his next trip because in the meantime he would like to have a son. After three years, the *Preceptor* returned and reminded him of his promise. The disciple thanked him for the personal care and attention he was receiving from his *Guru*, but asked him to excuse him until the next trip. He said that in the meantime his son would grow older and would be able to take care of his business. When the *Preceptor* returned again, the disciple expressed that he was very much obliged to the *Guru* for all his kindnesses, but wanted to be excused for a few more years, in the meantime his son would get married. The *Guru* never becomes careless in taking care of the disciples. The *Guru* returned again and reminded the disciple of his promise. The disciple told that he would follow his *Guru* after one year because he was expecting a grandson very soon and would like very much to see him before he left.

After a year the *Guru* returned to find that the disciple was dead and gone. The *Guru* immediately closed his eyes and made an astral journey, to find out that the dead disciple's soul was still in the same house. This time it was embodied in a kitten. The *Guru* contacted the disciple and reminded him of his promise. The *Guru* told the disciple, "Although you are in the body of cat, I can help you evolve if you just follow me." The disciple's astral body incarnated into a cat so that he could play with the grandson. The one-year old grandson liked to play with the kitten. The disciple, now embodied as a cat, replied that he would like to be excused for the next few years until the grandson grows older, because the grandson would be disappointed if he left now.

Again the *Guru* returned to find that the cat was dead and gone. The *Guru* closed his eyes and made an astral journey to find that the disciple was now embodied as an ox in the same house. The *Guru* appealed to him again and reminded him of his promise.

The disciple, now embodied as an ox, replied, "My son has only two oxen to harvest the crop. They have been working hard to make the crop ready for harvest. If I go with you, one ox cannot harvest the crop, therefore please excuse me till the next trip."

When the *Guru* made the next trip he found that the ox was dead since long ago because it worked too hard harvesting the crop. The *Guru* made another astral journey to find that the disciple was still in the same house. This time, he was a worm in a cesspool. The *Guru* reached him astrally and reminded him of his promise. The disciple replied that he had been so much attached to the material and physical and his family that he could not follow his *Guru*, and had to suffer tremendously in his past lives as a cat and ox. He further added that now he had many hundred sons, grandsons and great-great grandsons, all little worms which were following him in the cesspool.

He told the *Guru*, "When I had one son, I could not leave him due to affection and love, how could I leave this prosperous family of many hundred grandsons?" and he requested his *Guru* to excuse him for another trip.

To cut the whole thing short, the personal angel in the form of the *Guru* did not leave the embodied attachment and awakened it to his true soul until it liberated it from the worldly life in space. The soul was helped by the guardian angel to evolve mentally and spiritually till it was able to become an angel for the inferior souls who grope in the darkness of this world and in the life beyond, for help and guidance.

It is very important for an embodied soul on this earth to be receptive to the guidance and instructions of the *Preceptor*. If a student is not receptive, it creates a psychic barrier between the guardian angel and the embodied soul, and as such the soul does not derive the benefit of help. If you are hungry and somebody is giving you milk to drink, you must be able to receive it in the cup. If you hold the cup up-side-down, all the milk will be wasted and you will be still hungry. The personal guardian angel exerts its influence from afar or by standing close to the embodied soul in the hour of trial, always counseling the intuition of the embodied soul and encouraging it by its love and affection. But if the embodied soul is not receptive, the advice is never assimilated.

You must realize that there is a very close unity and bond of solidarity between the Invisible Beings who inhabit space and the embodied souls who live on this earth. Those who cut themselves off from the invisible world commit a great mistake which limits their understanding and progress. Man is nothing but a soul from space captive in flesh. Its true journey starts when it is released from its captivity. There is hierarchy in space which is determined by the state of advancement of each soul. The advanced souls guide the inferior and lesser ones. The soul is a center of light, a seat of joy, knowledge, love of one and all, and peace that passeth all understanding. The more evolved a soul is, the more it is awakened to its true qualities. The true nature of the soul can be perceived in your spiritual heart which is situated in your physical heart on its right side. The space of your spiritual heart is equal to that of the space of your thumb. If the heart is operated, you will find a cavity the size of your thumb, which is covered by sensitive membrane. This cavity to an ordinary person is a vacuum full of ether. To a person who has inner vision, this cavity is the spiritual heart, the seat of the soul, which is embodied in the human body.

Chapter 36 MIND'S AND SOUL'S LIFE IN SPACE

THE MIND AND SOUL survive the fall of death. The mind and soul are the parts of the human organism which do not disintegrate after the fall of body. The human body is an envelope which is discarded at death like an old dress. The vehicle for mind, emotion and Spirit is eternal and it accompanies the soul on its astral journey. The spiritual vehicle houses your true individuality, conscience and intelligence. At the time of death the mental body which connects the soul with the body starts to withdraw itself from the flesh, as a result of which the senses have difficulty in perceiving the world because the nerve currents which are transmitted from the astral senses to the physical senses become irregular and sometimes stop and do not carry the messages in and out. Then the astral senses draw inward and reach the mind asking for immediate help. The physical senses are only the instrument for the astral senses. The power to see, taste and hear is in the astral senses which are housed deep in brain tissues. Astral senses are only an instrument of perception used by mind. At the time of death, the astral senses find that the mind is unable to give them energy and help and as such they get disappointed in their request for help. As the astral senses don't receive help, they cling to the mind. In response to the request for help from the senses, the mind and the astral body rush for help to the spiritual body, which gives life to the astral every second. The spiritual body is housed in your spiritual heart. The mental body is also disappointed because it does not receive any help from the spiritual heart, and it clings to the spiritual body and does not return to its position in the brain.

The astral body contains in it all the impressions, filmed automatically, of your whole life on this earth. It contains, in seed form, all your feelings, emotions and desires. All life is drawn from every cell and nerve of the body. It is a painful process for those who are attached to their worldly possessions. One of the reasons for this fear is not the fear of death, but the fear of losing friends and possessions and the hard-earned money in the bank. Once the *Prana* (life) is withdrawn from the nerve cells and the organs, it cannot return, and finally the spiritual body, wrapped up in the astral body together with all the senses, mind, intelligence, and the determinative faculty, leaves the body for its astral journey. It is then that a man is pronounced dead. After death, immediately one awakens to astral life.

In the astral journey, a person is received by children, friends, relatives, parents, etc., who are still seeking your love. The process of separation of the soul from the body starts long before death sets in. When a person has been chronically sick for most of his life, and confined to a hospital, the separation of the soul from the body starts from five to ten years before the hour of death. In such cases, death is a very slow process.

In cases of sudden death, the soul does not separate from the body until after the body is pronounced dead. Sometimes, the soul continues to cling to the dead body for many days after death. Many people are surprised when a minister at the graveyard bids goodbye to the Spirit after addressing it in prayer. People think that there was no Spirit with the body at that time. In many cases, it accompanies the body in the grave till it completely disintegrates.

When a person, for example, is run over by a car on the street on the way to his office, the soul does not leave the body. Although respiration and pulsation stop, still the soul stays with it. It does not want to be left alone with the body, it wants to be in the house where it used to live amid friends and relatives. It does not like to be left alone in the funeral parlor until the date of burial. A person dying in an accident, dies all of a sudden without any prior notice. As such, the Spirit as well as astral body is most unwilling to leave the dead physical body. The astral body still has the desire to fulfill its wishes, commitments and make dreams come true in this earthly life through the now dead body.

For example, a person engaged to a girl and plans to marry very soon, then build a nice home in the country, buy a Cadillac, raise a number of children, etc., would have great difficulty in leaving the body if all of a sudden he is run over by a train. Mental and astral faculties still want to fulfill their sweet dreams of getting married and raising children, and therefore they try hard to enter the body and use it as an instrument for the fulfillment of the desires. The body, when run over by a train becomes unfit for the mind and the Spirit to live in it and use it. Still, they keep on clinging to the flesh in the hope that the body can help them in the fulfillment of their ambitions. The greater the attachment and desires, the longer the period during which the soul keeps clinging to the flesh.

On the other hand, people who are mentally and spiritually enlightened and use their worldly possessions as a means towards an end, rather than an end in itself, do not have much difficulty in leaving the body and proceeding on their astral journey. A person who is spiritually evolved already knows how to make astral journeys, and also knows about life beyond and man's true life in space. It is only those persons who are too much attached to the pleasures of this world who are not ready for the journey in the beyond and have to suffer much at the time of death, and grope in darkness for guidance on their astral journeys. In cases of heart attack, suicide, and other accidental deaths, tremendous pain and struggle takes place in the soul at the time of departure.

Since a soul carries its senses and mind with it on its astral journey, it continues to perceive and respond in return. Although it is no longer captive of flesh, it always aspires to the love and attention of those to whom it was attached on earth. If its friends and relatives on this earth do something which would displease it if it were still embodied, it will still get hurt and disappointed and it will respond. Thoughts from friends and relatives register on its mental body—the astral. These thoughts can make it either happier and cheerful, or gloomy and depressed.

The thoughts received by the soul in the life beyond bring a change in the colors which constitute its astral body. Thoughts of love, joy, guidance and wisdom generate positive and brighter color in its mental body, while negative thoughts of jealousy, hatred, etc. generate darker color in its aura. The more negative and darker the colors, the heavier becomes the astral body and the closer it comes to the earth. The brighter the colors of the astral body, the more rarefied and lighter it is, and the higher it moves into space. The higher the soul is able to rise in space, the more it is able to enjoy the Divine glory of the Divine beauty. The nearer the soul comes to the earth, the less it shares the Divine wisdom and beauty, and the more it suffers from worldly sorrows which afflict mortals. Just as a person in the physical body cannot jump high into space due to the law of gravity, similarly, inferior souls stay closer to the earth for the same reason. Developed souls leave the body immediately upon death and shoot into space right away at a tremendous speed into the infinite blueness.

Every single thought of yours has a form. The form exists in the shape of vibrations. Every thought is photographed in your astral body during your earthly life. All these photographs are preserved in your astral body. When the physical body falls, the Spirit bears your *Karmas* within it. *Karmas* are those actions of yours which must bear fruits in lives to come. Just as inside a seed there is a big tree with leaves and fruits resident in the seed, similarly, in your mental body, are the seeds of many, many lives to come. Underdeveloped and inferior souls appeal for help and advice. They are most receptive to sympathetic thoughts which register on the mental body like an electric current. Thoughts of love and harmony enlighten them and encourage them on the Path. The thoughts of relatives and friends, that they have not abandoned the soul, and that they still respect the wishes and desires of the soul, make its outlook happier and brighter.

The primary obligation in this world is to discharge these spiritual obligations. You have an obligation to your spouse, to your children, to your boss, to your friends and neighbors, to the people of your world and your country. Above all, you have your spiritual obligation, the obligation to the Spirit within you, which is obligation to yourself. The spiritual obligation is an obligation for mental and spiritual enlightenment while you live in this world. If you meet all other obligations but ignore the obligation to your Spirit, life is wasted. In order to achieve enlightenment, a person must find a spiritual guide to initiate him in the mysteries of Truth. Also, one has a spiritual obligation to the souls of dead parents. Unless you deny the existence of soul and mind, you must exert to know it. The soul is not far from you, it is closer than your own breath. It is within you. It is in your spiritual heart. Know your soul and become enlightened. Nothing comes without effort. There is fire in the firewood, but you cannot feel it. There is oil in the olive, but you can't see it. There is butter in the milk, but you can't see it. Similarly, there is soul in the body, but you cannot see it. The knowledge of soul and Truth is disclosed in inner research.

Chapter 37 DO MASTERS CONTROL WORLD DESTINY?

IN INFINITE SPACE, there are no confined places for the spiritual and mental body to live. According to its spiritual development, a mental body is able to rise high into space and is sustained at a specific height. The height at which such body continues to function and live is determined by its lightness in weight. The more a person is spiritually evolved, the lighter his mental and spiritual body is, and the higher it finds its place to reside.

Vast space consists of numerous solar systems. Each solar system has different life from the others. In vast space there are various constellations and solar systems. In each solar system, life on the various planets differs. In each group, there are seven solar systems. The earth on which we live is the fourth in the group of seven solar systems. Life on the three lower solar systems below this solar system is less developed and inferior, while life on the upper three solar systems is highly evolved in comparison to life on earth.

As a person evolves spiritually, his mental and astral body becomes rarefied and lighter, and consequently he gets liberated from one solar system and then another. Just as at the time of death the soul and mind are liberated from the flesh, and being too light are not held back to the earth due to the law of gravity, similarly, when the mental and spiritual bodies evolve on a higher solar system, they are liberated from the grosser part of the astral and mental body—especially the desires and cravings for the physical and material, which exist in the form of astro-mental images—and then they move still higher in space toward the solar system where more pure and Divine Beings reside. The purer the mental body is, the lighter and freer it becomes. Undeveloped souls are weighed down heavily by the weight and density of the fluid which constitutes their mental body. Due to this weight, the inferior and less developed souls stay closer to the earth where they lived.

The perception and happiness of a soul do not depend upon its environment. They are the result of the inner state of mind. The impressions of the past life which are imprinted on the fluidic mental body continue to project within the astral body and the soul continues to perceive accordingly. Thus each soul bears within itself its happiness or unhappiness irrespective of its environment. The more advanced a spirit is, the stronger its faculties of perception. A soul perceives through the astral senses. There is spiritual hierarchy in space. Souls which are more evolved reach a higher place, leaving the inferior ones behind, who are like blind persons who cannot find their way on the street in broad daylight. A blind person in mid-daylight stands and waits on the street for somebody to help him cross the street. Similarly, inferior souls without the guidance of evolved souls are unable to move in the astral world.

The sense of perception of the inferior world is very dim in comparison to that of the Great Masters who are very highly evolved. A person who is deaf cannot enjoy a concert in Carnegie Hall. Similarly, less developed souls with their blunted senses are unable to enjoy the most divine beauty of Nature and the music of the spheres. Inferior spirits, wrapped in heavy fluids created from their grosser desires, stay depressed, closer to the earth, and the molecules which constitute their fluidic body are closed to perceptions from the astral world.

Persons who have traveled in space and orbited the earth and made an effort to reach the moon and other planets, know and understand the inexpressible divine beauty and splendor which are enjoyed on one's journey in space. One watches the earth, sun and other planets moving in their orbits like a merry-go-round. The rank of each spirit is directly proportional to its fluidic constitution. The fluidic constitution is made as a result of the deeds and *karmas* of the past life of the soul on this earth. Developed spirits move freely in vast space, faster than sound, while inferior and less pure souls with selfish and impure desires, stay below. The Great Masters occupy the top-most solar systems. Between the two extreme states of souls are countless intermediate degrees in which the various souls stay according to their development. Birds of a feather flock together. Similarly, spirits which are of equal development are attracted to each other by their tendencies, thoughts and sentiments. Just as a person in the physical body cannot see through the physical senses those who live in the astral and mental body, similarly, inferior souls cannot see the Advanced Souls as they move around in space in and between them, because their power of perception through the astral senses is very limited.

The Great Masters, who are highly evolved souls, have tremendous power of perception through their astral senses. For them every color has a perfume, and scent becomes audible. They translate the music of the spheres into language and exchange their thoughts with equally developed souls, at a speed faster than light. Inferior souls continue to suffer in their mental bodies being upset by their instincts and desires. Their sufferings from emotions, worldly appetites and selfish desires are as intense as they were when they lived in this world. In the astral world they do not have a physical body through which they can satisfy their unsatisfied desires, and therefore their sufferings become more intense.

The Great Masters, on the other hand, keep themselves busy as a bee, exchanging ideas with the Heavenly Fathers and other Masters with bewildering rapidity as every thought registers on their fluidic bodies. The Great Masters are busy creating phenomena of the world and shaping millions and billions of solar systems, creating wealth and poverty to the nations, deciding war and peace between nations, and bringing evolution and involution to numerous planets, comets and other bodies.

All this is achieved by the Great Masters by the power of their will. The will can draw and unite together certain molecules, electrons and protons in the atmosphere, and create matter and life. Similarly, the power of will can also dissolve them and transform them back into energy. The will of the Great Masters to create things is pregnant with positive colors. On the other hand, the will for destruction and dissolution is pregnant with negative and darker colors. The Great Masters watch the various souls in various solar systems, having achieved the cycle of their planetary lives, and being purified, rarefied and evolved in their mind and souls by migrations through the various solar systems, and through the experiences gained in the period of their migrations and reincarnations. The people who live on this earth in a physical body are only a counterpart of those invisible beings who inhabit the astral.

On this earth, people live in the physical body, while on higher worlds people can live in mental and astral bodies alone. The density and constituents in space which surround the higher worlds are such that the thoughts of the Great Masters are able to penetrate them without materializing them into physical things. Once those thoughts enter the atmosphere of this earth, they start to create phenomena and materialize things. What controls the destiny of the world is not easy to understand for a person who is ignorant of the power of the Great Masters. Science has discovered that in the prebiotic age, matter and earth developed through invisible forces and finally life evolved from matter. The whole creation is the result of the will of the Great Masters, and the creation of the world is sustained by the same will, and will be dissolved only at their will. Yogis discovered in their inner research that the Great Masters exerted their mighty will over matter, bringing chemical changes by their will power and thus creating life on the earth.

The will of the Great Masters is pregnant with colors which can be divided into three parts: *Sattwa, Rajas,* and *Tamas,* which mean positive colors, a mixture of positive and negative colors, and finally, the negative and darker colors. Certain colors darken the fluidic body and transform energy into matter. Certain colors transform matter into energy by refining it. The other colors of intermediate degrees help sustain creation. Thus the Great Masters are able to control and direct creation, preservation and dissolution by the mighty influences of their will power. Their will power is released by their mere wish. It is purely a mental action. Just as you will to take another step while you walk on the street, similarly, the Great Masters will to do something and it happens.

The Masters are amused to see nations and countries making war and peace, and signing treaties over boundaries and lands, because the kings and nations all belong to the land. The land does not belong to them. Soon they will be all dead and buried deep in the earth, only to become a part of the earth. But they waste their time in useless discussions during their lives about possessing the land. The will of the Masters by means of reacting on the fluids in space is able to create great works which are incomparable and beyond analysis. It is by means of their will that the things of humanity are changed and reproduced.

The highly evolved souls distribute and send love to all men of the world without any distinction between rich and poor, from their place of abode, high in the astral. Higher still is the abode of the Ideal and Perfect Souls, which are a store of Truth, beauty, peace and love, radiating inspiration, encouragement and the peace that passeth all understanding.

Masters do incarnate on this earth by mere will to initiate the people of the world into the mysteries of Truth, and splendors of eternal beauty and Divine Truth. Masters, when incarnate on this earth, live as ordinary persons and can hardly be distinguished from an average person, except through their deeds. By his wish, a Master, while living on this earth, can make anyone here recognize him, that he is one of the Great Masters who have incarnated on this earth. Without their blessings and wish, no one can know that the Masters have incarnated on this earth, as they walk the street with mortal people only to help them and raise the moral and spiritual standards in their life, which will bring rarefication and purification of their mental and astral body and prepare them for their luminous journey in the astral.

Masters also, from beyond this world, watch and help the awakening of new lives upon the surfaces of numerous worlds, the growth of human life that inhabits those worlds, and through their vast power of perception they note that on each solar system that life, motion and activity are kept in harmony with the order of the Universe.

Masters receive orders directly from Cosmic Consciousness, which is the same as the Universal Mind. The language of Cosmic Mind is the most melodious vibration of the ether and music of the spheres, which they translate into language. Great Masters always see your actions on this world and maintain the bond of unity between life here and hereafter. Due to their spiritual development, highly evolved souls are not burdened with the weight of flesh, woes and sorrows, sickness and death, fear and worries.

Gorakhnath, Sadasiva, etc., are some of the highly evolved souls who lived on this earth. Masters can materialize on the earth by their mere wish. They can appear before you in a second and disappear in the next. It is these Masters who control the destiny of the world. At present there live on this earth seven Great Masters. One of them is in the United States of America. They work in close harmony with each other. One can know them and recognize them only by their Grace.

Long ago there was a person in India who was very highly evolved spiritually. He was very much attached to his son and at the time of death the last thought in his mind was to see his son before he died. Due to his unsatisfied desire for the son, he reincarnated again. His *Guru*, who was one of the Masters, continued to help this embodied soul on earth. The Adept was very anxious to see the Master as his *Guru* in a physical form. The Master made astral contract with the Adept and told him that he would be able to see him next day during the religious celebrations to be held in the Temple outside the village on the bank of the Ganges during *Kumbha Mela*. The Master conveyed to him that he would be dressed in rags and sitting on the side of the road begging for food and alms. He further stated that a lot of flies would be hovering over the bleeding wounds on his body. He said that he would be lame and too weak to walk. He also said that due to his being in a diseased and despicable condition, thousands of people passing the street on the way to the Temple would not even look at him. He further added that when the ceremony at the Temple came to an end, everybody would return to their homes, late in the evening, and there would be no one left on the street or in the Temple. There would be no sound from the gongs in the Temple, the only sounds would be that of the wild animals impatient in their hiding places to come out in search of prey.

"Then you come to me, I will be there, you will find me."

Such is the Grace and blessings of the Master by which alone a person can find and recognize a Master who incarnates in this world at will with a specific mission.

The Adept was the only person to recognize the Great Master, sitting on the roadside, while thousands of people passed the street without taking notice of this fact. As the Adept saw the only person sitting on the roadside at the end of the ceremony at the place he was told, his heart was full of joy. He ran and hugged him and carried him in his arms to the Temple.

The *Guru* transformed his old, sick body into the youthful and healthy body of a twenty-year old, gave him all the necessary guidance and instructions and once more raised his hand towards the disciple and blessed him before he disappeared. The *Guru* maintained invisible contact with the embodied soul until it had achieved its goal and was ready for its life in the astral.

Chapter 38 FALLING IN PSYCHIC RHYTHM

A YOGI IS ABLE to do miracles and create psychic phenomena and manifest tremendous powers by falling into psychic rhythm. Everything in this world has motion. Wherever there is motion, there is rhythm. When you fall in swing with the rhythm, you are able to accomplish greater results with less efforts. Yogis, in their inner research, discovered the higher rhythms of Nature, and they also worked out a scientific system of techniques to enable them to fall in swing with these rhythms mechanically, which enable them to draw the higher forces of Nature to them, which they can use in the creation of the psychic phenomena. Various techniques for the creation of psychic phenomena are based on the law of psychic rhythm. These techniques swing you mechanically into this rhythm of psychic powers. Once you are one with these higher forces, you feel free to draw as much as you want and need at a specific time. The various breathing techniques taught and practiced by the Yogis to help them fall into psychic rhythm are based on these principles.

The main purpose of these Yogic breathings is to control, direct and apply *Prana*, which is the vital force or force of thought. *Prana* is the sum total of all energy, mental as well as physical. Energies ethereal, electrical, as well as magnetic, are all part and parcel of *Prana*. Yogic breathings help you control the forces of *Prana* by operating on the rhythm of breath. If you can control one wave in the ocean, you will be able to control all the waves in the ocean. If you can control *Prana*, which manifests in your body through your breath, you will be able to control all physical and mental energies which fill space. Control of *Prana* through Yogic breathings opens the door of unlimited powers which will enable you to control and use the finer forces of Nature, and also to fall into psychic rhythm at your will.

Yogis discovered that *Prana* contains life and intelligence. *Prana* manifests in your body primarily through your breath. It is *Prana* which takes the breath into your lungs and brings it out, in your inhalation and exhalation. Whether you want to or not, the *Prana* makes the breath go into the respiratory organs. When the *Prana* ceases to manifest in the breath, a person is dead. You may say it is the air and oxygen which a person breathes which keeps him alive. If it was the oxygen which made a person live and breathe, then a lot of oxygen could be pumped into the nostrils of people lying in the grave, and next day they would all be walking on the street. Yogis discovered that *Prana* takes the oxygen in your lungs and makes the lungs expand and contract, which creates motion in your heart and pulse subsequently. Yogis perceived during contemplation that there is a special circulation under the skull in the cerebellum, the pulse rate of which is about twelve to fourteen counts per minute only. This pulse rate differs from the rate of your heartbeat or pulsation in any other part of your body, including the skin that covers your head. The pulsation in the cerebellum is determined by the rhythm of the breath at a specific time by a specific person. The rate of pulsation and heartbeat is determined by the pulsation in the cerebellum. Thus it becomes easy to understand that it is this *Prana* that gives life to your whole body.

The breath from the right and left nostrils are transformed into positive and negative currents by the olfactory organ which is situated between the two eyebrows. The positive and negative currents are transmitted into two important psychic channels known as *Ida* and *Pingala*, which I have illustrated in my book, *Yoga And Long Life*, figure 1, page 23. If there were no negative and positive currents, a lightbulb would not light. If there were no negative and positive currents running in your system, you could not stay alive.

From *Ida* and *Pingala*, the negative and positive currents are transmitted to smaller psychic channels, which are seventy million in number. The psychic channels are known as *Nadies*. *Nadies* are astral tubes which are made of gray and white ethereal substance. The negative and positive forces are stored in the psychic centers which are also known as lotuses or *chakras* in your spine.

The psychic channels and psychic centers are made up of fine etheric substance and therefore are not visible to the ordinary eye, but they can be perceived by those who have developed psychic vision or Divine perception. I have given the practical method for developing Divine perception in Chapter 40 of this book, "A Two-Year Course in Divine Perception," in detail. The psychic centers in the spine are the substations where the psychic energies are stored as they are drawn in through psychic channels when you fall in swing with the psychic rhythm. I have described in detail the psychic centers in my book, *Yoga And Long Life*, " Part III, Chapter VIII, page 129, and the illustration, figure 3 on page 130, shows the various psychic centers in the spine.

The rhythm in the Yogic breathings for the creation of the psychic phenomena arouses and sets psychic forces into activity. Yogic breathings have been recently tested by various scientists in the United States of America. A test held at the Michigan Medical Center, and another test held at an American laboratory in San Francisco, produced amazing results. It was discovered that during Yogic breathing, chemicals were created in the blood which were the source of energy in the muscles of the Yogi. In rhythmic breathings for the creation of the psychic phenomena comes a tendency of all the molecules of the body to move at a regulated speed in the same direction, which is exactly the definition of electricity. The Yogis perceived during contemplation that the will evolves into nerve currents, while practicing Yogic breathing, which are similar to electricity. Yogic breathings which generate *Prana*, have a specific rhythm, not due to vague and fanciful ideas of the Hindu Yogis, but because of the scientific results created by the rhythm in the Universe. Everything in this world moves in rhythm, the creation, evolution and involution of the world, the accent in your speech, the rise and fall in prices, the movement of planets around the sun, the ebb and flood of the tide in the ocean, the various seasons, one succeeding the other, work and rest, sleep and the wakefulness. By falling in swing with this rhythm, a person can save time and energy. Success is assured due to the use of the higher forces of Nature. It is this higher psychic rhythm which controls and directs all other motion and rhythms of the world. Yogic breathings help you fall in swing with this rhythm and thus enable you to draw the higher forces to help you create psychic phenomena.

A person who understands the rhythm of the ebb and flood of the tide will side with the ebb when he wants to go deep into the ocean. He does not have to exert himself, the retreating tide will take him deep into the ocean by its own strength. Similarly, when he wants to come back to the beach, he falls in swing with the flood of the tide and it will carry him to the beach. A person who does not know the rhythm of the ebb and flood of the tide may struggle hard and unsuccessfully, to go into the ocean. No matter how hard he struggles to get deep into the ocean when the tide is flowing towards the beach, he can never succeed. Similarly, if he tries to swim his way back to the beach when the tide is on the ebb, he can never succeed, no matter how strong he may be. Forces of Nature are far stronger than those of Man. When the forces of Man work against the forces of Nature, it is Man who loses the battle. People who know the rhythm of Nature and are able to fall in swing with the rhythm of Nature at their will, are always successful because the cause of success lies in the forces of Nature that carry the person to the goal of success, prosperity, happiness or any other thing he wants in his life. The rise and fall of prices is controlled by the same rhythm of psychic forces which are constantly released by the Great Masters. A business man who does not have the knowledge and understanding of this rhythm will buy things in the market when prices are too high, and also sell them at the wrong time, when the prices are too low. Therefore he does not get the benefit of the rise and fall in prices and loses his capital in the business.

On the other hand, if a person knows the working process of the rhythm of the higher forces, he is not unhappy when the prices go down, he waits happily to sell when prices rise. Similarly, he does not become impatient over losing an opportunity when prices are too high, he simply waits for the fall in prices when he will get things cheap. As a result of the knowledge of rhythm, a business man becomes successful and makes a fortune in the market.

Pingala, the psychic channel from the right nostril carries the positive current of *Pranic* energy and thought force, while *Ida*, the psychic channel from the left nostril carries the negative currents into the body. The use of one nostril at a time, and then the other, in a specific rhythm in the creation of the psychic phenomena, seems unimportant to an ordinary person in the West. When they understand the flow of positive and negative energy in the psychic channels, i.e., *Ida* and *Pingala*, they understand the reason for the practice of rhythm in the Yogic breathings. Due to the observance of rhythm in the practice of Yogic breathings for the creation of psychic phenomena, they are known as rhythmic breathings. Yogis discovered that the loss of harmony in the rhythm of breathing with Nature outside, brings physical as well as mental disharmony in the body, and the result is one or another kind of physical and mental ailments. By rhythm in breathing you can restore strength, energy, poise and harmony when needed.

The rhythm of breathing changes in every person unconsciously. At one time of the day you find the breathing from the right nostril is heavier than the left, while at another time you find just the reverse. Nature changes the rhythm of breathing during various parts of the day and night automatically. Rhythm in breathing is Nature's way to restore mental, physical and emotional balance in a person by the involuntary shifting of the breath from one nostril to the other, depending upon the hour of day or night. The rhythm in breathing maintains harmony between you and the forces of Nature and keeps you healthy, happy and prosperous. Due to the distractions of the modern world and present way of life in the iron age, it has become rather too difficult for Nature to restore harmony and rhythm in your breath, and this is the reason for lack in physical and mental health.

Yogis discovered the science of breath and therefore they do not wait for Nature to come and help them, rather they use the forces of Nature to achieve quick results. If a person is emotionally upset, a Yogi will simply make him do specific breathings with a certain rhythm, and very soon emotional stability is achieved and a perfect rhythm of harmony is established between him and the world outside. There are rhythmic breathings for cooling in summer, warming in winter, soothing the nerves, relaxing the body and mind, overcoming emotional upsets, breathings to calm the nerves and the mind, breathings for healthy respiration and circulation, etc. I have described in detail the cleansing breath, positive breathing, breathing to calm the mind and *Pranayama* in Chapter XIII of Part III of my book, *Yoga And Long Life*.

Rhythmic breathings are very useful for those who want to bring change in their physical condition by psychic healing. When the flow of *Prana* in any part of the body is less or more than normal, there is disease. When the flow of *Prana* is not normal in the hand, the hand is in a state of partial paralysis. *Prana* (energy) is needed in every part of your body for its normal and healthy function. Without the normal flow of *Prana*, the digestion, assimilation, elimination, pulsation and respiration, would not be healthy and normal. By the Yogic breathings known as *Pranayama*, an Adept is able to control the flow of *Prana*. *Pranayama* means control of *Prana*. Through rhythmic breathing one is able to direct the flow of *Prana* in any part of his body, and thus restore the normal flow of *Prana*. Health is restored naturally and psychic healing takes place.

By a specific rhythm in breath, one can produce and direct forces of thought and energy towards the creation of psychic phenomena. The use of *Prana* and thought force increases by many hundred times the mental powers of psychic healers as well as of those who create any type of psychic phenomena. When you have supplemented your thought projection with plenty of *Prana*, you can materialize your thoughts quicker. This *Pranic* energy is stirred, created and made available to you by practicing the prescribed rhythmic breathings. I have described in detail various rhythmic breathings for the creation of psychic phenomena in Chapter 39 of this book, "Two-Month Course in Psychic Phenomena."

Yogis believe that the body is a living battery of energy, and as such it should always be kept thoroughly charged with *Prana*, especially by those persons who want to create psychic phenomena. During the practice of these breathings the body should be kept polarized. The required polarization can be achieved by closing both the circuits. When you cross your legs you have closed one end of the circuit, and when you do *Jnana Mudra* you are closing the other end of the circuit. I have described and illustrated the *Jnana Mudra* in my book *Yoga And Long Life* on page 3. While visiting your friend, if you leave your car in the garage with the motor running, naturally the battery will be used up till you come back. You must shut off the engine when you are gone. Similarly, when you are charging your battery with *Prana* and psychic energy is being stored in your psychic centers in the spine, you must stop the leakage of energy so that your body is fully charged with *Pranic* energy without which the creation of the psychic phenomena is not possible. By closing both ends of the circuits you prevent the leakage of energy while you are charging your body battery with psychic forces. The Yogis are able to manifest unbelievable powers in creating psychic phenomena only after charging their body and psychic channels with the psychic and thought forces, by falling in swing with the psychic rhythm of the forces of Nature.

Once a disciple wanted to know if his *Guru* used psychic powers by his will, or whether these powers worked for him without his knowledge. One afternoon, while the *Guru* was asleep, the disciple lit a match and put it under the back of the *Guru*'s palm to see if the *Guru* would feel it or not. Due to psychic powers, the *Guru* while awake could do things without being affected by fire, like walking on fire, etc. The *Guru* woke up suddenly and asked the student what he was doing. He asked, "Did you intend to set fire to me? Why? Have I done anything unpleasant to you?"

The disciple was very much embarrassed. Finally he spoke, "I put the lighted match under your hand to see if the psychic powers are still working while you are asleep."

The *Guru* said that they work only by conscious effort, unless you have made previous arrangement for their functioning under the control and guidance of the subconscious mind. Thus, it makes it clear that in order to carry out the creation of psychic phenomena, you have to make conscious efforts. People who just sit idly accepting everything that comes to them in their life by saying this is their destiny (Karma) are completely wrong in their approach. The destiny can be changed and the *Karmas* can be reversed by your conscious effort when you learn the process of the creation of psychic phenomena. The lines in your hand which represent astrology and the science of palmistry only tell you what is going to happen next in your life, but by making an effort you can change the course of psychic phenomena, as a result of which the lines in your hand will change. The newly-formed lines in your palm will show that now you will be getting prosperity instead of adversity. You have the power and the ability to change the course of destiny according to your wish by the creation of psychic phenomena.

Chapter 39 TWO-MONTH COURSE IN PSYCHIC PHENOMENA

FOR A LAYMAN who wants to learn the creation of psychic phenomena, a course of eight weeks is given below. This course cannot give the full guidance in the techniques and practices of the process. A student should be personally initiated by the teacher into some of the techniques incorporated into this course, while some other techniques should be practiced in the company of the teacher repeatedly for some time before a student is ready to practice by himself. Due to these reasons, the greater details of some of the techniques could not be given in this course. The use of psychic powers needs responsibility and self-restraint on the part of a student to prevent them from being prostituted for selfish ends. This book will be available to all, even those who do not realize their full responsibility in the use of these powers. For efficient training, a student after reading this book, should find a teacher who will help him in working out the minutest details which will make him ready for the creation of the psychic phenomena. The book is like a driver's manual. You cannot drive a car by only reading the manual.

FIRST WEEK'S PROGRAM

In the first week, the student should practice the *Mantra* for Purification, and *Mantra* for Unification. I have already described in detail in the early chapters of this book, what the *Mantras* are, and how they create a state of mind resulting in physical phenomena. These *Mantras* can be repeated at any time, while you are sitting, standing, walking, or traveling in a taxi, bus, train or subway. These *Mantras* should be repeated mentally. When you are alone, you can repeat them aloud.

The *Mantra* for Purification aims to purify your psychic channels of their clogged inlets. Unless the psychic channels are clean, and the inlets choked with debris purified, you will not be able to use these channels for drawing psychic forces, or for releasing said forces for the creation of psychic phenomena. For example, if you have a lot of supply, unless the roads are open for travel, you will not be able to use that supply due to the roads being jammed with traffic, or anything else. The *Mantra* for Purification radiates vibrations which also purify the atmosphere around you as well as within you. If you repeat this *Mantra* in your apartment, every piece of furniture, paintings, clothes, even walls, will be fully charged with the positive vibrations, and they will start radiating them back towards you. Anyone who enters your apartment will feel the positive influences. If you go to live in a new apartment which was formerly occupied by people who were negative in their thinking, you will find that you are uncomfortable and restless due to the negative vibrations which the walls, furniture and every atom in it radiates toward you. By this *Mantra* you can neutralize all the negative vibrations and replace them by positive vibrations. The *Mantra* is equally good for changing the environment at your office where you work. When you create a positive environment around your place of work and office, you find that you can work better, and also you feel happier, brighter and stronger.

The second *Mantra* is the *Mantra* for Unification. This *Mantra* establishes a psychic rapport between you and the psychic forces in space by erecting a psychic astral tube in space. As you repeat this *Mantra*, the astral tube is constructed automatically. As soon as the astral tube is ready, the psychic forces start to flow from the space outside straight into your psychic channels. For the first two days, one should repeat only *Mantra* No. 1, the *Mantra* for Purification.

On the third and fourth days, one should repeat both the *Mantra* for Purification, and *Mantra* for Unification, in a proportion of 4-1.

On the fifth and sixth days, one should repeat the *Mantra* for Purification and *Mantra* for Unification in the proportion of 1-2.

And later on, one should repeat the *Mantras* in equal durations.

Remember: The *Mantra* for Purification should always precede the *Mantra* for Unification.

All the techniques given in this course should be practiced in the order they have been given in order to avoid any complications, and to ensure better results.

The *Mantra* for Unification should always be done in silence. The meaning of the *Mantra* for Unification is identical with the Word of God, which unites Man with God. The Word of God is in you, and you are in It. Similarly, you are in the *Mantra* for Unification, and the *Mantra* for Unification is in you. A person comes to life with the first repetition of this *Mantra* which starts with the first breath in life, and ends with the last breath in life. Once you are initiated in the *Mantra* for Unification, you have to close your eyes and concentrate on your breath, and try to hear the same *Mantra* in your breath on each inhalation and exhalation. The more and more you become aware of the *Mantra* being repeated in your incoming and outgoing breaths, the more and more you will rest in peace. You will find that your breath becomes very slow and steady, and your mind becomes quieter and quieter. The success of establishing an astral tube to enable the psychic forces to enter your psychic channels depends upon your awareness of this *Mantra* in your breath as it moves in and out.

SECOND WEEK'S PROGRAM

The first week's program should be continued while you start the program for the second week. You should repeat your *Mantras* for at least three to five minutes every day before you start your new course for the second week.

The *Nadi* Purifier *Pranayama* should be included in your program in the second week. The aim of this *Pranayama* is to expedite the purification of the psychic channels. One should not do more than seven *Pranayamas* at a sitting, in a day. The second week's program should not be started unless a person has completed his first week's program. The *Nadi* Purifier *Pranayama* consists of inhaling, retention, and exhaling, in a rhythm of 4-12-8. First, one should completely exhale from both nostrils; then one should inhale (both nostrils) to the count of four; and retain for the count of twelve, with right and left nostrils closed by right thumb and right ring finger respectively; then release the pressure on the left nostril, and exhale only through the left. There should not be a break while you practice this *Pranayama*. If you find you cannot do seven *Pranayamas* at a sitting, do three *Pranayamas* at a sitting, and then during the week, increase one *Pranayama* each day until you are able to do seven *Pranayamas* at a sitting.

For the first three days in the second week, you should confine your practice to *Mantras* Nos. 1 and 2, and the *Nadi* Purifier *Pranayama*.

From the fourth day, one should also incorporate the *Nadi* Stimulator *Pranayama*.

The *Nadi* Stimulator *Pranayama* stimulates the psychic channels and prepares them for use during the creation of the psychic phenomena. This *Pranayama* also creates a brighter and positive outlook in your mind by affecting your thoughts. It also creates a mood of happiness and cheerfulness, which is followed by natural beauty, handsomeness, and personality. In the *Nadi* Stimulator *Pranayama*, first you should exhale, then you should inhale, and when the breath is full, you should start creating the humming sound of a bee, concentrating on the sound. The sound should be prolonged as long as you can, to increase the effectiveness of the *Pranayama*.

In the *Nadi* Purifier *Pranayama* you should concentrate on the breath as you inhale and exhale. During retention of the breath, the concentration should be on the psychic eye, known as the Third Eye, the seat of metaphysical and occult powers. It is situated between the two eyebrows. The exhalation in this *Pranayama* should be so slow that you should not be able to feel it at 10-12 finger-width distance from your nose.

Concentration during the *Nadi* Stimulator *Pranayama* should be on the sound.

THIRD WEEK'S PROGRAM

During the third week, one should continue to practice the course of the first and second week, in the same order. In addition, one should incorporate in his program, the *Nadi* Vibrator *Pranayama*. This *Pranayama* releases tremendous psychic and mental powers into the psychic channels. It should be strictly learned and practiced under the guidance of a teacher. One should not do more than three of these *Pranayamas* at a sitting, and one sitting a day. One of the immediate effects of this *Pranayama* is that it prevents the externalization of the mind, and awakens you to inner awareness, leading to the use of the astral senses. The number of these *Pranayamas* are increased or decreased according to the reaction the teacher finds in the student. The *Nadi* Vibrator *Pranayama* can be seen in Illustration No. 2 of this book.

FOURTH WEEK'S PROGRAM

In the fourth week, one should continue the program of the first three weeks and should incorporate in it the practice of the Closed Circuit *Pranayama*. The Closed Circuit

Pranayama consists of a nine-cycle breath and its count is 3-12-6. Yogis believe the body is a living battery of energy, and therefore it should be kept fully charged, especially by the Adepts who want to create psychic phenomena. The purpose of this *Pranayama* is to charge your seventy-two million psychic channels with psychic energy. You should first exhale from both nostrils, then you should inhale with both to the count of three, and retain the breath for the count of twelve by closing both nostrils with the right thumb and the right ring finger, and exhale through the left nostril to the count of six. The concentration should be on the breath during inhalation and exhalation, and on the Third Eye during the retention of the breath.

Each *Pranayama* should be followed by a mental exercise. Breathing during mental exercise need not have any proportion of counts. Just breathe normally. The mental exercise consists of following your breath as you inhale and exhale. The breath has to be taken to the various parts of your body with your concentration and then brought back.

The first mental exercise consists of breathing through the right toes, taking it up to the top of the head, and then bringing it back to the right toes.

The second mental exercise consists of breathing in through the left toes, taking it to the top of the head, and bringing it back to the left toes.

The third mental exercise consists of inhaling through the right finger tips and taking it to the top of the head, and then bringing it back to the right finger tips.

The fourth mental exercise consists of breathing in through the left finger tips, taking it to the top of the head, and then bringing it back to the left finger tips.

The fifth mental exercise consists of breathing through the top of the head, taking the breath to your right toes, and then returning it back to the top of the head.

The sixth mental exercise consists of breathing through the top of the head, taking the breath to your left toes, and then returning it to the top of the head.

The seventh mental exercise consists of inhaling through the solar plexus, taking the breath to the top of the head, and then returning it back to the solar plexus.

The eighth mental exercise consists of breathing through the pores of your skin all over your body, directing the breath to the top of the head, and finally exhaling through the pores of your skin all over the body.

The ninth mental exercise consists of directing your concentration upward through the spine as you inhale, up to the top of your head, and then directing your concentration downwards towards the end of the spine as you exhale.

In order to achieve the full benefit of this *Pranayama*, the nine *Pranayamas* and nine mental exercises should be done without a break at one sitting. To start with, it will be difficult for a beginner to do all the nine *Pranayamas* in one stretch, and therefore he should have breaks of a couple of minutes after each two *Pranayamas*. In the fifth week he should have a break after each three *Pranayamas*. He should continue taking these breaks till the end of the seventh week, and longer if necessary. It is very important that one should not feel uncomfortable. One will be able to do these *Pranayamas* with greater ease and comfort as the proper and natural rhythm is established in his breathing by regular practice. Even if it takes eight months to establish the proper rhythm, one should not hurry. Nothing should be forced on the system, rather, the system should be allowed to develop naturally towards the proper rhythm.

FIFTH WEEK'S PROGRAM

During the fifth week one should continue the program of the preceding weeks and should incorporate the Psychic Current Concentration *Pranayama*. In this *Pranayama* the psychic currents which are generated in your seventy-two million psychic channels are stored and charged in your psychic centers, which are also known as the *chakras*, or Lotuses, situated in your spine. The seven psychic centers house astral organs. The illustration on page 23 of my book *Yoga And Long Life* very clearly explains the psychic centers and the currents which pass through them. These psychic centers correspond to your sacral plexus, prostatic plexus, epigastric plexus, cardiac plexus, pharyngeal plexus, Third Eye, and the Seventh Seal. This *Pranayama* should be learned under the direction of a teacher. Once the psychic centers are charged, the psychic energy-will be available for use when you want to create psychic phenomena.

In this *Pranayama*, as in all others, the rhythm of the *Pranayama* is of utmost importance. It is like tuning your radio; if you dial the wrong station, you will be tuning into the wrong program. Similarly, if you practice the wrong rhythm, it will make the mind radiate the wrong wavelength, thus making you tune into the wrong phenomena. The more successful you are in mastering the rhythm, the greater the efficiency with which you will be able to create psychic phenomena.

SIXTH WEEK'S PROGRAM

In the sixth week, you continue to practice the program of the former five weeks, and supplement it with the stilling of your mind. Unless and until your mind is still and calm, you cannot draw patterns in your creative mind which you want to materialize into material phenomena. If there are too many other thoughts in your mind, the new image in your creative mind will be dim and hazy, as a result of which the materialization will be ineffective or only partially effective. Therefore, it is very important that the slate of your mind should be clean before you draw new drawings on it. The drawings are the creation of a pattern in your creative mind which will help you visualize your thoughts. In other words, you will be seeing the things which are coming into your life in the form of thoughts which are made purely of vibrations. Once you develop the habit of ideation, you will be able to see any and all of your thoughts immediately as they come into your mind, as a result of which you will not have to make much effort in materializing your thoughts after you have practice in the techniques.

There are various methods for stilling the mind and they can be taught by the teacher according to the ability and readiness of the student. These techniques should be personalized to suit the individual, rather than given in a uniform shape for the people as a whole.

SEVENTH WEEK'S PROGRAM

During the seventh week you should continue practicing the program of the previous six weeks in the same order. When you have finished your usual program, you should start making efforts for psychic projection from your creative mind of the thought patterns which contain the things of your dream in the form of thought vibrations. With the projection of vibrations from your pattern in the creative mind, a sufficient amount amount of psychic energy and thought force should be released by the power of your concentrated will. It is a mental action which helps the release of the psychic forces from your psychic centers, as a result of which your thought patterns shoot into space and the process of materialization starts. After the projection into space, the thought pattern should be held in that position for the space of time required for the materialization of your thought into physical phenomena. As your projection is held firm in space, it continues to draw to itself atoms, electrons and protons, combining them with the specific currents of the ether, giving them shape and form as a preliminary step for materialization.

EIGHTH WEEK'S PROGRAM

During the eighth week you should start creation of an event or happening, or the creation of a phenomena you wish to create in your life. The practice of the whole technique described above is known as a treatment. The treatment can be given to any thing, happening, event or circumstance. You should give ten to twenty minutes for each treatment. Treatment may be given once a week. If things do not improve with as great a speed as desired by you, you can give two treatments in a week, at intervals of at least three days.

When you sit down for a treatment you should follow the whole process in the same order as I have described above. That is:

... first, the *Mantra* for Purification, 5 times

... then the *Mantra* for Unification, 7 times

... the *Nadi* Purifier *Pranayama*, 3 times

... the *Nadi* Stimulator *Pranayama*, 3 times

... the *Nadi* Vibrator *Pranayama*, 3 times

... Closed Circuit *Pranayama*

... Psychic Current Concentration *Pranayama*, which consists of seven cycles of *Pranayamas*, each *Pranayama* followed by a normal inhalation and exhalation

... then, still your mind for about two minutes

... then create patterns in your creative mind of the objects, things, and happenings, as you want them to objectify, materialize and happen in your life.

... then practice psychic projection to create the psychic phenomena desired by you.

It is very important to sit in a steady pose when you are creating the psychic phenomena, giving treatment, or practicing any of the techniques which I have described above during your eight-week course. A steady pose of the body helps create mental steadiness, which is indispensable for the creation of the psychic phenomena. *Siddhasana*, also known as The Auspicious Pose, is the best for the creation of the psychic phenomena. *Siddhasana* is named after the *Siddhies* (perfected psychic powers of the Yogis) which are acquired by sitting in this pose while practicing the above techniques, as well as the Yoga practice. *Siddhasana* can be seen in the illustration on page 114, Chapter 12 of my book, *Yoga And Long Life*. Women should not practice this *Asana* without consulting a teacher. Lotus Pose, Half Lotus Pose, and Sukhasana can also be practiced in creating psychic phenomena. Many people find *Vajrasana* (Adamantine Pose) very comfortable and easy to do. *Vajrasana* can be seen in illustration No. 1 in this book.

While creating psychic phenomena, and repeating the *Mantras* for Purification and Unification, and practicing any of the techniques of the above course, you must keep your circuits closed so that the energy generated during the practice does not leak. The method for closing the circuits has been described in the early part of the book.

Practice of Cleansing Breathing, Positive Breathing, and Breathing to Calm the Mind, will expedite one's success in practicing the *Nadi* Purifier *Pranayama*, *Nadi* Stimulator *Pranayama*, *Nadi* Vibrator *Pranayama*, and Closed Circuit *Pranayama* and Psychic Current Concentration *Pranayama*. If you practice the Cleansing Breathing, Positive Breathing, and Breathing to Calm the Mind five minutes every day, which I have described on page 122, Chapter 13 of my book *Yoga And Long Life*, you should not have any difficulty in the practice of the *Pranayamas* for the creation of psychic phenomena.

Chapter 40 TWO YEAR COURSE IN DIVINE PERCEPTION

SINCE TIME IMMEMORIAL, people of all ages interested in spiritual evolution, having retired from active worldly life, proceeded to the woods and holy Himalayas. There they used to develop themselves spiritually, and at the same time they used to teach the people of all ages who would come to them. People from wealthy, respectable families go to these *Ashrams* for spiritual evolution, including princes and kings. Many kings used to send their children to these *Ashrams* to be initiated in spiritual knowledge. The teacher was known as a *Preceptor*. They generally come from very respectable families. The *Preceptors* are very well acquainted with the worldly problems of the people, as well as with their spiritual needs. These *Preceptors* are completely detached from the world, fully disciplined in their life, masters of mind and senses. They live a very simple life. They have achieved perception of mind, astral body, the soul, the five sheaths which function as vehicles for thought, emotions, and other inner faculties. Generally, the students who go to study with a *Preceptor* live with him in the same *Ashram*, as an inmate of the *Ashram*. People from all walks of life and of all ages were able to quench their thirst for spiritual knowledge by living in these *Ashrams*.

It has not been easy for students to be selected as an inmate in the *Ashram*. Students were initiated into the inner teachings which would make them good citizens and nationals, as well as spiritually enlightened. Students are initiated into various *Mantras*, including the *Gayatri Mantra*, to prepare them for initiation into higher spiritual knowledge. Persons with their families also go to live in these monasteries, to achieve inner perception. To a greater or lesser degree, every student has to devote part of his time to *Japa* (the repetition of *Mantras*), *Tapa* (Yoga practice), and *Swadhyaya* (study of recommended books), before he is initiated into *Raja Yoga*. His body is purified by the practice of *Asanas* and *Pranayama*, and mind and heart are purified by the practice of *Yama*, *Niyama*, *Dharana* and *Dhyana*. The students give a part of their time to the personal service of their *Guru*. The students in the beginner state give 25% of their time to the service of the *Preceptor*, while the advanced students devote 50% of their time in serving the *Guru*. It is after this stage that the student was considered as a candidate for being selected to be initiated into the techniques of *Raja Yoga*.

Raja Yoga means the Yoga System for Kings. Primarily, *Preceptors* used to initiate kings into *Raja Yoga*, and through them these teachings were incorporated into the law of their land, and as such, everyone in the country was able to participate in those teachings simply by respecting and abiding by the law of the land. As time passed, ordinary persons achieved access to *Preceptors*, whose number grew with time. It was after training in an *Ashram* that a prince was considered fit to rule his country.

Yogis discovered in their inner perception that true happiness, peace of mind, and better understanding cannot be achieved without the realization of the Truth in inner perception. During contemplation, Yogis discovered that the awareness of an ordinary person is limited to the physical and material. They also discovered a process by which awareness can be channeled into the psychic channels which would bring inner perception. There are certain vital psychic channels known as *Nadies* which are closed in an average person. By practicing *Raja Yoga*, awareness is diverted into these channels, bringing self-realization and spiritual enlightenment. In the center of the spinal column is situated the spinal cord. The space between the spinal column and the spinal cord is filled with an oily fluid, as a result of which the spine does not strike against the inner wall of the spinal column. In the center of the spine is situated the *Sushumna*. In the center of the *Sushumna* is situated the *Chitra Nadi*. In the center of the *Chitra Nadi* is situated the *Brahma Nadi* (canalis central). When the awareness of a person is diverted through the *Brahma Nadi*, it brings spiritual enlightenment. All these *Nadies* are astral tubes made up of astral matter which is gray and white in color. These *Nadies* carry psychic currents within them. The *Brahma Nadi* has vacuum inside and its lower end at the root of the spine is closed in all beings except Adepts and Yogis. By practice of *Raja Yoga*, a person is initiated to divert the flow of awareness to the *Brahma Nadi*. As the awareness goes higher and higher and reaches the seven centers situated in the spine, one by one, the awareness of various planes of consciousness is achieved. By penetrating the centers in the spine, a person is able to penetrate the layers of consciousness, and therefore is able to achieve the knowledge and wisdom which lies beyond those planes.

Yogis discovered that all sensations and motions of the body are sent to the brain through nerve fibers, the result being perception. When perception is independent of the nerve fibers, it is extra-sensory perception. When awareness is channeled to the *Brahma Nadi*, a person progresses step by step towards extra-sensory perception. When a person succeeds in taking his awareness to the last center at the top of the head known as the Seventh Seal, he achieves full enlightenment, which is identical with Unity of Man and God Consciousness.

Yoga Sadhana and practice of *Raja Yoga* is the great wealth India has to offer to the people of the world. It is in these instructions that a student is taught the various steps which enable him to firm up his mental states by various techniques to make him ready for enlightenment. In the absence of such instructions, a student remains restless for guidance, especially if he has already tasted the nectar of spiritual progress. The students who seek spiritual enlightenment can be divided into three groups. Good students can achieve self-enlightenment and Divine perception in a period of two years by following this course. A fair student may achieve inner perception in a period of four years. No definite time limit can be fixed for the rest of the people who seek spiritual enlightenment. The time for self-realization will depend upon their spiritual background of past lives, as well as their purity of heart and mind, and their eagerness to achieve their goal.

The following Two-Year Course in Divine Perception is prescribed for the good students.

FIRST EIGHT MONTHS

In the first eight months, a student should practice as instructed by his *Preceptor*: *Yama, Niyama, Asana, Pranayama, Pratyahara, Dharana,* and *Dhyana* — which will lead him to *Samadhi*. These are known as the eight parts of *Raja Yoga. Asanas* and *Pranayama* I have explained in my book, *Yoga And Long Life*, and you are advised to refer to these illustrations. The practice of these techniques awakens the *Kundalini* (inner awareness), which will bring perception of *Pranamaya Kosa*. *Pranamaya Kosa* is the body of *Prana* (life).

FIRST PART—*Yama*

There are ten Yamas, known as:

1. *Ahimsa* (not hurting others).
2. *Satya* (speaking the truth).
3. *Asteya* (non-attachment).
4. *Brahmacharya* (celibacy).
5. *Chama* (forgiveness).
6. *Dhiraja* (patience).
7. *Daya* (kindness).
8. *Arjava* (politeness).

9. *Mitahara* (eating in moderation).
10. *Sauch* (hygiene, internal and external).

Mitahara plays an important part in spiritual enlightenment. When you eat food, it starts to disintegrate and in the process releases vibrations. Some vibrations create disharmony in the system and sometimes throw the mind off its balance, thus creating obstruction in the practice of *Raja Yoga*. The training in *Raja Yoga* is incomplete without the knowledge of basic principles of food. I have described the significance of food in Yoga practice in Part Four, Chapter 16 of my book, *Yoga And Long Life*.

A married person is considered celibate if he does not have any dealings with persons of the opposite sex other than the legally married spouse. A person who discharges all his obligations to the spouse in the married life, raising children, etc., is considered obeying the laws of Bramahcharya.

SECOND PART—*Niyama*

Niyamas are nine in number They are:

1. *Indriya Bus* (control of senses).
2. *Santosh* (contentment).
3. *Astikta* (religious nature).
4. *Dana* (charity).
5. *Ishwara Aradhana* (church worship).
6. *Sravana* (receiving instructions).
7. *Lajja* (respectfulness and modesty).
8. *Drdhata* (courage).
9. *Japa* (repetition of *Mantra*).

THIRD PART—*Asana*

The *Asanas* play a very important part in spiritual enlightenment, because a steady body helps to make the mind steady. I have described *Asanas* in detail in my book, *Yoga And Long Life*. It contains a course of *Asanas* for beginners, another course for intermediates, and another course for advanced students. A student should select a course of *Asanas* according to his physical condition and ability. As far as possible the guidance of a teacher should be taken in *Asanas*, especially if they belong to intermediate and advanced groups. There are 8,400,000 *Asanas*. A Yogi is always in one of the *Asanas*. While he sleeps he is in an *Asana*, while he walks he is in an *Asana*, while he sits he is in an *Asana*, while he eats he is in an *Asana*—no matter what he does he is always practicing Yoga *Asanas*. One can recognize a Yogi simply by seeing him, because he is always in some *Asana*. Out of the total amount of said *Asanas*, 84 are the important ones. Out of the 84, two are most important, which are often practiced by all Yogis. They are known as *Siddhasana* and *Padmasana*. For *Siddhasana*, you may refer to page 114, and for *Padmasana* to page 112, of *Yoga and Long Life*. By practicing *Asanas*, a person is able to restore radiant health, and also become ready for spiritual awareness. One can also practice *Virasana* if he is unable to practice *Siddhasana* and *Padmasana*. *Virasana* is illustrated on page 89 of my book *Yoga and Long Life*. Persons who find difficulty in attaining any of the above-stated *Asanas* can practice *Raja Yoga* while sitting in *Vajrasana* (Adamatine Pose) illustrated on page 3 of this book.

FOURTH PART—*Pranayama*

Through the practice of *Pranayama*, a person is consciously able to take his awareness in *Brahma Nadi* through various Lotuses till it reaches the Seventh Seal known as the *Sahasrara Chakra*, where full enlightenment takes place. *Pranayama* should be learned and practiced under the personal guidance of the teacher, *Pranayama* means the control of *Prana* (negative and positive currents of life).

FIFTH PART—*Pratyahara*

Pratyahara is the control of the senses. By *Pratyahara* an Adept is able to withdraw his mind from the physical senses and divert it toward the astral senses. When a person is successful in *Pratyahara*, the distraction of the senses and the world outside do not bother him. Just as a turtle, when it withdraws its four legs and head inside the shell, no matter how much you strike him, is not affected. Similarly, the world does not affect you.

Pratyahara helps neutralize all incoming and outgoing thoughts from your mind. Each thought is like a wave in the ocean. While there are waves in the ocean, you cannot see your face in it. When the ocean is calm, you will immediately see yourself reflected in it. Similarly, higher Wisdom and Truth reflects in your mind only when it is calm.

SIXTH PART—*Dharana*

Dharana is one-pointedness of mind, which is achieved by concentration on various psychic centers. *Dharana* brings awareness of the elements in subtle form.

SEVENTH PART—*Dhyana*

Dhyana means the inner perception of objects and things in their subtle form. *Dhyana* is of four kinds:

Padhastha (visualization of feet).

Pindastha (visualization of whole body)

Roopastha (visualization of full form with minor details)

Roopateet (concentration on formless).

Dhyana helps the student to achieve the awareness of *Annamaya Kosa* instead of maintaining his awareness of the physical body. In *Dhyana*, a person achieves inner perception of all subtle functions taking place in the body. Also, *Dhyana* enables the student to have the realization and perception of the functions taking place between the *Annamaya Kosa* and *Pranamaya Kosa*.

EIGHTH PART—*Samadhi*

Samadhi is the state of full enlightenment where the student becomes identical with the teacher as well as with Supreme Consciousness. Just as you mix the water of one glass with another, which cannot be separated again, similarly, in *Samadhi*, Unity is established between the Individual Soul and the Universal SOUL.

While a student practices the first eight-month course, automatically his mental and psychic powers start to awaken, and he starts to acquire and possess consciously perfected Yogic powers, as *Siddhies*. There are eight *Siddhies* which are acquired by the practice of this first eight-month course of *Raja Yoga*. The names of the *Siddhies* are:

Anima	*Prapatee*
Mahima	*Para*
Laghima	*Isita*
Garima	*Vasikarama*

By the use of *Siddhies*, a person can travel in space in invisible form, enter another person's mind, enter a dead body and restore life to it, make his body light or heavy according to his wish, move at will across vast space, accomplishing results simply by wish and achieve control over anything in the world. Many students, by achieving *Siddhies*, forget their ultimate goal of spiritual enlightenment and get involved in the psychic powers which help them attain worldly things by mere wish. Therefore a student should be very careful not to pay attention to these miraculous powers achieved by *Raja Yoga*. One should always keep in mind the ultimate goal of Divine Perception (Spiritual Enlightenment).

Before starting *Pratyahara*, a student should be able to sit in any one of the four above-recommended poses to practice *Pranayama*. When one can practice *Pranayama* for one hour without changing his pose, then only, should he start the fifth stage of *Raja Yoga*, known as *Pratyahara*. On an average, student should devote every day six hours to Yoga practice and six hours to the service of his *Guru*.

SECOND EIGHT MONTHS

During this period a student should give most of his time to higher perception. He can reduce the time practicing techniques of the first eight-month course by 25% to 50%, especially the time for *Asanas* and *Pranayama*. In this course, a student is able to penetrate the mental body which is situated in the Seventh Seal. When the perception takes place in the mental body, he is able to perceive the function of *Manomaya Kosa* and *Vijnanama Kosa*, which enables him to perceive how sensations are received by astral senses through nerve currents, and then how the astral senses present it to the mind, and the mind passes it on to the intelligence, and intelligence to the determinative faculty, and finally the decision is transmitted to the spiritual body which is situated in the spiritual heart. You will perceive that in the astral body the mind is in the center and the ten senses surround it on all sides. Five are the senses of perception, and five are the senses of action. The ten physical senses of action and perception are the counterpart of the ten astral senses. Mind attaches itself to each one of the senses, and as such is able to perceive, and accordingly it suffers or enjoys according to perception. Just as you can watch cars moving on the street through your eyes, similarly in this perception you see the function of all the ten astral senses together with the action and reaction between them and the mind. This is known as the awareness of *Manomaya Kosa*.

In this course you are also able to penetrate the *Vijnanama Kosa*, where you see the function of intelligence and mind, and how decisions are made. You also perceive the connection between the astral body and the mind. You will perceive that the astral body is made of five elements in subtle form. The five physical elements are the counterpart of the five subtle elements. This brings you the perception inside of your astral body which is situated in your Seventh Seal. You also get full perception of all the minute functions performed by the subtle body and its connection with the physical body. This course also includes the perception of various physical bodies, including the sun, moon, comets, planets, and millions and billions of other solar systems. In the second eight months, a student is able to perceive his astral body exactly in the form in which it leaves the physical body at the time of death, carrying with it all the five senses of perception, five senses of action, intelligence, and determinative faculty. On an average, the student should spend eight hours in Yoga Practice, eight hours serving the *Guru*, and the rest of the time in sleep and doing personal things.

THIRD EIGHT MONTHS

In the third eight-month course, a person achieves the highest awareness of the spiritual body. A student penetrates *Anandamaya Kosa*. *Anandamaya Kosa* is a body of Bliss. Awareness of this body makes a person live in bliss all the time, and all who come near him are influenced by the radiation of peace, joy and bliss emanating from his aura. During this period a student achieves perception of his spiritual body which is housed in the spiritual heart. Also he perceives the minutest details of functions taking place between the astral body situated in the head and the spiritual body situated in the spiritual heart. Action and reaction between these two bodies take place through the spine in the form of color vibrations emanating from them. Once you enter the spiritual heart which is the seat of the individual soul, as well as the Universal Soul, the next step is to realize the unity between the two.

An average person thinks he has only one body—a body made of flesh and bones—but that is not true. In inner perception the Yogis discovered that there are five bodies inside the physical body. Just as your physical body needs an apartment to house it, similarly, the inner five bodies are situated one inside the other to provide safe and normal physical and mental functions in every day life. The first body is known as *Annamaya Kosa*. It is made out of the food you eat. Every cell in your body has these five bodies one inside the other. The upper and grosser is made out of the juices from the food you eat. *Annamaya Kosa* has six bodies inside it. When a baby is born, he brings with him six sub-bodies which constitute the *Annamaya Kosa*. Three he inherits from the father and three from the mother. The three sub-bodies inherited from the father are white in color, and they are bone, marrow and seminal energy. The other three parts which are inherited from the mother are red in color, and they are skin flesh and blood.

The second body within every cell is *Pranamaya Kosa*, which is the body made of negative and positive currents of life. These currents of life, known as *Prana*, are carried by the elements of air. The third body is known as *Manomaya Kosa*. This houses your mind, ego, and intelligence.

The fourth body is known as *Vijnanama Kosa*, which houses your determinative faculty.

The fifth, and last, body within you is *Anandamaya Kosa*, which houses bliss and happiness. The true nature of Man is known in *Anandamaya Kosa*. Penetration into this body makes one perceive and realize his true nature is light, peace, truth, knowledge and bliss.

These various bodies serve as a vehicle for the expression of your mind. Sometimes it is expressed through your thoughts and other times through the ego, intelligence, physical body, or through any other of the above-mentioned bodies.

It is very important to maintain personal contact with the *Preceptor* during practice of *Raja Yoga* to achieve Divine

Perception, and therefore it is not possible to attain this goal through books, or even through this course. This course can help a person proceed on the Path until he finds a *Guru*.

During the practice of the third eight month course, a student should devote every day, on average, ten hours to Yoga practice, eight hours to serving the *Guru*, and the rest of the time in attending to his personal things. The time for Yoga *Asana* and *Pranayama* should be reduced to one hour each day.

During the third eight months course, student perceives unity in diversity. He realizes the bond of unity between the material and spiritual, visible and invisible, science and religion, physics and metaphysics. He is able to reach and use transcendental forces through his physical body. He realizes in Divine perception that visible and material objects are nothing but a semi-stable condition of energy, which is sustained in the form of visible things by spiritual forces. Life and matter are both manifestations of spiritual forces and as such, in their original form, matter and life do not differ from each other. In Divine perception you will find a threefold manifestation of spiritual forces.

1. Creation of visible phenomena, i.e., spiritual forces creating things anew by its every rejuvenescent molecular activity. By mastering these spiritual forces, you can rejuvenate your body and stay young as long as you want. Pundit Madan Mohan Malvia, the Vice Chancellor of Hindu University in India, was able to make all wrinkles on his face, like a spider's web, disappear, by practicing *Kaya Kalpa* (a new lease on life, replacing the old body by a new one). There were also signs of new teeth sprouting from his gums. He was seventy-six years old when he took a course in *Kaya-Kalpa* under the guidance of a yogi in India. Similarly, Yogi

Markandey lived for many hundred thousand years by keeping his body always sixteen years old.

2. Spiritual forces maintaining and stabilizing matter which is only a relatively semi-stable condition of energy from which matter appears and into which it disappears, i.e., maintaining creation.

3. The spiritual forces by their chemical action breaking up the combination of matter, the disintegration of all physical forms, including the human body, plants, animals, etc.

In Divine perception you realize the spiritual forces which stand behind the material front of the world, i.e., the material and physical are like puppets guided from behind the visible by invisible spiritual forces. The Divine perception once achieved is never lost. Divine perception will enable you to see the hidden wisdom and spiritual values in everything which is physical and material.

Patience and perseverance is needed on the part of the seeker to achieve this goal.

HARI OM TAT SAT

Illustration 6. The Author's Mahasamadhi Memorial.

Index

a

actions, physical *44, 131, 134, 158, 213–214*

action, power of *100*

Adept *viii, 53, 58–59, 63–66, 69, 77, 79, 85, 93, 106, 111–112, 128, 145, 147, 177–178, 210–211, 217, 231, 259–260, 267, 276, 285, 288*

Adepts *xxi, 181, 235*
  spiritually developed *235*
  Yoga *235*

advising *xxii, 142, 179, 184, 206, 286*

affirmations *89*

age (vows) *xxi*

akasha *50, 74, 101, 105, 235*

Akashic Records
  see records, etheric

alarm clock, psychic *xxiv, 173–178*

allergy *135, 203, 227–229*

alms *xx–xxii, 73, 259*

amulet *33, 36–39*

anesthesia, psychic *58, 60*

angel, guardian *xxv, 87, 241–242, 245*

anger *37, 41–42, 86, 88, 91, 93, 99, 111, 148, 173, 176–177, 184, 190, 201, 222, 229*

animation, suspended *59, 106*

anxiety *140*

asana *xv, 221, 280–281, 284, 286–288, 291, 294*

ascetic *73, 222*

ashram *73, 118, 283–284*

assimilation *41, 59, 105, 190, 221, 226, 267*

astrology *150, 183, 269*

Atharva Veda *xiv*

atoms *63*

attachment *xx, 103, 244, 249, 286*

attacks, psychic *xxiv, 93, 133, 135, 203, 207*

attraction
  mental, law of *28–29, 31, 45, 163–165, 187*
  psychic *28, 187*

aura *xxiv, 84, 93, 134, 183–184, 203, 206–207, 250, 292*
  psychic *xxiv, 84–85, 93, 99, 134, 183–184, 203, 206–207, 250, 292*
  spiritual *84, 206*

awareness *xxii, 54, 57, 61, 84, 170, 231, 284–285, 288, 291–292*
  inner *85, 212–213, 275, 286*
  of Annamaya Kosa *289*
  of an ordinary person

  284
 of body *60*
 of Mantra for Unification
  273
 of pain *57*
 of psychic vehicle *58*
 of the body *xxi, 57–58,*
  103, 125, 289
 of the Divinity of the Universe *223*
 of the elements *289*
 physical *103*
 planes of *170, 285*
 power of *61*
 spiritual *xxii, 58, 86, 88,*
  102–103, 288, 292
 three states of *xix*
 withdrawal of *60*

b

background, spiritual, of past lives *286*
balance, mental, physical and emotional *266*
bank, spiritual *95*
beauty
 Divine *250, 254*
 store of *257*
begging *xix–xx, 48–49, 73*
beings
 Divine *253*
 invisible *239, 241, 245, 256*
being, psychic (Man) *161, 182*
Bible *103, 129, 231*

blessings *ii, 92, 158, 258–259*
bliss *84–85, 237, 292–293*
blood *vii, 27, 41–43, 52, 60–61, 90–91, 108–109, 112–113, 135, 178, 190–193, 195, 225, 229, 263, 293*
 biochemical changes in *55*
blushing *60*
bodies
 celestial *169, 236, 256*
 of the *Valakhilyas* *236*
body *253, 255*
 as a living battery of energy *267, 276*
 astral *99, 226–232, 234, 241, 243, 247–250, 253–254, 258, 291–292*
 benefits of a steady pose of *280*
 cells and organs of *27*
 chemistry *41, 191, 226*
 chronic and destructive conditions of *vii*
 compared to carriage *225*
 curative effect of mind on *108*
 decrepitude of *102*
 effect of mantras on *90*
 effect of the mind on *vii*
 elements which constitute *99*
 emotional *84, 226*

eternal *74*
healing forces released into *174*
healthy *102, 260*
inner *51*
materialization into human *xiii*
mental *30, 50–52, 67, 77, 91, 182, 226, 236, 247, 250–251, 253–258, 291*
    of thoughts *84*
    see body, mental
physical
    after death *58, 249*
    as means towards end *220*
    as temporary vehicle *49*
    attachment to *103*
    awareness of *289*
    connection with subtle body *292*
    created from five elements *101*
    effect of mental state on *185*
    expression through *293*
    fall of *49, 87, 128–129, 146, 227, 230, 232, 234, 241, 247, 250*
    fed by psychic body *134*
    five bodies inside of *293*
    functions of *vii*
    materialization into *77*
    migration to another *232*
    of cat *243*
    of comets, planets and stars *236*
    of the moon *237*
    survived by astral body *226*
    transformed into energy *77*
    under law of gravity *250*
    use of transcendental forces through *294*
    usefulness of *220*
presiding deity of *235*
processes of *108*
psychic *58, 74, 134, 183, 193, 207, 266*
relaxation of, by breathings *266*
repair of, by higher mind *109*
resurrection of *72*
separation from soul *248*
    see death
spiritual *51, 84–85, 246–248, 253, 291–292, 294*
    disintegration of *87*

299

    perception of   *292*
  spiritual aspect of   *236*
  subtle   *75, 292*
  surgery on   *57*
  vehicle   *49*
  withdrawal of mind from   *57*

bond, spiritual, between disciple and teacher   *94*

brain   *29–30, 44, 49, 51–54, 109, 113, 115, 117, 124, 127, 168–170, 174, 185, 189, 207, 209, 211, 217, 225, 229, 238, 247, 285*
  center   *49, 53, 127*
  infinite   *169*
  tissues   *247*

breath   *273*

breathing   *262*
  calming   *266, 281*
  cleansing   *281*
  control of   *261, 267, 288*
  positive   *266, 281*
  purifier   *203, 274–275, 280–281*
  rhythmic   *203, 263, 265–267*
  stimulator   *203, 274–275, 280–281*
  vibrator   *203, 275, 281*

breathings, Yogic   *204, 261, 263–265, 267*

broadcasting   *x*
  mental   *x, 45, 108, 154, 210*

Buddha   *168, 179, 235*

business   *31, 42, 44–45, 108, 112, 130, 132, 140, 142, 148, 153–154, 157–159, 162–163, 175–176, 198, 215, 228, 242–243, 265*
  spiritual   *97*

Bhusunda   *74*

C

call   *152–154*
  mental   *45, 151–155*
  of Spirit   *222*

calls, psychic   *151, 154*

Canada   *xi*

cancer   *55, 135, 190, 192–193, 221*

capacity, mental   *214–215*

career, successful   *108*

celibacy   *286–287*

cell, activities of   *27–30, 108–109, 112–115, 117, 168, 174, 185, 204, 207, 229, 239, 248, 293–294*

centers
  astral   *230*
  nervous   *109, 170, 227, 230*
  psychic   *95, 149, 179, 206, 263, 268, 278–279, 289*

chakras   *230, 263, 278*

Chakra, Sahasrara   *288*

changes, physical   *96, 134, 189*

channels, psychic   *124, 179,*

204–206, 262–263, 265,
268, 272–276, 278, 284
charity   219–220, 223, 235,
287
  highest   219, 222
  spirit of   219
chemicals   30, 41–42, 61,
63, 90–91, 96, 108–109, 113,
133, 183, 191–192, 204, 214,
216–217, 229, 256, 263, 295
  poisonous   191, 195, 229
chidakasha   50
chitta   50–51, 54, 89
Christ   x, 49, 58, 129, 168,
179, 231, 234
Christian Science   143
Christianity   231, 233–234
Christmas   193
circulation, of blood   41,
60, 105, 190–191, 221,
262, 266
clean-shaven head (vows)
  xxi
cobra
  bite of   60
  venom   61
colds   135, 203
colors
  astral   146
  negative   146, 184, 257
  positive   146, 184, 256–
257
communion, holy   69, 92
see Samadhi
concentration   74, 86, 89,
212, 230, 275–277, 280–

281, 289
condition   94, 191
  mental   90, 158–159,
191, 200, 211
conditions
  physical   xxiii, 27, 39,
41–42, 44, 49, 53–54,
90, 93, 105, 107–109,
112, 135–136, 158, 183,
185–187, 189, 191–192,
195, 199, 211, 266, 288,
294–295
conscience   247
consciousness   84, 221
  absolute   220
  cosmic   xxii, 63, 102,
238, 258
  Divine   237
  of body   102, 125
  of God   285
  religious   223
  spiritual   85
  states or layers of   xix,
47, 50, 54, 128, 170,
285
constellations   149, 235,
253
Consulate, American   120–
121
contact   163
  mental   37, 86–87, 98,
160, 173, 178
  psychic   160, 177–179
contemplation   65, 167,
173, 178, 262–263, 284
  men of   149

control, of senses 102
Cosmic Being 28, 220, 241
creation of the world 28, 101
credits, psychic 157
cremation 70–71
currents
   negative 262, 265
   nerve 52, 247, 263, 291
   positive 262–263, 288, 293

d

darshan 78, 158
death 37, 51, 61, 70, 93–94, 99, 112, 146, 175–176, 193, 195, 226, 229, 234, 239, 241–242, 247–250, 258
   overcoming 70
   sudden 61, 248
debits, psychic 157
decisionmaking, power of 115
defense, psychic 131, 135, 203, 207
   power of 200
deficiencies
   astral 99–100
   spiritual 99
deity 235
depression 146, 230
destiny, of the world 78, 256, 258
destruction 34–35, 132, 183, 204, 221, 256

determinative faculty 231, 248, 291–293
development, spiritual ii, 37, 83, 88, 98, 173, 236, 253, 258
devotees xx, xxii, 84, 223, 239
devotion 158–159, 184, 197
dharana 74, 221, 284, 286, 289
Dhruva 239
dhyana 75, 221, 284, 286, 289
diabetes 158, 190, 226
diamond 63
digestion 41, 59, 105, 190, 221, 226, 267
disciple ii, viii–ix, xiv, xx–xxi, 34, 36–39, 66–67, 70–71, 73, 77, 83–85, 87–88, 90, 94, 97–100, 102–103, 118–120, 122–124, 130, 147, 154, 173, 181–182, 234, 243–244, 260, 268
discipline xxi, 36, 102, 222, 283
discrimination, power of 27, 29
disease vii, xxiv, 34, 37, 55, 99, 113, 189–190, 192–193, 195, 221, 233, 259, 266
   functional 191
   mental 135, 200
disorders
   physical 86, 135

disposition, mental *219*
dissolution *74, 101, 167–168, 256–257*
   of the world *74, 101, 167–168*
Divinity *220, 223*
doctrines, secret *xxi*
dream *xix, 47–48, 50–52, 58, 124–125, 143, 147, 153, 182–183, 220, 279*
dreams
   come true *124, 142, 144, 188, 215, 249*
   sweet *249*
drugs, poisonous *133*

e

earth *ii, xi, 27–28, 34–35, 53, 66–67, 69, 74, 95, 100–101, 105, 113–114, 129, 168, 170, 177, 183, 195, 201, 209, 231–235, 237–239, 241–243, 245, 248, 250, 253–259*
Eastern Hemisphere *xi*
ego *221, 235, 293*
elements *237*
   five *50, 71, 74, 95, 101, 291*
   mastery over *71*
   nutritive *191*
   of air *293*
   subtle *216, 289, 291–292*
elimination *41, 59, 113, 190, 226, 267*

emotion *xxv, 41–42, 48–49, 52, 54, 83–84, 159, 177, 184, 189, 191, 195, 213, 225–229, 232, 247–248, 255, 266, 283*
emotions *41*
   control of *225, 229*
   depressing *41, 52, 191, 230*
   negative *41, 54, 191, 229, 232*
energy *57, 60, 64–66, 74, 77, 83, 95, 101, 105, 167, 179, 188, 204, 217, 236, 247, 256–257, 261, 263–265, 267–268, 276, 278–279, 281, 293–295*
   hidden *101*
   in matter *101*
   into matter *66, 257*
   invisible *65*
   manifest *101*
   mental *279*
   negative *265, 288, 293*
   of muscles *100, 263*
   of nerves *100*
   physical *77, 236, 294*
   positive *265*
   psychic *268, 276, 278–279*
   saving *45*
   unmanifest *101*
   vibrations of *57*
enlightenment
   mental *222, 251*
   spiritual *xx, 37, 67, 77,*

  85, 219–220, 222, 235,
  251, 283–287, 290
environment *35, 39, 42,*
52, 78–79, 90, 101, 148,
161–162, 185–187, 254, 272
 control of *53*
 spiritual *78–79*
enzymes *52, 112, 225, 229*
ether *101, 167, 171, 230,*
 246, 258, 279
evils *157*
evolution *28, 37, 83–84,*
 87, 102, 133, 168, 220–
 221, 233, 256, 264, 283
 mental *83, 87, 233, 241*
 of the world *28, 133*
 spiritual *37, 83, 87,*
  102–103, 233, 241–242,
  245, 253–254, 283
  highest *50*
exercise, mental *276–277*
exhaustion, nervous *175,*
 227, 230
expression, power of *139*
Eye, Third
 see Third Eye

f

Ford, Henry *132*
faculties
 astral *249*
 creative *107*
 mental *220, 249*
  supernormal *xiv*
 spiritual *220*
failure, in life *132, 140,*
 215
fame and fortune *xxiv,*
 139–140, 142–143, 164
fame and success *142*
family, spiritual *97*
Father
 Divine *85*
 Spiritual *85–86*
  see Guru
fear *41–42, 78–79, 88, 140,*
184, 191, 194–195, 198, 220,
227–229, 248, 258
 cause of *228*
 color of *184*
 mental patterns of *195*
 of death *194, 248*
 of heights *229*
feelings *vii, 41, 99, 120,*
140, 158–159, 175, 184, 189,
219, 226–227, 248
film, mental *50, 52*
fire *xx, 71–72, 74, 83, 101,*
136, 174, 199, 239, 251,
268
food *xx, 41, 43, 48, 66,*
72–73, 83, 91–92, 104,
108, 112, 189, 198–199,
219–220, 223, 229, 237,
259, 287, 293
 not cooking *xx*
 spiritual *219–220*
 temptation of *198*
forces
 Divine *83*
 ethereal *207*
 gross *182*

304

healing   *107, 145, 174, 178, 204–206*
higher   *28–29, 38, 43, 63–64, 83, 105, 117, 128–129, 132, 136, 143, 145, 165, 185–187, 214, 261, 264–265*
inner   *198, 201, 212*
invisible   *64–65, 129, 153, 161, 232, 256, 295*
lower   *222*
mental   *43, 86, 157, 192, 214–215*
    control of   *107, 191*
    development of   *107, 192, 214–215*
negative   *29, 133*
of prana   *261*
of thought   *65, 267–268*
of will   *212*
positive and negative   *263*
propelling   *212*
psychic   *63, 107, 133, 136, 158, 160, 162, 178, 186, 204–207, 210, 261, 263, 265, 272–273, 279*
    charging body's battery with   *268*
    protective   *207*
reserve   *205*
spiritual   *83–86, 216–217, 294–295*
subtle   *231*
force, primal   *105*

forgiveness   *69, 141, 219, 286*
formula, psychic   *38*
form, subtle   *38, 50, 83, 91, 216, 289, 292*
fragrance, ethereal   *64*
friendship   *v, x–xi, 43*
    between India and USA   *x*
frustration   *99, 214, 233*

g

Gandhi, Mahatma   *43–44*
Ganges River   *ii, xx, 71, 73, 78–80, 223, 259*
Germain, Saint   *168*
glands   *41–42, 54–55, 90–91, 170, 185, 190–191, 211, 225–227, 230*
Glory, Divine   *250*
goal
    higher   *173, 221–222, 233, 242*
    spiritual   *87*
goals   *37*
God   *236*
    love of   *36, 219*
    taking refuge in   *70*
    Will of   *28, 213–214*
    Word of   *101, 273*
gold   *63, 223*
    mansion of   *67*
Gorakhnath   *73, 103, 258*
Grace   *103, 259*
Great Master   *71, 258–259*
    known as Vishnu   *239*

Great Masters   *x–xi, xiv, 28, 58, 64, 67, 73, 78, 87, 168, 210, 239, 254–259, 265*
   astral journeys of   *231*
   power of   *73, 256*
   psychic powers of   *67*
growth, spiritual   *34, 87*
see development, spiritual
guidance   *ii, viii, xiii, xx, xxii, 37, 79, 86, 130, 134, 149, 160, 165, 171, 177, 181, 184, 201, 221, 233, 242–243, 245, 249–250, 254, 260, 268, 271, 275, 285, 288, 294*
   Divine   *xxii*
   spiritual   *37, 177, 181, 242*
guide   *35, 251*
see Guru
gunas   *101*
Gupta Dynasty   *193*
Guru   *ii, xiii, xix–xx, 33–38, 49, 66, 72–73, 83, 94, 97–104, 130, 159–160, 173, 176–177, 243–244, 259–260, 268, 284, 291–292, 294*
Guru Mantra
   see Mantra, Guru

h

handicaps   *99*
happiness   *51, 54, 88, 99, 148, 192, 219–222, 254, 264, 274, 284, 293*

   inner   *54*
   secret of   *219, 221*
Harsha Verdhan   *235*
hatred   *41, 88, 140, 146, 148, 184, 201, 220, 250*
healer   *91, 178–179, 267*
healing   *107, 109–111, 113–114, 145, 151, 177, 204–206*
   faith   *xi, 107*
   mental   *107*
   psychic   *viii, xxii, 107, 151, 177–179, 203–204, 206, 266–267*
healing treatment, dangers of   *206*
health   *ii, ix, xxi, 34, 36, 41–42, 45, 48, 52, 93, 95, 101–102, 107, 109, 112–113, 135–136, 179, 189–192, 195, 198, 200, 204–206, 209–211, 220, 229, 260, 266–267, 288*
   by mantra   *94*
   by talisman   *34, 36*
   mental   *34, 41, 101, 113, 136, 179, 229, 266*
   physical   *ii, 34, 36, 41–42, 55, 93–94, 101–102, 107, 109, 112–113, 135–136, 179, 189–192, 195, 198, 205–206, 211, 220, 229, 260, 266–267, 288*
   ruin of   *205, 229*
heart
   attack   *249*

cells obey the orders of the *115*
cells of *115*
failure *221*
function of *229*
of hearts *157*
physical *102*
spiritual *xiv, 51, 70, 102, 245–247, 251, 291–292*
    location of *51, 245*
    love of God in *36*
    purification of *284*
    purity of *242, 286*
heartbeat *43, 105, 108, 225, 262*
  suspended animation of *106*
Heavenly Fathers *87, 236, 241, 255*
help *214*
heritage, spiritual *97*
hierarchy, spiritual *254*
Himalayas *ii, 72, 77–79, 91, 118, 155, 163, 176, 193, 210, 222, 228, 283*
Hindu *x–xi, xix, 31, 89–90, 94, 145–146, 177, 200, 204, 223, 242, 294*
    Scriptures *xiv*
    Yogis *xi*
Holy Man *70, 79, 111*
  company of *54*
hormones *41, 52, 90, 113, 225*
hygiene, internal and external *287*
hypnosis *58–59, 145, 210–211, 233*

i

ida *262–263, 265*
images
  astral *131, 133–135, 183–184*
  astro-mental *34, 253*
  mental *34, 178, 253*
imagination *100, 146, 154, 211*
immunity, psychic *133, 135*
impressions, mental *191–192*
impulse
  for wrongdoing *xxiv, 197–201*
  psychic *94, 201*
  quickening *83–84*
  spiritual *83–84*
impulsion *149*
incarnation *235, 239, 242–243, 257–259*
income, psychic *xxiv, 157–160*
India *ii, v, viii, x–xi, xiii, 44, 48, 54, 60, 65–66, 69, 71, 74, 77–80, 84–85, 90–91, 93–94, 111, 118–122, 130, 145–147, 163, 173–174, 177, 190, 193, 204–205, 222–223, 234–235, 237, 239, 242, 259, 285, 294*

cultural treasures of *x*
Indriya Bus 287
influences
　astral 183
　astrological 34–35, 183
influence, psychic *vii, xxiv,*
　37, 107, 115, 136, 145–149,
　201, 203–204, 206–207
　harmful 35, 200, 203,
　　207
initiation *xix*, 38, 221, 283
　into spiritual mysteries
　　103
insecurity 41, 140, 184,
　220, 227, 229
institutions, mental 135,
　199–200
instructions, spiritual 176,
　219
intelligence 28, 53, 65, 95,
　109, 112–114, 134, 169,
　214, 230–232, 247–248,
　262, 291–293
　of cell 113
intuition 102, 245
Ishwara Aradhana 287

j

jealousy 41, 88, 140, 146,
　148, 158, 201, 250
Jnana Yajna 222
John the Baptist 128, 233
journeys, astral *xxv*, 170,
　231, 233–234, 241–244,
　247–250

k

Kabir 69–70
Kailashananda Mission *ii,*
　xx, 77–78, 81, 222
kalpa 239
karma 34, 51–52, 87, 91,
　102, 234–235, 250, 255,
　268
kaya kalpa 112, 294
Khatkhatananda, Swami
　66
kidneys 115
knowledge 100, 293
　ancient 124
　enduring 234
　infinite 125
　inner *x*
　inner research as a base of
　　65
　intuitive 53
　matter as a base of 65
　occult *xi, xiv, xxi*, 133
　of basic principles of food
　　287
　of psychic immunity
　　200, 207
　of psychic rhythm 265
　of the soul 102, 219, 251
　of the Vedas *vii*
　of Yoga 73
　power of 100
　seat of 245
　spiritual 123, 184, 219–
　　222, 243, 283
　　dissemination of
　　　123, 222, 242

    thirst for   *283*
  superconscious   *128, 285*
  transcendental   *53, 74*
  true   *234*
Kosa
  Anandamaya   *292-293*
  Annamaya   *289, 293*
  Manomaya   *291, 293*
  Pranamaya   *286, 289, 293*
  Vijnanama   *291, 293*
Kumbha Mela   *71, 73, 259*

l

law
  natural   *33, 63, 66, 111, 153, 185*
  psychic   *185*
life   *27, 108, 115, 169, 178, 204, 216-217, 235, 237*
  after death   *241, 248*
  ascetic   *222*
  astral   *226, 241, 248, 260*
  bare necessities of   *37*
  big decisions in   *125*
  breath of   *220*
  created by the will   *256-257*
  currents of   *288, 293*
  earthly   *249-250, 253*
  end of mortal   *247-248*
  eternal   *233*
  eternal existence of   *28*
  evolution from matter   *256*
  forces of   *203, 294*
  from matter, theory of   *27*
  from prana   *262*
  goal of   *222, 233*
  growth of, in human beings   *258*
  here and hereafter   *258*
  in cell activities   *27, 112*
  in every atom   *188*
  in iron age   *266*
  in matter   *30*
  in mind   *204*
  in plants, animals and human beings   *153*
  in prana   *262*
  in space   *241, 253*
  in the beyond   *87, 242, 245, 249-250*
  kept in harmony by Great Masters   *258*
  long   *36, 262*
  married   *287*
  material   *235*
  mind in   *108*
  necessities of   *78*
  of adjustment   *53*
  of invisible beings   *241*
  oneness of   *88*
  past   *51, 87, 227-229, 254-255*
  philosophy of   *220*
  planets of   *237*
  progress in   *221*
  relive experiences of   *57*
  restoration of   *290*

retirement from worldly *283*
spiritual *85*
spiritual forces of *294*
stirred by brain waves *189*
transfer of *73*
walks of *69*
way of *x*
    American *xiii*
withdrawal of *248*
lifelessness, non-existence of *188*
lifespan *229*
light, inner *86*
Lincoln, Abraham *168*
Linga Sarira *101*
  see body, physical
liver *115, 191*
lotuses, psychic *230, 263, 278, 288*
love *36, 84, 128, 141, 146, 148-149, 154, 159, 190, 210, 219, 221-222, 244-245, 248, 250-251, 257*
of one and all *222*
thoughts of *111*
luck *136*
lungs *105, 109, 113, 115, 229, 262*
luxury *234*

m

mahakasha *50*
Mahatma Gandhi *179, 200-201, 235*
Malvia, Pundit Madan Mohan *294*
Man
  definition of *213*
  true nature of *293*
Mantra *xxiii, 38, 89-102, 104, 236, 271-274, 280-281, 283-284, 287*
achieving full benefit of *94*
Guru *xix* *xix, 94, 97-102, 104*
power of *xxiii, 89*
Markandey *295*
Master
of Science of Pranayama *74*
of the four stage of Meditation *75*
presence of *85*
search for a *86*
guidance of *154*
master, of your destiny *148*
mastery
over cell mind *117*
over material objects *117*
spiritual *181*
materialization *28, 30, 44, 51, 63-66, 79, 108, 213, 278-279*
of thoughts *63*
space as an instrument for *63*
Matsyendranath *73*
matter

as a base of evolution
   220, 233
as a base of knowledge
   65
as ethereal substance   *64*
as vibrations   *64*
astral   *100, 152, 226,
   230, 285*
cause and source of   *167*
constituents of   *204*
control of   *27, 217, 256*
creation of   *65, 105, 241,
   256*
development of   *256*
difference between mind
   and   *27*
dissolution of   *295*
from energy   *66, 257*
from invisible forces   *65*
in vegetation   *101*
into energy   *64–65, 77,
   101, 217, 256–257, 295*
maintenance of   *295*
non-differentiation from
   life   *216, 294*
orginal state of   *106*
polarization of   *33*
rarefication of   *64, 216–
   217*
stabilization of   *295*
subservience to spirit
   216
Maya   *vii*
meditation   *ii, 65, 72, 75,
84, 86, 89, 92, 167*
   successful   *86*

memory   *51, 168, 229*
metaphysics   *185, 294*
Milarepa   *74*
mind
   and astral senses   *291*
   as place of suffering   *58*
   astral images in   *131*
   attaching and detaching
      57, 291
   balance of   *287*
   beyond the reach of   *181*
   body processes guided by
      108
   brain   *29, 115, 117, 174,
      178, 207*
   calming   *266, 273, 278,
      281, 289*
   calmness of   *289*
   capacity of   *159*
   cell   *185*
   changing positions of   *xix*
   cleaning the slate of   *278*
   connection with astral
      body   *291*
   conscious   *108–109, 113,
      117, 125, 128–130, 133,
      139, 160, 165, 187, 213,
      216, 268*
   conscious withdrawal of
      57
   control of   *57, 59, 74,
      84–85, 158*
   cosmic   *28*
   creative   *105–106, 187,
      278–280*
   definition of   *27, 29, 43,*

57, 59, 105–106, 108–109, 115, 128, 131, 159, 170, 174, 214–215, 226, 231, 247, 258, 278, 291
driving   83
effect of the body on   vii
Eternal   128–130, 132
eternal existence of   28
ethereal nature of   74
evolution of   220, 256
evolving the powers of   31
existence of   251
forces of   136, 158, 192, 203, 214–215, 217, 232
functioning
    independently of the body   xix
    through the body   xix
functions of   204, 225, 231, 291
harmful and negative thought in   210
harmful influences in   203
higher   viii, 28–29, 31, 43, 53, 108–115, 117–118, 124–129, 132, 139–140, 142–143, 148, 160, 165, 186–187
higher forces of   214
higher powers of   44, 124, 128, 187
higher vehicles of   215–217
housed by Manomaya Kosa   293
human   27
impulses of   201
in all objects   27, 29
in blood   27
in crystals   30
in food   108
in invisible form   28
in life   27
in matter   27, 30
in parts of the body   28
in physical objects   28
in space   28
in the body   108
indwelling   30, 129, 169, 187, 189
inferior   27, 29, 33, 115, 139
instruments of perception for   247
knowledge of   231
last thought of   259
law of   28–29
liberation of   253
life in   108
life in space of   xxv, 241, 245, 247, 249
location of   27
long ago thoughts projected from   119
lower   188, 215
mastery of   181, 283
necessity of, for life   108
negative   115, 191
negative thoughts in   41

of an owned object *33*
of animate beings *117*
of cells *27–30, 112–115, 117, 204, 207*
of inanimate objects *117*
of matter *27, 29*
of objects *145, 153*
of organs *27, 115, 204, 278*
of the heart *115*
of wild animals *111*
one-pointedness of *86, 289*
over matter *27, 29, 108, 192*
over mind *xxiii, 27, 29, 108, 111, 192*
peace of *49*
polarization of, in gold or silver *33*
polarization through *33*
power of *27, 29–31, 43–45, 53, 58, 65, 105, 111, 113, 129, 163, 181, 214–215, 217*
    expressed through a violin *30*
preventing externalization of *275*
processes of *200*
psychic *31, 111, 117, 124, 132, 140, 160, 165, 173–174, 179, 181, 203–204*
psychically advanced *111*

purification of *242, 256, 284*
purity of *286*
rate of vibration of *226*
reading *148*
relaxation of, by breathings *266*
reproduction of thoughts in *30, 146*
screen of *50*
shaping the body *77*
spiritual nature of *74*
state of *47, 54, 61, 96, 189–190, 225–226, 254, 271*
    boredom *88*
steadiness of *287*
stilling *278–280*
strong desire in *100*
subconscious *vii, 109, 268*
subduing *84*
Supreme *214*
survival after death of *247*
therapy for *107*
thoughts arising in *158*
thoughts entering into *134*
thoughts received by *45*
thoughts released by *45*
thoughts shooting from *134, 139*
training of *86*
Universal *105, 127, 258*
using higher powers of

313

    215
  value of *159*
  vehicle for expression of
    293
  vehicle of *213–216*
  vibrations of *128, 204,
    279*
  wavelength of *278*
  withdrawal of *58*
    from senses *288*
mindlessness, non-existence of *188*
mind-stuff
  see thought waves
miracles *x, xxiii–xxiv, 27, 151, 261*
monastery *84–85*
monk *ii, xvii, xx–xxi, 36, 73, 120, 130*
monsoon *60*
moon *77, 95, 98, 100–101, 105, 124, 149, 167, 183, 231–234, 237–238, 254, 292*
muscles, power of *107*
music, of the spheres *128*

n

Nadi *xvi, 203–204, 206, 263, 274–275, 280–281, 284–285, 288*
  Brahma *285*
Nature
  agents of *241*
  beauty of *241, 254*
  forces of *x, 38, 264, 266, 268*
  healing power of *109*
  higher forces of *43, 63–66, 71, 105, 107, 111, 117, 128, 132–133, 136, 143, 145, 148, 153, 158, 160, 165, 185–186, 232, 261–262, 264*
  higher powers of *viii*
  invisible forces of *153*
  language of *128*
  lower forces of *222*
  mysteries of *47, 100, 128, 170–171, 233*
  power of *132, 264*
  protection of *199*
  rhythm of *261, 264*
navel *230*
needs, spiritual *283*
nerves *52–53, 112, 114, 185, 214, 229, 266*
  calming *266*
New Thought *107*
Nivritti Marga *xx*
Niyama *157, 221, 284, 286–287*
nostril
  left *262, 265, 274, 276*
  right *265–266*
nostrils *262, 274, 276*

o

obligations
  moral *98*
  spiritual *98, 251*
observation, power of *229*

Oneness in All *88, 221*
ordination *xxi*
organs
  internal *42*
  involuntary *42, 109, 192, 225–226*
Orient *x, 145*
  Wisdom of the *xi*

p

Padmasana *288*
pain *48, 58, 107, 189–190, 199, 215, 222, 248–249, 272*
  awareness of *57*
  immunity to *57–58*
  of an operation *57*
palmistry *269*
parivrajaka *xxi*
partnership, spiritual *97–98*
path, spiritual *37, 75, 77, 85, 88, 98–99, 104*
patterns *30, 41, 53, 191–192, 278–279*
  mental *vii, xxiii, 28, 30, 33, 38, 41, 44, 53, 63, 117, 129, 189–193, 195, 212, 216, 278–280*
    wrong *87, 141, 193, 210*
  psychic *38, 53, 63, 193, 279*
peace
  between nations *256–257*
  inner *221*
  message of *222*
  of mind *42, 54, 88, 133, 284*
  of the Preceptor *84*
  perfect *222*
  radiation of *292*
  rest in *273*
  store of *257*
  that passeth all understanding *54, 102, 219, 221, 245, 257*
  thoughts of *111*
  world *145, 210*
penance *ii, 222*
perception
  as reproduction of past sensations *50–52, 183*
  astral *127, 129, 182–184, 231, 234, 254–255*
  changing *47*
  Divine *xxv, 263, 283, 286, 290, 293–295*
  extra-sensory *47, 53–54, 285*
  higher *291*
  in knowledge space *53*
  in mental space *53*
  inner *128, 235–237, 239, 283–284, 286, 289, 291–292*
  instrument of *247*
  of astral body *283, 292*
  of celestial bodies *292*
  of mind *283*
  of subtle body *292*

of thought waves *54*
physical *50, 232*
    discarding *53*
power of *255, 258*
psychic *xxiv, 49, 53, 127, 183*
sense *100, 103*
sense of *254*
supersensory *xxiii, 47, 49–50, 53*

perfume *65*
Perfume Saint *65*
perseverance *213, 295*
person
    highly spiritually evolved *259*
    most successful *215*
    spiritually evolved *249*
phenomena
    astral *170, 233*
    psychic *vii–ix, xxiii, xxv, 91, 105–107, 111, 117–118, 132–134, 136, 141–143, 179, 201, 204–205, 207, 209–212, 217, 231, 241, 261, 263–265, 267–269, 271–272, 274, 276, 278, 280–281*
philosophy, of life *88, 220–221*
phobias *227*
physics *x, 185, 294*
physiology *185*
pictures, astral *xxiv, 131, 134–135*
    see images, astral

pingala *262–263, 265*
plane
    astral *137, 170–171, 182–183*
    ethereal *169*
    psychic *183*
planets *95, 101, 124, 149, 167, 183, 232–233, 236–239, 241, 253–254, 256, 264, 292*
pleasure *58, 162, 249*
plexus *109, 227, 277–278*
    cardiac *278*
    epigastric *278*
    pharyngeal *278*
    prostatic *278*
    sacral *278*
    solar *277*
poison *41–42, 61, 190–191*
    neutralizing *55, 90–91*
Polar star *169, 239*
polarization *xxiii, 31, 33, 36, 115, 267*
positivity *54, 190, 201, 206*
postures, Yogic *ii, 159, 290*
poverty *88, 256*
power
    creative *139*
    healing *114, 206, 237*
    infinite *125*
    invisible *83, 92*
    magnetic *187*
    Supreme *237*
    spiritual *xxii, 100, 102, 104, 181*
    to resist impulsive urges *201*

to see *49, 127*
to synchronize mind *89*
unlimited *viii*
powers
   higher *114, 118*
   mental *159, 230, 267, 275*
   miraculous *27–28, 33, 106, 171, 290*
   occult *275*
   of endurance *74*
   of mind *111, 124, 128, 130, 142, 171, 187, 230*
   of subconscious *117–118*
   perfected *67*
   psychic *107, 120, 136, 185, 290*
      achievement of *181*
      as result of spiritual enlightenment *67*
      astral tube created by *152*
      awakening of *87, 213, 290*
      by use of will *268*
      control of *43*
      development of *xiv, 107, 143, 181*
      difficulties in manifesting *183*
      ease of use of *181*
      food materialized by *73*
      for fame and fortune *139–140, 142*
      functions of *204*
      generation of *179*
      in amulet form *37*
      job created by *147*
      law of *45*
      levitation by *71*
      manifested through Mantra *95*
      man's endowment of *53*
      materialization by *80*
      miraculous results of *71*
      need for self-restraint when using *271*
      of advanced minds *111*
      of an Adept *69*
      of Great Masters *67*
      of Guru Gorakhnath *73*
      of Hindu Yogis *x*
      of Holy Men *111*
      of Siddhas *77*
      of Swami Khatkhatananda *66*
      of Tirimolu Nayanar *74*
      of Trilinga Swami *71–72*
      of the Yogis *281*
      of Yogi Gupta's Guru *72*

of Yogi Matsyen-
dranath *73*
of Yogis *69, 261*
on reverse *43*
opening channels for
124
plans guided by
124
renunciant's vows
concerning *xxii*
renunciants' vows
concerning *xxii*
rhythm of *261*
set into operation
71
similarity to thought
process *42*
taught by the Great
Masters *x*
teachings and devel-
opment of *xi,
31*
timeless wisdom of
143
to access etheric
records *168*
to change circum-
stances *147*
to protect and de-
fend oneself *132*
to transform crimi-
nals *112*
universal dynamic
127
used by salesmen
108

spiritual *34, 84, 159*
unbelievable *268*
unlimited *261*
yogic *xxiii, 69, 73*
prana *100, 105–106, 139,
203, 205–206, 212, 262, 293*
at time of death *262*
body of *286*
charging the body with
267–268
control of *106, 261, 267,
288*
for thought projection
267
generating *206*
generation of *263*
imbalance in the flow of
266–267
in life *262*
normal flow of *267*
parts of *261*
transmission of *206*
use of, in psychic phenomena *267*
withdrawal of *248*
pranayama *ii, xvi, 74, 221,
266–267, 274–278, 280–281,
284, 286, 288, 290–291, 294*
pratyahara *221, 286, 288–
291*
pravritti marga *xx*
prayer *89, 145, 223, 248*
universal *145*
Preceptor *35, 83–88, 90,
94, 97, 181, 200, 243, 245,
283–284*

see Guru
    accepting help from   86
    administering of vows
        concerning the use of
        mantra   91
    as guardian angel   242
    aura of   84, 206
    awareness   84
    company of   85, 197
    essential help of   86
    evolution of   84
    family   204, 242
    guidance of   viii, xx, 83–85, 87–88, 103–104, 134, 149, 171, 181, 184, 188, 201, 204, 221, 233, 242–243, 245, 275, 288, 294
    help in life beyond from   87
    human foibles of   88
    impulse from   83–84, 86
    in India   84
    increasing numbers of   284
    instructions from   286
    maintaining personal contact with   293
    mental contact with   85, 87
    powerful thoughts of   87
    presence of   86
    psychic exchange with disciple of   85
    relationship with the student   85
    service to   284
    spiritual inheritance from   104
    spiritual powers of   83–84
    study with   85
    teaching mantras by   91
    training of the student for meditation   86
    virtues of   88
Preceptor
    Yogi Gupta   130
    see Yogi Gupta
prices rise and fall   264–265
primal force   95
privacy, mental   178
process, mental   xxiv–xxv, 189, 191, 225, 229
progress
    in life   xxi, 221
    individual   219
    mental   219
    physical   219
    spiritual   83, 93, 98, 100, 219, 286
projection
    mental   xxiv, 171, 209, 211–212, 215
    psychic   169, 209, 235, 279–280
Prophets   231
propulsion, psychic   xxiv, 209, 211–212, 215
prosperity   34, 37, 43, 93, 98–99, 108, 157, 164, 220, 234–235, 264, 269

psychiatrist *142*
psychoanalysis *227*
psychologization *33–35, 107–108, 115, 143, 145*
psychology *30, 107, 185, 189*
publisher, successful *139*
pulsation *105, 221, 225–226, 248, 262, 267*
purification *64, 233, 242, 258, 271–274, 280–281*
purity
  of heart *242, 286*
  of mind *242, 286*

r

Rama Krishna, Swami *84*
rapport, psychic *272*
rarefaction *64*
Rashis *238*
realization, of Truth and Spirit *222*
records, etheric *xxiv, 167–171*
reincarnation *102, 234, 256*
relationship, spiritual *85*
relaxation *ii*
religion *31, 143, 151, 223, 234, 294*
renaissance, spiritual *223*
renunciation *ii*
resistance, weak *203*
respiration *41, 43, 221, 226, 248, 266–267*
responsibility, spiritual *97*
results, spiritual *93*

resurrection *xxi, 234*
  of the spirit *70*
rhythm
  of breathing *225, 265*
  of nature *264*
  psychic *xxv, 261–264, 268*
ring-pass-not, psychic *35, 112, 203, 207*
Rishikesh *ii, 73, 77–78, 118, 122*
robe, orange *xx*
rosary *xix, 104*

s

Sadasiva *69*
sadhana *72, 91–92, 285*
saint *vii–viii, xxiii, 65–66, 69, 71, 84, 98, 168, 210*
salesman, successful *215*
samadhi *viii, 54, 69, 74, 221, 286*
Samadhi->foreignword *289*
samadhi *290, 296*
samskara *102*
sanatorium *ii, 78–79, 190, 193, 228*
Sanskrit *90*
sanyasa *xx, 36*
satsang *98*
Satsankalp *79*
Satya *286*
science *294*
  Divine *xi, 107*
  mental *xi, 83, 193*
  modern *41, 49, 63–64,*

90, 104–105, 135, 150,
167, 185–186, 192, 195,
211, 217, 236, 256
   of creation of psychic phe-
      nomenon   132
   of living   ii
   of physical development
      83
   of pranayama   74, 266
   perfect   54
   Western   x, 195
security   41, 133, 140, 184,
220, 227, 229
   absolute   222
self protection, power of
204
selfishness   184
   abolition of   88
selfless service   92, 222
Self-Illumination   102
Self-Realization   36, 284,
286
senses   xix
   astral   xxiv, 47, 49, 127–
      130, 170, 182, 216,
      230–231, 247, 254–255,
      275, 288, 291
   five   292
   of action   231, 291–292
   of perception   231, 291–
      292
   physical   47, 49, 52, 127,
      129–130, 170, 231, 247,
      255, 288, 291
   power of   127, 247
Seventh Seal   278, 285,

288, 291–292
   see Chakra, Sahasrara
Shakespeare, William   49,
168
Shakti   95, 100
   Gyana   100
   Iccha   100
   Kriya   100
   Kundalini   95
Shaw, Bernard   168
shock, mental   190
sickness   xxii, 42, 99, 135–
136, 159, 190, 192–193,
200, 205, 258
Siddhas   77
   power of   74
silence   54, 78, 129, 139,
149, 273
skin   112–114, 127, 164,
185, 193, 247, 262, 277,
293
sleep   xix, xxi, 43, 47, 54,
58, 74, 109, 123, 158, 164,
174, 183, 264, 268, 288,
292
   lack of pain in   58
snakes, poisonous   177
solar systems   149, 167,
169, 231–232, 234, 239,
241, 253, 255–256, 258,
292
soul   245
   advanced   245, 255
   advancement of   245
   at peace   49
   born in a family   97

brightening *36*
connection with the Guru *97*
departure from dead body *146*
earthbound *241*
embodied *242, 245, 259–260*
existence of *251*
freedom of *88*
happiness of *254*
hierarchy of *255*
highly evolved *241, 254–255, 257–258*
immortality of *220*
individual *290, 292*
inferior *241, 245, 250–251, 253–255*
inquiry into nature of *48*
knowledge of *102, 251*
life in space of *xxv, 247*
location of *51, 213*
of dead parents *251*
past lives of *255*
perception of *254, 283*
Perfect *257*
position in space *250, 255*
purification of *242*
seat of *246*
separation from body *248–250, 253*
spiritual impulse from *83*
spiritually evolved *236*
starvation of *219–220*
survival after death *247*
therapy for *107*
true nature of *245*
types of *235*
Universal *290, 292*
Soul, taking refuge in *70*
sound, eternal *101*
space
  infinite *253*
  knowledge *50, 53*
  mental *50, 53*
  outer and ordinary *28, 34–35, 183*
  spiritual hierarchy in *245, 254*
spine *xxi, 109, 174, 263, 268, 277–278, 284–285, 292*
Spirit *77, 85–86, 213, 248–251*
  brightening *36*
  inquiry into nature of *48*
  knowledge of *219*
  awareness of *58*
spirits
  developed *255*
  inferior *254*
  of equal rank *255*
  rank of *255*
stability, emotional *41–42, 266*
standards, spiritual *258*
state *225*
  mental *41, 90, 93, 106, 108, 158–159, 185, 189–191, 204, 285*
  of dream *xix, 54*

psychic   *204*
substance
  astral   *63*
  ethereal   *37, 63–65, 105, 134, 167–168, 170–171, 212, 231–232, 236, 263*
success   *43, 273, 278, 281*
  after success   *140*
  carried to   *264*
  cause of   *264*
  in business   *37, 44, 108, 157, 175, 265*
  in life   *xxiv, 31, 132, 143, 152–153, 157, 198, 213–215*
    secret of   *214*
  material   *37*
  through use of higher forces   *264*
suffering   *58*
Suggestive Therapeutics   *107*
Sun   *x, 65, 74, 95, 100, 105, 124, 148, 167, 169, 178, 183, 189, 197, 231–238, 254, 264, 292*
supernatural   *63, 111, 152, 185*
Supreme Consciousness   *290*
Supreme Power   *214*
swami   *36, 66–67, 71–74, 84, 111*
switchboard, mental   *59*
S.O.S., psychic   *xxiv, 151–154*

system, nervous   *42, 106, 109, 191–192, 225–227, 229*
  autonomic   *192, 225–226*
  parasympathetic   *109, 225*
  sympathetic   *42, 109, 192, 225*

t

talisman   *33–36, 38*
taste, power of   *103*
teacher, spiritual   *ii, 151*
  see Guru
teachings
  esoteric   *vii, xi, xiii*
  higher   *102, 118*
  inner   *283*
  occult, Western interest in   *xi*
  Rosicrucian   *xi*
techniques, Yogic   *105, 107, 119, 170, 188, 204, 230*
  of breathing   *261*
telegram
  mental   *161–162*
  psychic   *xxiv, 161–163*
telepathy   *x, 182, 189*
telescope, astral   *xxiv, 181–182*
Third Eye   *230–231, 275–276, 278*
thought
  body   *51, 189*
  force   *265, 279*
  pattern   *30, 33, 117,*

    189–190, 212, 279
    process   42, 211, 229
    transference   x, 45, 189
    waves   35, 44–45, 53–54,
        89, 117, 134, 146–147,
        164, 186
thoughts   vii, x, xxiii, 41,
    107, 139, 143
    as internal action   44
    as vehicle for expression of
        mind   293
    attracting similar
        thoughts   140
    backed by will   214
    becoming things   xxiv,
        185, 188
    bundle of   226
        see body, mental
    color of   146
    conscious   139
        raising to higher
            mind   117
    contagious   41–42, 135,
        200, 210
    control of   57, 83, 137
    controlling body chem-
        istry   41–42
    correlation with things
        216
    creative   44, 63, 117,
        119, 139–140, 142, 148,
        152, 185–188, 213, 216
    depressing   41
    distracting   179
    effect on brain particles
        185

    effects of   57
    energized   38, 90–91
    expressed through world
        brain   214
        see will of God
    form of   146
    good, bad and neutral
        see gunas
    harmful   112, 143, 186,
        203, 210
    higher   213–214, 216
    immortality of   135–136
    influence on objects   185
    invisible   87, 107, 127
    materialization of   50,
        63–64, 80, 105, 108,
        187, 267, 279
        into action   148
    nature of   44, 146
    negative   vii, 35, 41, 54,
        131, 133, 135, 140–141,
        146, 190, 210–211, 250
    neutralization of incoming
        and outgoing   289
        see pratyahara
    of a Yogi   181
    of average person   139
    of celestial bodies   236
    of Divine Blessings   210
    of deceased   34, 183
    of Great Masters   255–
        256
    of guardian angels   242
    of happiness   210
    of higher mind   139
    of love and harmony   251

324

of others *134*
of peace *210*
of relatives and friends *251*
of Yogis *210*
one-pointedness of *89*
penetration of *171*
positive *111, 140, 146, 186, 274*
power of *42–43, 64, 108, 117, 139, 171*
process of registration of *57*
see mind, definition of
projection of *119, 169, 178, 182, 186, 209–211, 267*
reading of *148*
reality of *44, 193*
reception of *147*
   by deceased *250–251*
recording of *167*
release of *37, 63*
reproducing in others *43, 45, 141, 145–146*
silent *149*
translation of *148*
transmission of *54, 146–147, 171*
uncontrolled *141*
under emotional upset *226*
vibrations of *35, 49, 131, 139, 145, 192–193, 217, 279*

visualization of *279*
weak *140*
tie
   sacred, with the Guru *97*
   spiritual *97*
Tiger Swami *111*
Time, Wheel of *237*
time
   of death *127, 175, 226, 247, 249, 253, 259, 292*
   saving *45, 142*
   to buy *215*
   to sell *215*
Tirimolu Nayanar *74*
training, spiritual *72*
treasure
   spiritual *98*
   see wealth, spiritual
treatment, psychic *viii, 173–174, 185*
Trilinga Swami *71*
Truth *133*
   and the role of the Guru *100*
   awareness of *xxi*
   consciousness of *xix*
   dissemination of *132*
   Divine *258*
   finding *100*
   higher, reflected in the mind *289*
   highest *vii, 220*
   inner mysteries of *49*
   knowledge of *251*
   mysteries of *100, 133,*

222, 233, 251, 257
realization of   xx, 221,
    234, 284
reverence for   197
search for   181   181
secret of   219
seekers of   71, 78
speaking   286
    see Satya
Statements of   89
store of   257
voice of   200
tube, astral   152, 178, 204–
    206, 231, 263, 272–273, 285
see Nadi
twice-born   xxi

u

ulcers   142, 158, 192, 211
unawareness   61
understanding   85, 128,
    148, 219, 222, 237, 245,
    257, 265, 284
United States   ii, v, viii,
    x–xi, xiii, 45, 65, 79–80,
    114–115, 118–122, 124,
    173–174, 234–235, 258,
    263
Unity in diversity   88, 221–
    222, 294
Unity of Creation   220
Unity of Man   285
universe   169, 220, 223,
    242, 258, 264
    responsibilities of   242
upset, emotional   54, 226–

227, 229, 266
uranium   64
urges, impulsive (neutralizing
    them)   xxiv, 162, 197–
    201
Uttanpad   239

v

Vajrasana   xv, 281, 288
values
    spiritual   88, 98, 237,
        239
        values   295
    wisdom   37, 88, 98, 295
Veda of Psychic Powers   xiv
see Atharva Veda
Vedas   vii
vehicle
    astral   58
    eternal   247
    spiritual   84, 217, 247
vibrations
    mental   204
    of color   99, 231, 292
    of light   169
    positive   35, 272
    spiritual   77, 80
Virgin Mary   168
virtues   88–89, 157
virus   135, 203
Vishnu   239
vows, of Hindu monk   xx,
    91
Vrittis   54
    see thought waves

w

waking *xix, 54*
war *222, 256–257*
Milton, John *49*
water *xx, 66, 69, 74, 77–78, 87, 90, 92, 97, 99, 101, 105, 125, 128, 189, 198, 205–206, 238, 290*
   streams of *74*
   transformed into butter *67*
wavelength
   mental *54, 117, 134, 151–152, 161, 163–165, 170, 278*
   psychic *151–152, 163–165*
wealth *37, 48–49, 92–93, 98, 103–104, 142, 163, 219–220, 235, 242–243, 255, 283, 285*
   spiritual *72, 92, 94, 98*
Western Hemisphere *xi, xiii*
will
   Divine *xxii*
   in hypnosis, weakened *145*
   of God *214*
   power of *37, 59, 63, 66, 95, 100–101, 134, 154, 201, 206, 211–212, 231, 236, 256–257, 279*
      for materialization *63–64*
wisdom *xi–xii, 95, 98, 100, 124, 128, 130, 146, 184, 219–220, 237, 239, 250, 285*
   dissemination of *132*
Wisdom
   Divine *250*
   higher, reflected in the mind *289*
wisdom
   of the East *ii*
   of Yoga *73*
   spiritual *88*
work *36, 99*
world
   invisible *28, 38, 87, 242, 245*
   physical *38, 97, 128*
worldly possessions *248–249*
worry *42, 92, 118, 158, 201, 211*
worship, church *287*

y

Yama *157, 221, 284, 286–287*
yantra *38*
year, successful *215*
Yoga *ii, 36, 38, 72–73, 83, 85, 91, 98, 106, 112, 243*
   Hatha *ii, ix*
     see postures
   Karma *234*
   practice *72–73, 83, 85, 88, 91, 98, 281, 284, 287, 291–292, 294*
   Raja *ii, 221, 233, 243,*

284–288, 290–291, 293
 sadhana   285
 student   225, 228
 types of   ii, 36, 233
Yoga and Long Life   ii, viii, 262–263, 266–267, 278, 281, 286–288
Yogi   viii, x, xix, 64–65, 111, 288, 294
 aura of   54
 blessings of   92
 company of   54
 control of environment by   53
 family   177, 204
 guidance of   294
 highest achievement of   50
 in dream of king   48
 non-attachment of   217
 Perfected   84
 psychic battery of   179
 psychic powers of   71
 respect for   92
 thoughts of   79, 181
Yogi Gupta   ii, iv, vii–viii, x–xi, xiv, 130
 birthplace   ii
 system of developing psychic powers   xiv
Yogi Gupta New York Center   ii, xii
Yogi Gupta Society   iii–iv, vi, viii

Yogis   x–xi, 65–66
 see contemplation, men of
 asanas practised by   288
 astral journeys of   231, 233–234, 237
 effort for spiritual mastery of   181
 family   204
 Hindu   264   xi
 inner contemplation of   167, 178, 263, 284
 inner perception of   284
 inner research of   27–28, 44, 57, 89, 173, 181, 225, 256, 261–262
 levitation by   71
 Perfected   77
 see Siddhas
 process of awakening the astral senses of   182
 psychic pass-not-ring   112
 psychic powers of   67, 69, 71, 171, 268, 281
 reliance on astral senses   128
 respect for   91
 thought transmission of   147
 will power of   59

Z

zodiac   236, 238

Printed in Great Britain
by Amazon